Mass Communication Law and Ethics

Mass Communication Law and Ethics

Contributors

Joergen Oerstroem Moeller et al.

AURIS
Reference

www.aurisreference.com

Mass Communication Law and Ethics

Contributors: Joergen Oerstroem Moeller et al.

Published by Auris Reference Limited

www.aurisreference.com

United Kingdom

Mass Communication Law and Ethics

ISBN: 978-1-78154-736-6

British Library Cataloguing in Publication Data
A CIP record for this book is available from the British Library

Printed in the United Kingdom

Exclusively distributed by CBS Publishers & Distributors Pvt. Ltd.

Contents

List of Abbreviations

APT	Association pattern technique
BBS	Bhutan Broadcasting Service
DAP	Democratic Action Party
DPM	Deputy Prime Minister
GDP	gross domestic product
HVM	Hierarchical value map
HVMs	Hierarchical value maps
ICT	Information and Communication Technology
PKR	People's Justice Party
SSCI	Science Citation Index Social
SNSs	Social network services

List of Contributors

Joergen Oerstroem Moeller
Visiting Senior Fellow, ISEAS Yusof Ishak Institute, Singapore
Singapore Management University & Copenhagen Business School, Singapore
Honorary Alumnus, University of Copenhagen, Copenhagen, Denmark

Kurt Lang Gladys Engel Lang
University of Washington

Lhamo T
Public Policy Program, National Graduate Institute for Public Policy, Tokyo 106-0032, Japan

Oyama T
Professor of Public Policy Analysis, National Graduate Institute for Public Policy, Tokyo 106-0032, Japan

Feifei Han
Department of Sci-Tech Communication and Policy, University of Science and Technology of China, Hefei, China

Zhangzhi Ge
School of Public Affairs, University of Science and Technology of China, Hefei, China

Rongting Zhou
Department of Sci-Tech Communication and Policy, University of Science and Technology of China, Hefei, China

Célestin Messanga Obama
Department of Advertisement, Advance School of Mass Communication, University of Yaoundé 2, Yaoundé, Cameroon

Brittany L. Pavolik
Department of Communications Media, Indiana University of Pennsylvania, Indiana, PA, USA

Mark J. Piwinsky
Department of Communications Media, Indiana University of Pennsylvania, Indiana, PA, USA

Lacey A. Fulton
Department of Communication, Clarion University, Clarion, PA, USA

Sara Chinnasamy
University Technology Mara, Selangor, Malaysia

Izyan Roslan
University Technology Mara, Selangor, Malaysia

Jean-François Nguegan
University of Yaoundé II, Advance School of Mass Communication (ASMAC), Yaoundé, Cameroon

Thomas Essono
University of Yaoundé II, Advance School of Mass Communication (ASMAC), Yaoundé, Cameroon

Jingqian Tang
Library of Jinan University, Guangzhou, China

Denise Avancini Alves
Pontifical Catholic University of Rio Grande do Sul (PUCRS), Porto Alegre, Brazil
Federal University of Rio Grande do Sul (UFRGS), Porto Alegre, Brazil

Maria Helena Weber
Federal University of Rio Grande do Sul (UFRGS), Porto Alegre, Brazil

Valene Bummara
School of Journalism & Mass Communication, Texas State University, San Marcos, TX, USA

Jinbong Choi
Department of Media & Communication, Sungkonghoe University, Seoul, South Korea

Sang Hee Kwon
Sungkyunkwan University, Seoul, Korea

Min Kyung Cha
Sungkyunkwan University, Seoul, Korea

Seo Young Lee
Yonsei University, Seoul, Korea

Marianne Paimre
Department of Law, University of Tartu, Tartu, Estonia

Fatma Gürses
Department of Journalism, University of Kastamonu, Kastamonu, Turkey

Tai-Li Wang
The Graduate Institute of Journalism, National Taiwan University, Taiwan

Kazi Nazmul Huda
Department of Business Administration, Southern University Bangladesh, Chittagong, Bangladesh

Abul Kalam Azad
Department of Communication & Journalism, University of Chittagong, Chittagong, Bangladesh

Israel Udomisor
The Department of Mass Communication, University of Maiduguri, Maiduguri, Nigeria

Anthony Paul Udoh
The Department of Communication Art, University of Uyo, Uyo, Nigeria

Preface

Mass communication is the study of how people and entities relay information through mass media to large segments of the population at the same time. It is usually understood to relate newspaper, magazine, and book publishing, as well as radio, television and film, even via internet as these mediums are used for disseminating information, news and advertising. The text *Mass Communication Law and Ethics* focuses on new legal cases and emerging issues in mass communication law and ethics. First chapter discusses about economics forged by mass communication and scarcities. Second chapter offers a brief overview of both the origins of the concept of mass and its subsequent refinement by French, German, and American sociologists into the mid-1930s. Third chapter aims to assess the impact and influences of mass media as one of the key factors that shapes society, its culture, and values by investigating the growth of the media. Fourth chapter focuses on reconfiguration and empirical study on the evaluation system of Wechat communication effect of sci-tech periodicals. Fifth chapter deals with the normativity and the problem of look in the emergence of citizen journalism. Sixth chapter examines immediate recall and long-term retention for a local television newscast. Seventh chapter presents strategies used by the two major political parties, Barisan Nasional (BN) and Pakatan Rakyat (PR) in Malaysia to achieve their electoral goals. Ethnomethodological perspective on the conflict between magistrates and journalists in Cameroon has been focused in eighth chapter. Quantitative analysis on the science citation index social (SSCI) theses from 2005 to 2014 has been used in ninth chapter. Tenth chapter analyzes the social merchandising, an approach given to international human trafficking in entertainment venues of television, especially, from the telenovela Salve Jorge. Eleventh chapter explores the effectiveness of distracted driving public service announcement (PSA). Twelfth chapter compares the hierarchical value maps (HVMs) for portal sites, smart phones, and social network services (SNSs) according to means-end chain theory. Thirteenth chapter focuses on issues highlighted in national and international drug reports such as drug addiction, drug related crime, spread of HIV among addicts, drug-induced deaths, drug problem in schools etc. Fourteenth chapter aims at examining the relationship amongst democracy, citizenship and local press using the local media Boulder, a city in Colorado State of the USA, as a case study. Last chapter establishes a comprehensive behavior model of video-sharing websites, which is helpful both for online media research and business practice.

Chapter 1

ECONOMICS FORGED BY MASS COMMUNICATION AND SCARCITIES. NEW THEORETICAL FRAMEWORK —NEW POLICY PRESCRIPTIONS—NEW SCIENTIFIC THINKING

Joergen Oerstroem Moeller[1,2,3]

[1]Visiting Senior Fellow, ISEAS Yusof Ishak Institute, Singapore

[2]Singapore Management University & Copenhagen Business School, Singapore

[3]Honorary Alumnus, University of Copenhagen, Copenhagen, Denmark

ABSTRACT

Economics does no longer deliver analyses and solutions to problems confronting the global economy and contrary to expectation it does not move towards general equilibrium. Two big transformations take place: Mass consumption is replaced with mass communication—the era of plenty is replaced by scarcities. Economic models have so far proven inadequate to tackle the turnaround from growth & distribution of benefits to burden sharing leaving policy makers without advice and guidelines. The idea of economic thinking (homo oeconomicus) introduced by Adam Smith does not reflect realities in the beginning of the 21st century. Concentration of economic activities in the hands of relatively few operators rules out competition in the sense of a free market. Distribution of income and wealth is steered by a mismatch between supply and demand of skills rewarding those who by chance have the "right" skills. The concept of work is changing fast as is the notion of companies with jobs being performed outside companies eroding the well-established Theory of the Firm. Bringing in other social sciences it becomes clear that people are less motivated by economic incentives than presumed, which makes it necessary to broaden economic analyses and policy making. Interdisciplinary and intersectoral thinking incorporating human behavior crowds out pure economic reasoning. In a longer term perspective the way ahead may be to base economic thinking and models on big data analyzing how data are linked to each other without any prior assumption of theory. The future for economics may therefore be to go from deduction to induction.

INTRODUCTION

Adam Smith's "The Wealth of Nations", published in 1776, intercepted the impact on the human mind-set of the industrial revolution grasping the swing from feudal thinking—mainly societal status, honor and dignity—to money (homo oeconomicus). Since then economics has wrestled with the question about explaining what is happening (descriptive), telling how to do things better (instrumental) or weighing into politics (normative).

Economics and economists missed the Wall Street crash in 1929. Indeed one of the greatest economists of that time, Irving Fisher, published shortly before the crash a thesis saying "Stock prices have reached what looks like a permanently high plateau". The same happened to the great depression in the 1930s, the oil price crisis in the 1970s, the Asian financial crisis in 1997, the 2008 global financial crisis and the subsequent recession in 2008-2009.

Economists find it difficult to find out what the science is about. The classical school reigned until the 1930s. It focused exclusively on production capacity, capital goods, investment and interest rate theories. In economic terminology the supply side was the only thing that mattered. This edifice collapsed with the great depression in the 1930s. John Maynard Keynes stepped forward with his "General Theory of Employment, Interest and Money" saying that the demand side—in reality consumption—was the core of economics adding that the public should steer total demand by spending in recessions and saving in boom times. This worked well for some decades but growing inflation opened the door for Milton Friedman who in the early 1960s advocated control of the money supply combined with free markets, and rejected any role for the state.

Theory tells that the system moves towards general equilibrium. As anyone can observe this is wrong; the system is in perpetual disequilibrium. In the 1950s the global economy saw unemployment, growing demand pressure ruled the agenda in the 1960s, stagflation (stagnation and inflation at the same time despite economics swearing that this could not happen) paralyzed economic policies in the 1970s, and deregulation of markets was the magic words in the 1980s. After a brief interlude with stability in the 1990s two major financial crises struck in the first decade of this century.

The purpose of this paper is to analyze the state of economics as a science. Established theories do not corroborate what is happening and it would be a grave mistake to dig in and expect realities to adjust to theory. Instead a diagnosis of discrepancies should be applied as a start to redraw the theoretical framework. Failures and shortcomings of existing policy prescriptions (economic policy) explain why the global economy despite strenuous efforts is still wobbling. Maybe the time has come to move forward and acquiesce to a new kind of economics or even the era of non-economics emphasizing the importance of other social sciences and why big data may force deduction out and induction in.

THE BIG TRANSFORMATIONS

The global economy transits a transformation not seen since the industrial revolution. Mass consumption is giving way to mass communication. Knowledge must be shared to enhance productivity; people are only willing to do so if replicated by fellow human beings. Abundance of resources is replaced by scarcities—in some cases physically and in other cases economically pushing prices up. Burden sharing takes over from distribution of benefits; people are only willing to enter this social game provided that fellow human beings do likewise. The common denominator for mass communication and scarcities is analogous values connoting mutual trust pushing people to co-operate in groups. Utility theory, economic incentives, and homo economicus do not deliver because it supposes rationality and logic while it becomes more and more clear that human behavior is irrational, emotional and intuitive.

Knowledge is produced in enormous quantities. The impact depends on how easily accessible it is and the skill of the persons using it. More open societies benefit while closed and introvert societies struggle. Not only mutual trust among individuals, but trust between authorities and the people determine how knowledge is integrated in economic transactions. People want to share knowledge, but do authorities want them to do so and are authorities ready to share with the people?

No genuine theory exists explaining what it cost to produce knowledge. Normal concepts like marginal utility and marginal costs are non-applicable. Except for initial investment, which in most cases is small, it does not cost much to produce. People are willing yes eager to produce knowledge and place it at the disposal of others (Wikipedia!). Furthermore knowledge introduces a much higher propensity to rent instead of owing. People get access to user facilities via the net and pay for the time they use a product or a service. Examples are Uber, Airbnp and "unlimited streaming" paying for access to catalogues.

Business have managed to turn an otherwise free good into a commercial product—profit seeking mode—by an alliance with the public sector smelling potential tax revenues. As the many examples of imaginative citizens demonstrate they operate on borrowed times; compressing a free good or service into a business model straitjacket does not look viable.

Firms/Corporations are explained by lower transaction costs—it is cheaper to gather workers, machinery and resources in one place than having them dispersed. It does not work quite like that in the era of mass communication. The prime factor dominating competitive advantage is fast becoming skills and competences. Knowledge and mass communication offer access to skills/competences irrespective of geography mobilizing skilled people wherever they are. Precisely the same tendency is visible looking at innovation. Corporations are allocating research to companies or persons outside the firm and connect them to the activities of the firm via the net. The advantages reaped outshine what loss in transaction costs if any is encountered by not having people at the same geographical place. The result is breaking up of the firm. Corporations/firms embark on structuring activities around digital networks kept together visually and not physically. The repercussions for costs and management are seminal; in reality mass communication heralds a new business model.

Scarcities have been announced many times. In 1798 Thomas Malthus [1] predicted that population increase would outpace food production resulting in famine and the Club of Rome launched its study 'Limits to Growth' in 1972 [2] . The difference is that currently we actually have scarcities/shortages. The Food and Agricultural Organization of the United Nations (FAO) [3] point to food shortages in 40 countries. The commodity index is falling, but despite technology and lower global growth still 50 percent higher than ten years ago. Countries and regions face water stress and in some cases severe stress that does seem to get worse (e.g. Southern California and Sao Paulo).

For the production function durability, reuse, regenerate, remanufacturing and recycle must be taken more into account. Product cycle defined as the total use of resources for goods or services replace the narrow minded view of solely looking at energy use. Resources are used producing a new good and disposing of the obsolescent one. Total use of resources over the total life of a product (life cycle) will be included in profitability. There has been much talk of 3-D manufacturing as a revolution in manufacturing. The genuine revolution will be 3-D disaggregation allowing an obsolescent product to be disassembled for the components to be recycled. Garbage and waste becomes precious not only looking at disassembling, but finding landfills to recycle resources now their weight worth "in gold".

The consumption function undergoes similar transformations. Durability turns into a competitive parameter making it impossible for companies to produce and sell products with inbuilt obsolescence as is the case nowadays in certain sectors especially electronic products. Consumers will expect "hardware" capable of exchanging "software" prolonging the life of the product ? cell phones, fridges, and computers. 3-D may play a role in this. The change in values and attitudes may have a spillover effect on consumption. If a consumer postpones buying a car there is no guarantee that the car can be used in the same way five or ten years later. Restrictions may have been introduced limited the opportunities to use the car. People will focus more on happiness and well-being achieved through communication, services, doing something with others and for others growing out of mutual trust rooted in common and shared values (non-materialistic consumption). In the US the young generation is far less attracted by car driving than their parents. Surveys show that people in Asia look at companies' policy to give something back to society as an important part in branding. Physical well-being, tangible goods, and worldly possessions (materialistic consumption) yields as the main factor defining 'happiness'.

IMPLICATIONS FOR ECONOMICS

Students of economics learn that prices are set by supply and demand in a market. That may have been correct in the early days of economics, but no longer. In reality prices are set by a limited number of large corporations in a market with few players and limited competition (oligopolistic market). 1318 corporations control 80 percent of global business transactions ? 147 control 40 percent [4] . In 1995 the Big Six US banks—JPMorgan, Bank of America, Citigroup, Wells Fargo & Co., Goldman Sachs Group, and Morgan Stanley—had assets worth 17 percent of US gross domestic product (GDP). In 2005 the share had grown to approx. 50 percent [5] . After the global financial crisis it jumped to 60 percent. The two largest carriers in U.S. wireless Verizon Communications Inc. and AT&T together control around 70 percent of the nationwide market. Add Sprint Corp. and T- Mobile and the share goes up to 90 - 95 percent [6] .

This concentration allows the companies to play their own game. In the financial sector sophisticated financial instruments benefitting banks solely instead of oiling the economy are issued. The U.S. financial sectors share of GDP has risen from two percent in 1950 to eight percent before the financial crisis. This means that it encroaches on production without contributing more to growth. In the telecommunications sector companies commercialize what would otherwise be a cheap or even free good ? knowledge.

Distribution theories focus on labor versus capital. The latest in the line of hundreds of books looking into this is Thomas Piketty's "Capital in the 21st Century" [7] who argues that over time the rate of return on capital tends to be higher than economic growth tilting income distribution to the advantage of owners of capital. This is a typical industrial age analysis neglecting the skill factor. Skills of those operating machinery perceived in a broad sense determine marginal product. A premium is paid to those with a higher performance than those not having the skills in demand and consequently a lower performance. If a mismatch exists between supply and demand of skills this premium can be very high as seen over the last two decades with introduction of Information and Communication Technology (ICT) resulting in an almost explosive growth in inequality. Those having skills not in demand are crowded out of the high end job market forced to compete with middle level skills workers depressing the wage rate for this segment of the economy. Over the last decade the share of long term unemployment has grown rapidly in most industrialized countries while at the same time around 1/3 of U.S. businesses cannot fill vacant positions.

Since industrialization relative factor prices ? in this context wage rate versus commodity prices—has steadily favored the wage rate making it profitable to save labor and use resources without any cost inhibitions. In the future scarcities and higher resource prices change relative factor prices to favor resources and depress wages. The first consequence is that production will be more labor intensive and less resource intensive. The second one is a lower share of GDP going to labor. Statistics show that Labor's share has fallen in the U.S. from 59 per- cent in 1980 to 55 percent in 2012 [8] .

Industrial society benefitted from a kind of symbiosis between owners and workers both depending on the enterprise for prosperity. Now obscure and nontransparent funds take over ownership pursuing short-term profit goals primarily of financial character with little or no interest in the long term future of the enterprise. They hike the share price to resell or split the enterprise in separate divisions. This break-up of age old owner-worker relationships is followed by a similar break-up in business-society ownership with business' transferring costs to society. The financial crisis disclosed that financial institutions having lent recklessly transferred much of bad debt to the public sector—in economic jargon deleveraged debt while public sector debt rose. Redundant workforce is retrenched shifting the burden of taking care to the public sector. Many public services have been privatized and in some cases that may be good, but there are too many stories of privatization used to take money out of such companies e.g. in telecommunication and transport to feel comfortable—is it good for society? The taxpayers?

From the point of workers the corporation is becoming distant. The web and the cloud make it possible for workers to offer what they produce instead of their working capacity. As they can and do shift from company to company they, like the owners, lose interest in the long term future for the company. Tomorrow they can sell their product to another company.

Out of this comes an anonymous ownership and impersonal relations to companies breaking up the firm as we know it and introducing a business model much more focused on short term profit seeking and less interested in contributing to society.

WHAT DO OTHER SOCIAL SCIENCES SAY?

Anthropologists say that behavior is learned by watching other human beings. What is learned is cumulative in a generational sense—one generation passes it on to the next generation. Social environment—groups—becomes important because individuals learn inside a cultural framework. The more people seek together in groups and the better they function the more individuals learn and the more they pass on to future generations.

Homo oeconomicus is synonymous with individuals behaving selfish and seeking profit, but this theory is not upheld by studies outside economics such as psychology. Economists have defended their stand by saying that people may be generous only if they expect to be rewarded at a later stage, but neither this second line of defense is confirmed by studies outside economics. On the contrary, people are generous even if there is no prospect of later reward. Apparently generosity is built into our genes making it natural to share and help fellow human beings. One study looked at babies and concluded that watching people they showed a preference for figures that helped others.

Sociology comes to similar conclusions. The survival of the individual depends on the group he/she belongs to. Inside the group individuals may behave selfishly, but there is a clear recognition that cooperating and supporting each other enhances the survival prospect of the group and each member compared to groups where such behavior is less dominant.

CONCLUSIONS

The combination of economics' current problems and findings in other social sciences undermining or outright contradicting economic theory leaves no other option than bringing in interdisciplinary and intersectoral analyses. This kind of thinking highlights ability to combine and mix, predict consequences of doing something in one sector on other societal sectors and multitasking. Social networking finds its place by offering technology to combine information and knowledge without a deeper analysis and understanding. In short: A move from specialization to multitasking and combinations. The loser in this game is basic research and objectivity. The winner is multitasking and subjectivity.

When things are "normal", future behavioral patterns can be deducted from past behavior. In the midst of transformation things are not "normal" so people change behavior, making past behavior inconsequential. What we learn by watching other people and recalling our own reaction lose accuracy because past behavior was guided by events and surroundings not existing anymore. In "normal" times belief and observations coincided, reinforcing each other stabilizing the behavior of the individual. In changing times the opposite happens; the individual cannot handle events contradicting belief—what is termed cognitive dissonance blurs the picture paralyzing individuals.

For economics this makes modelling—the plinth of modern economics—close to a useless instrument. Modelling presumes cause-effect relationships to be stable or predictable repeatable which is only the case if past behavior is repeated and in times of change that is not the case—hence wrong forecasts from economic models.

Big data may provide the bridge to a new way of thinking by obliterating shutters isolating each social science in its own ivory tower. Utilizing big data reveals interdependence among various factors without a prior theory. Currently deduction confines economists to form a theory to be tested through appropriate economic tools. From theory to test to realities. Big data reverses that order starting with realities to be tested by common sense is followed by a theory if the interrelationship holds and passes the test.

We move from deduction having ruled social sciences to induction. Deduction narrows possibilities or alternatives as they need to conform to theory while induction is not constrained by a theory.

The swing around from deduction to induction combined with interdisciplinary and intersectoral analyses would provide us with much better tools to predict and forecast for the very reason that they will be much better to read and interpret human behavior.

REFERENCES

1. (2008) An Essay on the Principle of Population (Oxford Classics). Oxford Paperbacks 2008, Oxford Paperbacks, Oxford (First published in 1798).
2. Meadows, D.H. (2004) Limits to Growth: The 30-Year Update. 3rd Edition, Chelsea Green Publishing, London (First published in 1972).
3. FAO (2006) 40 Countries Face Food Shortages Worldwide. 9 October 2006, Rome. http://www.fao.org/Newsroom/en/news/2006/1000416/index.html
4. Welt (2011) Diese Firmen Bestimmen Schicksal der Weltwirtschaft. http://www.welt.de/wirtschaft/article13680359/Diese-Firmen-bestimmen-Schicksal-der-Weltwirtschaft.html

5. Johnson, S. (2012) Big Banks Are Hazardous to U.S. Financial Health. Bloomberg, 2 September 2012. http://www.bloomberg.com/news/2012-09-02/big-banks-are-hazardous-to-u-s-financial-health.html
6. Reuters (2014) Top Four U.S. Wireless Carriers Increase Control of Market, Review Finds. 18 December 2014. http://www.reuters.com/article/usa-wireless-fcc-idUSL1N0U22PR20141219
7. Thomas Piketty (2014) Capital in the Twenty-First Century. Belknap Press, Harvard.http://dx.doi.org/10.4159/9780674369542
8. Economist (2014) The Third Great Wave. 4 October 2014. http://www.economist.com/news/special-report/21621156-first-two-industrial-revolutions-inflicted-plenty-pain-ultimately-benefited

Chapter 2

MASS SOCIETY, MASS CULTURE, AND MASS COMMUNICATION: THE MEANING OF MASS

Kurt Lang Gladys Engel Lang

University of Washington

INTRODUCTION

The concept of mass goes back a long way to characterize a society that consists of people somehow connected by communication while, at the same time, also dispersed in space and essentially detached from one another. Mass has also been a pejorative for critics of modern capitalist society and its culture. In the years after World War II, this latter use of the term became the target of a broadside attack by several highly credentialed scholars, who questioned its value as an analytic tool. This paper, starting with Ferdinand Tönnies, offers a brief overview of both the origins of the concept of mass and its subsequent refinement by French, German, and American sociologists into the mid-1930s. Distinguishing between its ideological connotations and the analytic use of the term helps us to focus on the most general and persistent effects of mass communication: expanding the range of common experience and making people more responsive to distant events. This effect is magnified by the ubiquity of mass media; practically no one, not even those who scorn them, can altogether escape their influence. As a scholarly discipline matures, aficionados begin to review its history less to gain new insights than to retrieve a past in danger of getting lost. So it is that in this paper we focus on the significance and history of "mass" in order to highlight its original meaning. The appellation does indeed go back a long way before its employment not only as a modifier of communication, but also as a means to express one's dislike of modern capitalist society and its culture. Yet, while its meaning, to be sure, has always been somewhat problematic, it was only after World War II that the concept became the target of a broadside attack by several highly credentialed scholars, who challenged its appropriateness as a descriptor of modern society, its culture, and its media audiences. These scholars cited certain facts that "mass society theorists" were said to have ignored. Examination of the literature on "mass" suggests that their criticisms had a distinctly ideological component, and that quite different versions of the concept had been painted with the same broad brush and occasional careless readings of text — small wonder that they found inconsistencies and some all-too-obvious exaggerations in the writings of these "mass society theorists." Rather than present a point-by-point refutation, we first examine the intellectual and political context that fueled their criticisms, and then follow this with a highly condensed overview of both the origins of the concept of "mass" and its refinement from the end of the 19th century to the mid-1930s, at which time the political Left was about to develop its own view of mass, mass society, and mass culture to counter that of conservatives. Our aim is to salvage the sociological meaning of the term "mass" from the surrounding ideological rhetoric with a focus on insights still relevant for today's study of mass communication. We begin with a quick look back at how "mass communication" came to denote characteristics that today most everyone takes for granted. When people speak of the media, they usually have in mind corporate bodies or government agencies whose access to modern technology enables them to disseminate the same uniform content to a geographically dispersed multitude. At first, this capability was confined to cheap print, and then later expanded to motion-pictures, both of which were still dependent on physical transport. This limitation did not extend to either radio or television, which, given their wide reach, were destined to become the media of mass communication par excellence. But to develop into mass communication, the new technology had to be employed to reach a large audience. As late as the end of the 1920s, Ernest W. Burgess (1886-1966), a University of Chicago sociologist whose interest was mostly in human ecology, could still write about the conquest of space by new forms of transportation and communication, such as the automobile, the motion picture, the airplane, and the radio, without even a single reference to the expansion in the size of audiences and its consequences (1929, p. 1072). Two years later, David O. Woodbury devoted a book (1931) to "communication at a distance," grouping mass media with personal communication forms, such as letters that rely on carriers, or with those which do not. Distance-communication nowadays would surely include networking via the Internet, which, when compounded and saturated with particular content, can reach the multitudes sought out by propagandists and public relations specialists. Be this as it may, Harold D. Lasswell (1902-1978), in his introduction to a voluminous bibliography on propaganda and promotional activities, noted that "[b]efore cheap printing and general literacy, before moving pictures and radio, the possibilities of applying stimuli simultaneously to masses were extremely restricted" (1935, p. 17). The Internet, though open to many uses, has this potential. The point we want to make is this: It took a while for scholars, concerned as they were with propaganda and its consequences, to embrace the idea that "propaganda regardless of definition, must be regarded as a special form of mass communication," one with rather invidious connotations (Willey, 1935, p. 195). The generic label offered by Willey, however fitting, proved to be a sleeper, taking more than a decade to come into general use.

From a sociological perspective, the most striking feature of modern communication technology is its capacity to expand social relations beyond the clan, the tribe, and the local community. While ancient empires were built on military force and the loyalty of a small number of chieftains to a central authority, the typical social unit today covers far more territory and embraces more people than could once have been thought possible. This expansion is not just a matter of size, but also one of density. Individuals different in background, orientation, and skill, clustered in and around urban centers, have become more interdependent, and also, though only indirectly, more active participants in political life. The centrality of communication in the development of a common identity was, of course, a tenet of the Chicago School, a group whose influence extended beyond the University of Chicago. It drew heavily on the writings of Ferdinand Tönnies (1855-1936), the first to attempt a systematic formulation of what was new and unprecedented about modern society. His classic treatise revolves around two fundamentally different types of relationships — Gemeinschaft and Gesellschaft. These two types could co-exist in the same society, but the balance between them was changing. As Tönnies described the change, the smaller, more natural community (Gemeinschaft), whose solidarity was based on consanguinity, was giving way to society (Gesellschaft), which exists as "a circle of people who, as a community, live and reside peacefully near one another but are not quintessentially connected but substantially detached and, while on the one hand they remain connected despite their detachment, they remain, on the other, detached despite their connectedness" ([1877] 1922, p. 39).2 In this kind of social unit, each person acts essentially for him or herself, yet remains dependent on others by way of exchange rather than by gift giving. As consanguinity ties weaken, social relations become ever more instrumental, voluntary, and consensual while the unity of the society revolves more and more around common territory, language, or shared history propagated first through print and subsequently through other forms of communication that mediate across great distances. Theodor Geiger (1891-1952), a Danish sociologist who, albeit erroneously, is often classified as a critic of the mass society concept, summed the consequences of technological development even more succinctly and more eloquently: "Today mutual dependence . . . exists among people, most of them strangers and personally indifferent to one another. What connects them are not the bonds of sympathy but the necessities of life" (1955, p. 79).3 Appeals to sentiments of sympathy to strengthen social solidarity no longer made sense to Geiger. The more pressing need was for people to recognize intellectually their objective interdependence; education had to be directed toward this goal. Restated in cultural and political terms, communication technology has led to a greater involvement of the masses, previously confined to the periphery of society, in the activities and ideas of its central institutions (Shils, [1962] 1975). Or, as Daniel Lerner (1957) put it, media exposure develops a capacity for empathy, without which participation in the thought life of a geographically extended society would be severely limited.

The new media have also affected culture. There has been a far-reaching transformation of the general way of life, particularly in how people spend their leisure hours and how they take part in celebratory occasions. Traditional folk art and customary recreational activities have been partly replaced by an unprecedented flood of symbolic goods produced for the market or sold to media organizations for dissemination to their audiences. The viability of artistic creations today is less dependent on aristocratic or state patronage than so-called "high" culture had been in the past. Without momentous advances in communication technology, such a transformation would have been inconceivable. In sum, "mass" has served as a sociologically meaningful and analytically useful category for describing certain audiences, kinds of society, and forms of cultural production. In what follows, we back this claim by reference to works in an intellectual tradition that many contemporaries seem to have forgotten or may never have known.

THE CRITICS OF "MASS"

The preceding sketch of the direction of social change, whether or not it finds universal acceptance, can serve as a background against which to judge the criticism that the concept of mass attracted in the 1950s. Knowing that controversy is the heartbeat of academic engagement, what nevertheless strikes us as mildly puzzling is the vehemence of this attack, with such respected scholars as Daniel Bell ([1956] 1959, 1962) and Edward Shils (1957, [1962] 1975) along with Raymond and Alice Bauer (1960) in the vanguard, on the usage of "mass" to characterize modern society and some of its cultural productions. Our questions are the following: What gave rise to their attacks, and why were they quite so impassioned? One answer, but only a partial one, can be found in the general sense of well-being that had taken hold, especially in America, after nearly two decades of depression and war. To be sure, areas of deep poverty remained even in the United States of America. Yet, no objective observer during this postwar period could have failed to recognize the rise in the general standard of living, the increase in home ownership, and the significant gains in the well-being of parts of the working-class — gains that came to a level where one could even speak of the "affluent worker" (Goldthorpe, 1968). Industrial expansion also facilitated the absorption of new arrivals displaced from the countryside or from abroad, many without special skills or unaccompanied by family, so that they were apt to feel lonely, even altogether lost, in an unfamiliar urban environment. Their predecessors, the ones who had provided the raw material from which the images of the mass had been constructed, had nearly dropped out of sight, and as living conditions improved, revised images became applicable. Especially important in reinforcing expectations of upward mobility were the generous benefits made available to returning war veterans. They opened new opportunities for higher education and, over time, led to higher rates of political participation and more sophisticated cultural consumption. These same years were also a period of relative domestic tranquility. Threats to public order from wildcat strikes, illegal seizures of property, demonstrations culminating in violent clashes with the police, and acts of terrorism had decreased significantly from peaks reached after WWI and during the Great Depression. All these had been harbingers of what Bell (1960) predicted, perhaps a bit prematurely, would be the end of ideology. In any event, the model of nameless masses on the margins of society no longer quite fit.

Second, a new and possibly greater perceived threat than civil strife came with the onset of the Cold War, a threat that persisted, in varying strength, for decades until the dissolution of the Soviet dictatorship. Theories of mass society came to be seen in a new light. Explanations of the vulnerability of politically and industrially advanced societies, such as Nazi Germany, in terms of rootless and restless masses as easy prey for agitators (see Lederer, 1940; Fromm, 1941) lost relevance while apprehension about Soviet expansion grew. In the meantime, social scientists remained on call in the ongoing propaganda contest, much as they had during the war against the Axis, and a good many, gradually and over time, were to tone down the highly critical views they had previously held of their own society. The clear superiority of Western democracy, hapless and messy as it might be, was invoked to counter the promise of equality and other arguments used by communists to win over the downtrodden everywhere. Marshaling evidence on the rich social relationships, the responsiveness of government, the exceptional achievements in science and technology, and the free reign their country had given to artistic creativity was a project in which those who took their citizen duties seriously were happy to participate. Third, perhaps their most convincing refutation of "mass society" was based on a cumulation of research findings about the continuing relevance of primary groups and personal networks, even for relationships believed to be dominated by an impersonal cash nexus or subject to rational management. Studies conducted quite independently of one another and in a variety of settings — such as the factory work floor (Roethlisberger & Dickson, 1934), urban slums (Whyte, 1945), the military (Stouffer et al., 1949; Shils & Janowitz, 1948), or bureaucratic organizations (Blau, 1955) — highlighted interpersonal relationships and group norms as influences on behavior strong enough to override, at least on occasion, formal organizational controls. Other studies of the voting public and of mass audiences subject to a plethora of persuasive communications depicted recipients neither as isolated nor as hapless captives of propagandists (Lazarsfeld, Berelson, & Gaudet, 1948; Bauer, 1958). Numerous small-group experiments, a genre just coming into its own, offered further evidence of the strength of group influences. Summaries of such research findings appeared in a Shils monograph on the "present state of American sociology," in which he hailed the rediscovery of the primary group (Shils, 1948), and in the literature review provided by Elihu Katz as a theoretical underpinning for findings, albeit less than conclusive, about the effect of personal influence on decisions people make in everyday life (Katz & Lazarsfeld, 1955). A parallel shift took place in the dominant paradigm for macro-politics. Sociologists, as well as political scientists, embraced pluralist models, in which power appears more dispersed than in the traditional dichotomy of élite versus the population at large. It led William Kornhauser (1959) to redefine mass society as nothing more than an abstraction that postulated a mass of isolated and alienated individuals whose relation to an authority, such as a totalitarian state, was the only bond to unite them. A mass society in this pure form exists only as the theoretical extreme on a continuum. It surely does not provide a true picture of American democracy, where élites are open to influence from a variety of competing interest groups with varying amounts of citizen participation, and where no one group has a monopoly of power. Post-war critics attacked the "mass society" concept by depicting all its exponents as subject to the same misconceptions. Daniel Bell, quite rightly, discerned inconsistencies in the meanings given the term by various authors and went on to charge that the "theory" had no "organizing principle — other than the highly general concept of 'breakdown of values' — that put the individual elements of the theory together in a logical, meaningful — let alone historical — manner" ([1956] 1959, p. 22). What the theories articulated were the dissatisfactions of conservatives still yearning for an orderly past while neo-Marxists, as Shils (1957) had pointed out, developed their own version of the ills found in modern society. Many formulations about mass society — on both the Right and the Left — did indeed carry considerable ideological ballast. But so did the critiques. Bell's was first presented at a conference sponsored by the Congress for Cultural Freedom and then published, somewhat shortened, in Commentary magazine — both venues indicative of the Cold War mentality that had helped to inspire them. Pointing this out is not meant as a rebuttal of Bell's criticisms, but only to underline the ideology behind his argument, which he adorned with citations lumping together a variety of theorists, as if there were no space between, on the one hand, efforts by sociologists — such as Georg Simmel, Karl Mannheim, and Herbert Blumer — to specify the nature of a "mass" and, on the other, the philosophical and social pessimism to be found in the writings of Nietzsche, Spengler, Ortega y Gasset, Marcel Gabriel, and other conservatives, not even to mention Adorno and others of the Frankfurt school. Differences and contradictions within so heterogeneous a collection are what one would expect. Concerning at least one sociologist, Herbert Blumer, Bell was off the mark, when he took him to task for a sentence he quoted out of context. The mass, reads the quotation, "has no social organization, no body of custom and tradition, no established set of rules or rituals, no organized group of sentiments, no structure of status roles and no established leadership" (Blumer, [1936] 1951, p. 186, cited in Bell, [1956] 1959). What Bell missed, or misread, is that, for Blumer, the mass referred not to the whole society nor the "masses," but to a specific form of elementary collective behavior within society, limited in time and directed toward some object of attention. The object that can attract a temporary mass typically

arises outside the domain of local group life. . . . The mass that behaves . . . is made up of detached individuals. These individuals, to be true, have their own local attachments, share in convivial association, belong to primary groups, live and act to a great extent in accordance with conventional patterns, but [only] insofar as they belong to a mass, is it as alienated individuals in a new area of life not [adequately] covered by local group tradition. (Blumer, 1935, p. 118) There is not even a hint that Blumer, in defining a "mass," meant to depict American society or modern society in general as "atomized" and its people as estranged from one another. His intent was to distinguish between the behavior of a crowd and the behavior of a mass audience. The criticisms of the Bauers were more focused on the model of communication that they imputed to the "critics of mass society." They challenged three premises that, implicitly or explicitly, underlay a model abandoned by researchers cognizant of the cumulation of evidence. The premises were "(1) that informal communications play a minor role, if any, in modern society; (2) that the audience of mass communication is a 'mass' in the sense of being socially 'atomized'; (3) that content and effect may be equated" (Bauer & Bauer, 1960, p. 13). As to the first, obviously absurd premise, one can only wonder whosoever would claim that people had stopped conversing. As to the second premise, the quotation from Blumer, just cited, should suffice as a refutation while, as to the third, surely, recognizing that content matters and that messages can be framed to maximize impact falls far short of "equating" content with effect. Taken together, the three, as stated by the Bauers, seem little more than a strawman all too easily knocked down, even without research evidence. On the related issue of mass culture — whether the stream of entertainment available via the media has lowered taste — the Bauers judged the question still open, because data about the past sufficiently reliable for a comparison would be hard to find. They did, however, make a reasonable case that there is more "high" culture today than in earlier historical periods, even if it might be overwhelmed by a still greater increase in mass-produced popular culture. The last issue is the one that also troubled Edward Shils ([1962] 1975), who railed against the image of a "homogeneous" mass, leveled downward to the lowest denominator, alienated from society, egotistic, amoral, and without any serious beliefs and loyalties beyond an occasional zealous attachment to some radical movement or ideology. His argument, highly theoretical, is tightly reasoned. The indisputable decline in the sacredness of authority and the dispersal of primordial ties, formerly the basis for social solidarity, have gone hand in hand with a clear movement toward inclusion of the entire population into society. The mass of people today, he opined, indubitably experience greater affinity with the central institutions of their society than they did in the past, and the élites, for their part, have come to share many objects and standards with the multitude. These three developments have, together, shifted the center of gravity toward the individual. Shils did not specifically mention the role of communication in this shift, but apparently had it in mind when he acknowledged that, while there is today "perhaps a greater homogeneity than in the much less loosely integrated societies of the past," the complexity of modern society precludes that complete homogeneity perceived by the critics of "mass society" (1975, p. 101), a term he abhorred, but for which he was unable to find a satisfactory substitute.

Origins of the Term

To explicate the meaning and significance of "mass," we turn first to the work of Gustave LeBon (1841-1931). Why start with LeBon, whose writings are no longer taken very seriously? And why not go farther back: to de Tocqueville, who warned of the threat of equality to liberty; to Karl Marx and his characterization of the proletariat in capitalist society; to John Stuart Mill's concerns over the rise of mediocrity; to Matthew Arnold's apprehension over the decline of standards, to Hippolyte Taine's inquiry into the motivations behind mass movements, or to any number of others? The answer is that, even without a mention of LeBon's name, his descriptions of the mass in La psychologie des foules, first published in 1895, and in some subsequent writings, have pervaded disputes on the subject ever since. Specifically, his warning that "the age we are about to enter will in truth be the era of crowds" ([1895] 1916, p. 3) resonated widely, coming as it did at a time when working class parties were gaining ground and Western societies were still reeling from the turbulence that came in the wake of rapid industrialization and mass migration to cities. His book went through 26 printings and was translated into many languages. Although generally remembered as a treatise on crowds, and mostly cited in that connection, it is as much about the advent of mass society as it is about crowds, riots, and mobs. LeBon, to be sure, couched his explanations in psychological terms — contagion, loss of individuality, and regression to a more primitive mental state were his favorite terms. What qualifies the book as a treatise on the mass is LeBon's conflation of crowd behavior with that of the larger mass, as when he, for example, allows that "thousands of isolated individuals may acquire at certain moments, and under the influence of certain violent emotions — such, for example, as a great national event — the characteristics of a psychological crowd." The mere agglomeration of people, however, is not sufficient to cause the disappearance of the conscious personality and turn the feelings and thoughts of a multitude in the same new direction ([1896] 1926, p. 26).4 Nor is "their simultaneous presence on the same spot . . . indispensable. The action of contagion may be felt from a distance under the influence of events which give all minds an individual trend and the characteristics peculiar to crowds" ([1896] 1926, p. 144). Crowds are recruited from an already rebellious people; a local uprising, as it spreads, develops into a mass movement. For LeBon, the proximate crowd and the diffuse crowd are generically similar. Participants in both are slaves to the impulses they receive ([1896] 1926, p. 41), some so ephemeral that they scarcely exist for more than a day, and even "the more important ones scarcely outlive a generation" (1926, p. 167). This is where communication enters. LeBon assigned primary responsibility for the fickleness of opinion to mass circulation newspapers. The attention for which they typically clamor moves them to monitor and, at the same time, court and reflect the opinion of their readership. They act as the vehicle through which ordinary people (i.e., the "masses") exert influence on statesmen, whose fear of ever-shifting public opinion, "des opinions populaires," is so great that the press tends, more and more, "to become the supreme guiding principle in politics" ([1896] 1926, p. 170) and also, by implication, in other sectors of society. "Contagion," once having done its work among the lower classes, reaches the higher ones, so that in the end, "every opinion adopted by the populace always ends in implanting itself with great vigour in the higher social strata" ([1896] 1926, p. 146). With this last statement, LeBon seems to anticipate Shils, albeit with one huge difference: LeBon sees everyone and everything, including culture, dragged down in the process. More deserving of continuing attention, though largely overshadowed by LeBon, is Gabriel Tarde (1843-1904). He had a less psychological and more sociological view of the role of the mass in society. The main question addressed in his writings is this: What is the nature of the social bond that unites a multitude of individuals who "do not come in contact, do not meet or hear each other; [but] are all sitting in their own homes scattered over a vast territory, reading the same newspaper?" This is essentially the same question that Tönnies had framed and sought to answer in terms of the shifting balance between Community and Society. Tarde looked for answers in a different direction. For him, the bond that forged some kind of unity among a mass of geographically dispersed inhabitants lay "in their simultaneous conviction or passion and in their awareness of sharing at the same time an idea or a wish with a great number of other men [sic]" ([1898] 1969, p. 278). His resort to "imitation" as the all-pervasive social mechanism behind every meeting of minds, friendly or hostile, should not distract us from his perceptive diagnosis of the "currents of opinion." They emerge, definitely not from imitation between people meeting on the streets or at a public square, but within a population whose individual members, while sitting in homes that are scattered over a wide territory, are reading the same newspaper. Without a mass readership, there could be no public opinion other than in salons and cafes, plus sporadic input from crowds limited to the range within which a human voice can be heard. Tarde looked upon the press as the major medium of public communication,5 but he never claimed that it could ever substitute for the direct informal discourse within families or among neighbors, friends, and working associates. Rather, three mutually auxiliary inventions — printing, the railroad, and the telegraph — had enabled the multitude to interact more intensively and "combined to create the formidable power of the press . . . that prodigious telephone which has so inordinately enlarged the former audiences of orators and preachers" and in the course of it, allowed all sorts of publicists and promoters to exercise leadership over the public. Here, Tarde may seem to be echoing LeBon, but he certainly was not. In describing the present as "the era of the public or publics," he was envisioning a more pluralistic society. He firmly rejected his predecessor's formulation about this being the era of crowds while describing the present as "the era of the public or publics, and that is a very different thing." One can, and always does, belong simultaneously to several publics, but one cannot be part of more than one crowd at one time, so that "the gradual substitution of publics for crowds . . . is always accompanied by progress in tolerance" ([1898] 1969, p. 281). On some occasions, to be sure, an overly excited public deteriorates into a crowd, but such a "fall from public to crowd, though extremely dangerous, is fairly rare . . . [and] it remains evident that the opposition of two publics, always ready to fuse along their indistinct boundaries, is a lesser danger to social peace than the encounter of two opposing crowds" ([1898] 1969, p. 282). One of the great achievements of the press was to move conversation beyond small talk to "bigger" things, to persons and images, as we might say today, that have caught the public's attention. Tarde was among the first to recognize that, to quote him once again, the "increasing similarity of simultaneous conversations in an ever more vast geographical domain is one of the most important characteristics of our time for it explains for the most part the increasing authority of opinion versus tradition and even of reason." He also recognized in the growing dissimilarity of conversations that follow one another both one cause of the instability of opinion and a counter-weight to its power. And these opinions, as he stated by way of a footnote, be they stable or changing, testify to the immense social progress in recent years. Classes and professions coalesce, and the nation becomes "real" only on the day when a sustained conversation between individuals belonging to quite different professions and classes becomes the societal norm ([1898] 1969, p. 312; [1898] 1904, p. 104).

The press takes on the additional role of mediating between legislative institutions. Being in continuous and instant touch, reflecting the ongoing and reciprocal action and reaction within a population far larger, and more dispersed, than the local constituency of a member of parliament or the residents of a capital city, like Paris, the press brings together the multiplicity of opinions across the country and, over time, consolidates them into the composite that comes to stand for the collective opinion of the entire country ([1898] 1969, p. 77). Notwithstanding such an achievement, clearly unprecedented, some things remain the same. No matter how many "artificial" groups (Tarde's term) rise to defend some common interest — of an industry, a region, an occupation, a political tendency, or whatever else — their existence does not diminish the social value of the deep attachments most people have to their family or locality. Anyone who doubts this, so Tarde contended, would be committing a grave error: "Far from it: to become civilized is to find more affinities with others each day. The increased social field requires a better human heart, greater and more tender, just as a larger garden requires more abundant water" ([1898] 1969, p. 130). The power of family ties remains undiminished, even as these new groupings gain importance. Surely, Tarde's concept of mass has little, if anything, in common with the parody of "mass" that some critics of mass-society theory have used to discredit it.

Mass Society: Further Development of the Concept

By addressing the concept of mass and the role of the public in the management of mass society in the way he did, Tarde charted a path for others to follow. Brief sketches of various efforts to build and elaborate on his work are grouped here under four headings: society and collective behavior, the rebellious masses, masses and public opinion, and the turn to propaganda.

Society and Collective Behavior

Tarde's most immediate successor was Robert E. Park (1864-1944), whose name is closely linked to the Chicago school of sociology. Collective behavior, as Park defined it, subsumes the processes and interactions that give rise to certain recognizable, usually ephemeral, social formations — crowds, masses, and currents of public opinion. From this perspective, crowds form as a spontaneous coming together of people into more than normally intense interaction, and they should "be viewed as the result of a specific sociological process whose general characteristics are those which generate collective attention" (Park, [1902] 1972, p. 45). He notes, taking cues directly from Tarde, that whereas a crowd is limited in size "by the length to which a voice will carry or the distance that the eye can survey," a public develops through contagion without direct contact (Park & Burgess, [1921] 1969, p. 868). This lack of contact does not mean that the individuals who make up a public are isolated, that they exist only as part of an anonymous mass. Quite the contrary:

In the larger realm of politics and in the small world of intimate social life, certain general concerns that dominate thoughts and conversation are always present. . . . Thus collective attention appears as a process in which the group acts upon itself. (Park, [1902] 1972, p. 46) Even modern advertising achieves its "desired effect more from interaction between people than from direct suggestion" (ibid., p. 45).

Here again, Park adopts Tarde's concept of the public as developing out of several diffuse "crowds" of people or groups. Participants are transformed into self-conscious partisans by the opposition they encounter. Viewed as a form of collective behavior, so-called public opinion is generally nothing more than a naive collective impulse which can be manipulated by catchwords. Modern journalism, which is supposed to instruct and direct public opinion by reporting and discussing events, usually turns out to be simply a mechanism for controlling collective attention. The "opinion" formed in this manner shows a form that is logically similar to the judgment derived from unreflective perception: the opinion is formed directly and simultaneously as information is received. (ibid., p. 57) In this respect, a public is quite unlike a crowd that does not move beyond a common awareness. The words and actions expressed in public opinion, insofar as they result from discussion among individuals with opposing positions, will be based, more or less, "upon the presentation of facts" (ibid., p. 57). And finally, what is ultimately accepted as public opinion does not have to be "acceptable to each individual member of the public to the same degree. It is much more an opinion or an attitude which is external to every individual and which is viewed as something objective" (ibid., p. 59). It is, to paraphrase Park, more like an abstract norm to which people concede, much as, for example, they accept without much question the validity of scientific discoveries about which they themselves may know very little. Along a somewhat different line, Charles Horton Cooley (1864-1929), of the University of Michigan, noted that, with the expansion of consciousness and rational cooperation, tradition, which has a long extension in time but covers very little space, has to compete with thought and practices that arrive "sidewise, as it were, from contemporaries . . . [but] may endure only for a day" ([1909] 1929, p. 335). The unity so produced suggested to Cooley a form of collective behavior distinct from that of either a crowd or a public; in short, what others have called a "mass."

German sociologists sought to define a crowd or mass not as a process or in behavioral terms, but formally, as a basic sociological category. This holds especially for Georg Simmel (1858-1919), whose major interest was in the formal characteristics of social relationships, not in the dynamics stressed by Tarde and some others. Simmel's definition of a mass turned on numbers, and numbers alone. He saw these as having the same consequences in all settings. The unity of an organization, political party, social movement — it does not matter which — derives from some similarity in all the individual participants. Because "what is common to many must be accessible even to [the] lowest and most primitive among them," the more widely the common property that unites them is shared, the more it is destined to be the simplest, lowest, most primitive, least valued — inferior to the richness of the individual personality ([1908] 1950b, p. 93). This explanation makes obvious that individuals, when part of a mass, respond only to simple ideas, are more moved by emotional appeals than reason, rarely reach consent on a positive aim but prefer instead to unite in opposition to something (1950b, p. 397), and differ sharply from aristocracies that never include more than a minority. And, for Simmel, whatever is true of a mass or a mass organization holds true even more so for people crowded together in close physical proximity.

Passages such as the above have induced some critics of "mass society theory" to locate Simmel in the same conservative camp as LeBon. A more careful reading of texts reveals that he actually saw in the "mass" a liberating influence: its unity, by virtue of its size, consists "not of the total individualities of its members, but only of those fragments of each of them in which he [sic] coincides with all others" (1950, p. 33). Since small groups absorb more of their members' personalities than larger group, every increase in size grants individuality more latitude. Simmel went farther still in his embrace of modern "mass" society when, in an altogether different context, he lauded the individualism fostered by a monetarized economy: "Money, for its part, inasmuch as it converts impulsive-subjective procedures [Verfahrensweisen] into impersonal ones that are subject to objective norms is still a breeding ground for economic individualism and egotism" (Simmel, 1907, p. 490). Money also opens new opportunities for individual development, although those opportunities are limited to the intellectually motivated or the economically comfortable. Both economic and non-economic individualism were also being fostered by the more impersonal lifestyle that flourished in the modern metropolis ([1903] 1950a, p. 423). Because of Simmel's many-sided mix of opinions and observations, he does not quite fit into the category of "mass society theorist" as depicted by some critics. Among other efforts at defining the mass (see Vleugels, 1926), the most ambitious is an article by Gerhard Colm (1897-1968), published in the famous Archiv für Sozialwissenschaft und Sozialpolitik. This seldom-recalled sociologist endeavored to replace the loose colloquial notion of the mass or the masses with a theoretical construct devoid of ideology. References to the mental unity of members which, in some form after all, characterizes every kind of grouping, do not suffice for Colm because they fail to define the special nature of the bond around which a mass forms. His definition singles out the cumulation of shared experiences [Wir-Erlebnis] — disappointments, deprivations, grievances, etc. — that may ultimately unite people to whom most other channels for pursuing some objective or general goal, often poorly stated, are closed. He does not mention numbers as a determinant and actually seems closer to Park than to Simmel, neither of whom he cites, in observing that the feelings of identity in a mass are vague in comparison with other group formations. It is when the mass as a whole moves into action that the momentum inherent in this collectivity is superimposed on the individual (1924, p. 688). Other attributes of this mass are its homogeneity, its lack of structure, and its inability to accomplish very much. The mass as a mass, he explains, cannot bargain or strike a deal without the leaders who really act outside the mass. Masses typically form in historical circumstances where the recent shattering of social relationships has left many people adrift. Mass action directed against existing authorities then, in most instances, gains in appeal (1924, p. 692).

Rebellious Masses

Mass uprisings, disruptions of public order, and demonstrations causing the fall of governments — events that had spurred the diatribes of LeBon — presented a challenge to social scientists. Colm did not proceed beyond recognizing the mass as a reservoir for crowds during uprisings against existing authorities. It remained for Theodor Geiger (1891-1952) to offer a sociologically grounded analysis of the actions the mass carries out. He begins by distinguishing between the "mass" and the "masses," declaring that the two are not identical, and that the term "masses" had become an over-used epithet for the working class, which was indeed the recruitment reservoir for the "mass." Rather, the mass had to be viewed as a "collectivity [sozialer Verband] supported by the destructively revolutionary multitude, for which up to now there has been no other name" (Geiger, 1926, p. 37). Such a mass arises not only in conventional politics; it also has to be understood as a protest directed toward community and against society — as in the meanings Tönnies assigned these terms (1926, p. 168). The unity of purpose of the mass is evidenced in demonstrations, protests, strikes, seizures of property — actions that, although local, are nevertheless conditioned by the existence of a larger, more dispersed mass, encompassing a diversity of individuals, all of whom, being similarly situated in society, have experienced similar frustrations and grievances. Class conflict provides the context. Robert Michels (1876-1936) and, subsequently, Hendrik de Man (1885-1953), two other sociologists of the Left,8 explicitly warned against imagining that the followers of the socialist parties were "nothing but a large homogeneous, uniform gray mass ignoring the many gradations and specialties" (Michels, [1926] 1987, p. 89). Only through organizations do these working-class people, who may not even be fully familiar with the platform or program of their party, develop a tolerably homogeneous ideology. As Geiger put it, "no revolution is carried solely by the mass — rather the mass has only one function conferred on it — destruction" (1926, p. 57). This conception of mass movements and mass action developed with reference to working-class opposition accords with the negativity Simmel imputed to a mass. It also seems to fit the category of elementary collective behavior as defined by Park, but otherwise, it is of no great help in clarifying the nature of the mass as it functions within the context of mass communication.

Masses and Public Opinion

With the epithet of the Great Society, Graham Wallas (1858-1932) meant to evoke an image of a social universe expanded to the point where people "find themselves working and thinking and feeling in relation to an environment, which, both in its world-wide extension and in its intimate connection with all sides of human existence, is without precedence in the history of the world" (Wallas, [1914] 1917, p. 3). It is simply too diverse, too heterogeneous, to be held together or to act in accord by feelings of sympathy between people. For any consensus or unity of will to emerge, there must be some meeting of minds among people separated not only in space, but also by time. This could be achieved, Wallas averred, only through intellectual activity that "sharpen[s] the mental picture which every member of the Great Society forms of that larger multitude of his contemporaries, whom he will never see, but whose lives he must necessarily influence" (1917, p. 154). Leaders, too, must learn how to gain support from constituents. The complexity of social organization and our expanded environment require that policies be more consciously shaped. No longer can we rely on the vague impulses to which people — in crowds or in an agitated mass — ordinarily react from day to day; nor can we rely on the simplistic ideas that parade as genuine thought but really are nothing more than some by-product, whether of religion, of tradition, or of someone's copyright, administrative position, or private wealth. These are, after all, what generates wild electoral contests, war fevers, and other negative outcomes. They can only be countered by what Wallas called the Organization of Thought (1917, p. 227). Framing the issue of public competence — the very issue that would later preoccupy Walter Lippmann, John Dewey, and Karl Mannheim — in positive terms, Wallas distanced himself from the contemporary crowd psychology expounded in Britain by William McDougall and Wilfred Trotter. The Individual Thought, which takes place in silence and solitude, relying only on personal memory and imagination, no longer worked. The solution of problems required the Organized Thought, which includes the entire stock of knowledge in which social arrangements are grounded and only develops by way of discussion and communication. The requirement for participation is to have a large body of knowledge in common, . . . be familiar with the peculiar strength and weakness of each of the others and, above all, . . . be influenced by the same desire to follow the truth 'whithersoever the argument may lead.' (Wallas, 1917, p. 242) Every adult member of the Great Society belongs, to some degree, to the vast impersonal Thought Organization that has been created by modern means of communication. That our more personal Thought-Organizations work even tolerably well is, indeed, mainly due to the fact that the members of Parliament, Municipal Councillors, Government Officials, and Company Directors bring to their meetings minds already saturated by those statements and arguments about the world beyond the reach of their senses, which reach them through newspapers and books. (Wallas, 1917, p. 280) Although people in general look to these same sources to set the framework for some conversations, Wallas cautioned against confusing the two levels of public discourse: [the] impersonal Organisation [of Thought] with the personal communication which takes place when men who live in the same street or travel in the same conveyance, converse with each other; and to speak, for instance, of the 'public opinion' of a new suburb, where no one knows his neighbor and each season-ticket holder reads his newspaper in silence in the morning train, as if it were due to the same process as the 'public opinion' of an agricultural village on the day after some event which every householder has discussed with every other. (Wallas, 1917, p. 281) It would help more if society were better able to provide education for ordinary citizens as a precondition for more popular participation in the larger public discourse.

The Turn to Propaganda

Wallas completed The Great Society before the mass disillusionment that followed the senseless slaughter during four years of warfare had taken hold. That WWI should have enjoyed popular support as long as it did, and even been welcomed at its outset by some of the more educated as actually liberating, raised questions about the competence of the multitude. How could people have been initially so aroused, and then held captive to a cause that squandered their countries' resources and drained them of their young manpower? Critics of the war fixed on a new culprit — propaganda. There was an outpouring of exposes concerning monstrous falsehoods about enemy atrocities and the patriotic appeals that had emanated from the people's own government (see Nicolai, 1920; Bornecque, 1921; Baschwitz, 1923; Lasswell, 1927; Ponsonby, 1928). Among the most thoughtful of this genre were two books — Public Opinion (1922) and The Phantom Public (1925) — both by Walter Lippmann (1889-1974), who had studied with Wallas. The point of departure for Lippmann was the simple psychological proposition spelled out in Public Opinion, the earlier of his two books, that people make decisions and act on the basis of information about the world. The proposition applies no less to decisions in the public sphere than to those in private life. Yet, the world that people confront is altogether too big, too complex, with too many things happening all at the same time to give them the William Jamesian "direct acquaintance" with anywhere near all relevant facts. No one, even under the best of circumstances, is positioned to experience more than a tiny slice of the events that rivet national attention. In order to navigate their way through the larger universe, people construct a rudimentary model, some sort of mental map, from what they read in the press and, increasingly since Lippmann wrote, from the newer mass media. All of us — eminent leaders, statesmen, and law-makers no less than ordinary citizens — piece together our picture of the environment from what other people have observed and reported, supplemented by what each imagines for him or herself. Lippmann coined a new word, stereotypes, to stand for the pictures that people carry in their heads. Once they take shape, stereotypes act like a screen that inserts itself between people and the more complex reality, including the light in which group actions and public events are perceived. The resultant picture is always refracted, not only by propaganda and manipulation of the news through formal and informal censorship, but equally by omissions and misunderstandings on the part of recipients. These are caused "by physical and social barriers [to communication] . . . by scanty attention, by the poverty of language, by distraction, by unconscious constellations of feeling, by wear and tear, violence, monotony" (1922, p. 76). This list, meant to be merely illustrative rather than exhaustive, anticipates the "mediating factors" that members of a later generation, believing that they had come on something new, would cite in support of a theorem about the limited effects of mass communication. Lippmann further surmised that the direct and immediate impact of what people see, read, or hear about may be small, but the emotions stirred by these impressions tend to persist, especially when attached to some symbol — a name, a slogan, a cause, or a party — that serves as the rallying point for some multitude. The power of such a mass, or whatever one calls it, is nevertheless limited. People, if there are enough of them agreeing to act together, can occasionally, through strikes, boycotts, or mass demonstrations, resist what they do not like or coerce those who obstruct what they desire. But by mass action nothing can be constructed, devised, negotiated, or administered. . . . The limit of direct [mass] action is for all practical purposes the power to say Yes or No on an issue presented to the mass. (1922, p. 229).

Implementing what people clamor for and making sure that they reap the full benefits of any concession remains a task for leaders and spokesmen with special skills. To believe otherwise, as Lippmann put it most forcefully in The Phantom Public, is to subscribe to a "false ideal of democracy," based on a misleading fiction that all citizens can think and act as if they were office holders. They clearly cannot. Noble as it may be as an ideal, detailed input into policy by everyone is unrealizable, not because citizens are incompetent, but because of the unbridgeable difference between insiders, located where they have information on which they are positioned to act, and outsiders, who, while they may observe and judge though only from a distance, are too preoccupied with other things to develop expertise on the many complex issues government agencies deal with from day to day. And when the people do intervene, they are often manipulated for some partisan end (1925, p. 155). The "engineering of consent" and the proliferation of professionals skilled in its techniques were a great concern to Lippmann. He believed that the public, if only people were to use their limited knowledge correctly, could exercise some real power in public affairs without falling victim to propagandists. Lippmann, it seems, was not as unmitigated a pessimist as some take him to have been. An alternate, but not inconsistent, explanation of the ease with which masses can be misled was offered by Karl Mannheim (1893-1947), a refugee sociologist from Germany clearly perturbed by the strong electoral showing of the Nazis and the apparent mass support they were enjoying since their takeover of his industrially and politically advanced country. Mannheim's diagnosis stressed the effect of technology, not only on communication, but on society generally. Demands for specialization increase the interdependence among its component parts; for such a complex social system to work, the cogs have to mesh. Reason applied to technology, he argued, is primarily functional, focused only on the adaptation of means and tasks to an already determined objective. It trumps a more genuinely creative substantive rationality necessary for an evaluation of the ends and of the principles that shape them, so that "[with] each new act to fit in, the average person gives up a part of his [or her] intellectual autonomy . . ." (1935, p. 36). It is not, Mannheim was careful to say, that the world has become less rational, only that "irrationality" used to be more confined to the private sphere, but, given the fundamental democratization that modern societies have undergone, it is no longer so confined (1935, p. 19). Now that they have the franchise, the general populace — the once passive masses — play a more active role in politics than ever before. Their all-too-evident susceptibility to emotional propaganda signals the disproportionality between requirements of rational governance on the one hand, and an absence of organizations to mediate between the élites and the population at large on the other. Older, more "organic" publics have been replaced by a public that is "atomized" — not to the degree imputed by the mass society critics, but only in the very specific sense of lacking the dense network of organizations through which the people in liberal democracies (he cites England as an example) make themselves heard. The more such mediating groups are short-circuited, the easier it becomes to rally the multitude behind some vague cause.

Certainly, by the end of the 1930s, if not sooner, propaganda defined as "the manipulation of symbols to control controversial attitudes" (Lasswell & Bienenstock, 1939, p. 10), was recognized as indispensable, even in a democracy, for achieving any — self-serving or laudatory — political end.9 More and more leaders, whether of business or citizen associations, had their own public relations staffs. Socalled experts in persuasion made full use of the tools that a new breed of empirically-oriented social scientists were putting into their hands. Psychologists, sociologists, political scientists, practitioners — even historians and journalists — all contributed to an understanding of how propaganda worked. Many of these studies were "defensive," intended to alert people to its presence and, above all, to inoculate them against falsehoods and tricks used to mislead a gullible public. A major center for this research was the Institute of Propaganda Analysis in New York City. It sponsored studies of content and how messages were crafted to exploit the vulnerabilities of audiences, but it was less involved with the empirical investigation of actual effects. The same fears fueled studies of propaganda during WWII, which later supplied grist for a misleading fiction: that communication scholars had falsely depicted the mass media as "all-powerful" persuaders and manipulators of rootless and alienated individuals. Actually, as noted by two researchers involved in research on psychological warfare during the war, the nature of government propaganda shifted away from overtly moralistic and emotional appeals and toward more factual presentation (Kris & Leites, 1947). The trend confirms the power of Lippmann's insight about the power of information that is experienced only via the media. "Factual" misrepresentation can be hard to detect, even by experts, and still more so by the multitude of lay people, the bystanders to the political conflicts played out on the narrow arena that the media of mass communication provide.

Mass Culture

Culture has to do with the content and quality of collective life. A distinction between esteemed culture, with its rich and subtle meanings requiring cultivation, and the culture that succeeds on the market has long been recognized. The latter is often maligned by literati as "merely popular," hence destined to be soon forgotten, which has, in fact, been the fate of many such creations and performances. "Mass culture" has come into wide use as a term deprecating the value of commercially marketed arts and entertainment packaged to appeal to people in particular demographic categories. Media managers are inclined to perceive their audiences as a statistical mass, paying little attention to people's vital needs or capacities for development. Much criticism of mass culture has expressed a concern, most prevalent among conservatives, about the influence of the masses and their alleged propensity to intervene in just about everything, imposing their own vulgar views on others while neither making any demands on themselves nor respecting, or even showing proper regard, for the standards of a more discriminating minority. Germans designate this state of affairs as Vermassung — massification would be an English equivalent, but is too awkward to enter parlance. Attacks on contemporary culture from the Left have taken a different tack. These once were aimed at the deficiency of cultural opportunities for the working class, given a system where everything, including standards for recreation and leisure, are largely set by people focused only on profits. Capitalism and Its Culture by Jerome Davis (1891-1979), a Marxist sociologist and exponent of this viewpoint, exemplifies this genre. It contains not even a single reference to "mass culture" (Davis, 1935). The traditional Left, looking ahead to the development of a genuine working-class culture, had pinned its hopes on variants of the Proletkult, as practiced for a while in the Soviet Union, to encourage workers to be culturally creative, and to push writers, movie-makers, and visual artists to feature proletarians as chief protagonists in their works. Not until the 1940s did the neo-Marxist Left, led by the refugees of the Frankfurt school of sociology, but also harking back to the nearly forgotten Antonio Gramsci, fashion its own radical critique of mass culture as the product of a cultural industry. Few intellectuals propagated the élitist view quite as doggedly as the renowned José Ortega y Gasset (1883-1955), an outspoken conservative whose name has often been linked to that of LeBon. Ortega y Gasset openly expressed his disdain for the unschooled, whom he saw enamored by cultural objects with no real worth. To him, "mass" denoted not a particular social class, but a certain kind of person found among all classes, who, among other shortcomings, had no real appreciation of art: [T]o the majority of people, aesthetic pleasure means a state of mind which is essentially undistinguishable from their ordinary behavior. It differs merely in accidental qualities, being perhaps less utilitarian, more intense, and free from painful consequences. But the object towards which their attention and, consequently, all their other mental activities are directed — people and passions — is the same as in daily life. By art they understand a means through which they are brought in contact with interesting human affairs. Artistic forms proper — figments, fantasy — are tolerated only if these do not interfere with the perception of human forms and fates. ([1925] 1968, p. 9) People in the mass depended on sentimental intervention; they remained preoccupied with the human content in a work. Theirs was not the true artistic pleasure, of which, Ortega y Gasset believed, not many were capable. And while there had always been an abundance of such "mass" persons, they used to be scattered around the world and "lived a life, to all appearance, divergent, dissociate, apart. Each individual or small group occupied a place, its own, in country, village, town, or quarter of the great city" ([1929] 1930, p. 13). Insofar as cultural success remained in their hands, they dragged everyone and everything down toward their level. Actually, concern over a dilution of taste started long ago with the growth of a literature aimed at a broader audience. As early as 1817, the critic, William Hazlitt (1778-1830), a shrewd observer of the literary scene, deplored the "diffusion of public taste" promoted by public institutions and artificial means that were not synonymous with its elevation: The principle of universal suffrage, however applicable to matters of government, which concern the common feelings and common interests of society, is by no means applicable to matters of taste. . . . The highest efforts of genius, in every walk of art, can never be properly understood by the generality of mankind, . . . [whose taste is incapable of even gradual improvement]. ([1817] 1930a, p. 163) Public incompetence, Hazlitt believed, would also affect creativity. It hung like "a millstone round the neck of all original genius that does not conform to established and exclusive models" ([1818] 1930b, p. 96). In vying for popular applause, as some writers were tempted to do, they abandoned their own standards and became willing to pander to those "of the public for novelty and extraordinary effect" ([1816] 1877, p. 85). With these and other comments, Hazlitt anticipated the critics of mass culture by noting its effects on poets in a literary world that still encompassed only a small readership of relatively educated persons. That situation — a literary world of moderate size — no longer exists. Literary critics have had to broaden their perspective and, without abandoning concerns over mass competence, had to come to terms with the consequences of an unforeseen flood of entertainment and education via the media of mass communication. Nowadays, more people than ever participate, partake in, or have available so much material, so easily, and so quickly. New genres develop and old ones are adapted for mass distribution. The problem has been redefined somewhat. Criticism has been more focused on the erosion of literary tradition than on the alleged incompetence and interventionist posture of individuals that Ortega y Gasset had emphasized. In comments on mass civilization and minority culture, F. R. Leavis (1895-1978), a defender of the humanities against the onslaughts of mass culture, illustrated the shift by advancing a psychological Gresham's law. Content "debased for mass distribution," he asserted, drove out better quality information and culture (Leavis, [1930] 1969, p. 9). Among the symptoms of this debasement were the abridgment of canonic works and their adaptation for movies, or even for comic strips. The same nefarious consequences extended beyond literature to all of leisure and social life. Where advertising slogans and journalistic hype have become pervasive, linguistic versatility is bound to decline, and people's lives are accordingly impoverished. The main defense, following Leavis, is to keep literary tradition alive. Much commentary about the "culture" disseminated by the media does not specify exactly what is new and unique to it. The one characteristic of mass culture just about everyone should be able to agree upon is its lack of roots in a hallowed local tradition. It is not an expression of people's everyday life, certainly not in the same way that folk culture is. Instead, the content — the creations, artifacts, and performances that constitute mass culture — is received from somewhere else. A second feature, a consequence of the decline in aristocratic and older forms of state patronage, is the pressure on the creators and distributors of these contents to find or build audiences sufficient for economic viability. To maximize appeal, productions are suffused with marketing stratagems. These include packaging, sensationalism, cross-media promotion, a star system, going after records, offering prizes, novelty, and rapid obsolescence. There is a premium on being the "latest" and most up-to-date. Whether all these stratagems necessarily result in a "dumbing down" to the lowest possible level, as the Bauers contended, remains an open question. The most sought audience seems more nearly to represent some kind of a "middle mass," the largest possible number of those who could be at least minimally satisfied. And, finally, mass culture is near ubiquitous, its contents so pervasive that hardly anyone within reach can altogether escape its influence. It absorbs even the avant-garde. The fundamental issue having to do with mass culture is not its quality, but how it functions. Karl Mannheim emphasized the absence of institutions that connect producers with recipients and the consequences of such a situation. Audiences that represent organized groups were said to react differently than an unorganized mass, the kind that has taken over as the arbiter of success. Without a requisite stable institutional structure, popular sovereignty, in culture as much as in politics, can have messy results, as for example, in the literary world, where, Mannheim surmised that, in earlier days "an author, after he or she had once gained an audience, could expect to retain it for at least a generation. In the fluid mass society [of today] this stable audience, selectively recruited from the higher status groups, is replaced by an audience that has just gathered, one that, in the typical case, comes solely for the sake of one particular play. There is no permanent theater group with a distinctive repertoire but only a cast assembled for the one play. Such an impermanent fluctuating audience needs new sensations to reassemble," a condition bound to result in an increasing number of initial successes with no seconds or thirds,10 because the audience attracted when the playwright first bursts on the scene would already have disintegrated. Lacking a loyal circle of followers, authors and other cultural producers turn directly to the "open mass and, in this way, are more subject to the laws of mass psychology than they would be where there is an organic or socially evolved structure to serve as a cushion" (Mannheim, 1935, p. 74). Among the alternatives that Mannheim had in mind was a theater designed for the working-class and run by the unions or some organized entity to act as a brake on this tendency, rudimentary forms of which already existed in England and other liberal democracies.

Claims that the influence of mass culture is entirely negative are hard to sustain. Instructive on this issue are inferences about mass responses that Herbert Blumer (1900-1987), a student of Park, drew from queries to youthful movie-goers at a time when movies were even more important entertainment than they are today. He documented how movies provided youths with images of life unknown to them. Such an audience's importance becomes greater when these images operate against traditional forms. Blumer believed that, by tapping into, and exploiting, basic human values — common emotions, passions, and sentiments universal in humans beings — and placing them in a novel setting, motion-pictures turned the attention of individuals outward, beyond locally defined life. Like all agencies of mass communication, "they make what has been remote and vague, immediate and clear. By reason of this ability they are especially effective in establishing stereotypes. The effectiveness is greatest where the initial familiarity with the object is least, for in such situations the object now shown in a definitive and familiar way becomes a norm" (Blumer, 1935, p. 125). Blumer does not depict the mass of movie-goers as entirely passive recipients. They still select what to see and what to pay attention to. The power lies with the culture industry. Highly sensitive to the varying tastes and desires of its clientele and lacking a clear cultural program of its own, it sets in motion an impetus to something of an interplay between the convergent selection of the mass and offerings of producers, which, over the long run, helps channel popular tastes, creates all kinds of expectations, raises aspirations, and has some influence on how people prefer to live. Blumer conceptualizes this kind of audience as a mass: It consists of individuals with the most heterogeneous background — differences in families, in communities, in local cultures, and in class affiliations. This mass [like every other mass] has no form or organization. It has no program, no rules, no tradition, and no culture. It has no group consciousness, no we-feeling, no bonds of loyalty. In it, the individuals are anonymous, have no social positions, no designated functions. (1935, p. 122) A multitude of movie-goers constitutes a "homogeneous" mass, but only, as Blumer makes clear, with respect to the particular behavior. In this case, all of them having gone to the movies makes them part of that mass audience, and of that audience alone. Only in this context are they perceived as identical units, while in all their other "extra-mass activities they are highly heterogeneous . . ." And they are also, but only within this mass, "anonymous." They do not all know one another, but they still have their own local attachments, share in convivial association, belong to primary groups, live and act to a great extent in accordance with conventional patterns, but insofar as they belong to a mass, it is as alienated individuals in a new area of life not covered by local group tradition . . . ," (1935, p. 118) which is where audience members are most open to influence from the mass media. The concept of mass, so defined, does not refer to a particular stratum of society any more than mass culture refers to an impoverished human existence. It denotes a specific form of elementary collective behavior distinct from the emotional crowd, from the discourse that takes place in the public sphere, and from mass movements with varying degrees of organization. The limits of media effects cited by Blumer are equally noteworthy: he expected effects on youngsters, given their more limited experience, to be greater than on adults, but the images that a movie conveys are apt to be recast, and possibly even rejected, after further experience with the media or in actual life. Blumer was very aware that the influence of a picture "is dependent not solely upon its content but also upon the sensitivity and disposition of the observer.... Sometimes the meanings which movie-goers may get from the same picture are diametrically opposite" (1933, p. 180). Nor does being part of a mass eliminate group influences. Conversation certainly plays a role in defining what an individual will see in a picture — the aspects that he [or she] will select to pay attention to. An individual's sensitivity and perception are built very frequently in response to what his [or her] associates think and say. . . . [T]he different interpretations which are made of pictures are replicable to some degree in terms of the interests of one's group. (1933, p. 186) Companions or associates can also be barriers to media influence when they "look askance at a certain kind of picture, make depreciating remarks about it, ridicule its character and term one's interest in it as childish. One's attitude is likely to change by adopting the attitude of the group toward the picture" (1933, p. 134). Given these qualifications regarding media influence, the title of Blumer's article "Moulding of Mass Behavior through the Motion Picture" turns out, regrettably, to be somewhat misleading. His main claim for the media is that they help move children into the adult world and masses out of their provincialism.

Mass Revisited

Our review of the social science literature on "mass," albeit selective, has tracked its evolution into an analytically meaningful concept devoid of the ideological connotations seized upon by its critics. We also point out that the ensuing controversy over "mass society" or "mass culture" theory touched on interests and commitments not only inside, but also beyond academia. By showing that people in general were better off, less exploited, more able to resist manipulation, that they enjoyed warmer social relationships, and so forth, than predicted in either the Right or Left version of the theory, the critics did raise some valid objections, however misguided their blanket condemnations might have been. There was also, as we tried to point out, an important subtext behind their objections, one that has occasionally spilled over into the narrower field of mass communication to support the validity of the "limited-effects" theorem strongly promoted by researchers in, or with connections to, the Bureau of Applied Social Research at Columbia University. This new paradigm of mass communication, which was about to become conventional wisdom, was an obvious boon to the media industry. Research findings that emphasized the dependence of media effects on factors, including personal influence, that "mediate" between content and response, rather than on content alone, gave the First Amendment arguments of media conglomerates freedom from onerous regulations with this additional backing from science. The typical discourse in the academy revolves more around scientific issues than politics and policy. Our review of the sociological literature on mass refutes claims by critics that developments in survey research had laid the concept to rest once and for all. This is not to overlook or downplay their documentation of the various ways in which individuals respond to communication and of how messages are screened, relayed, or reinterpreted in their passage through interpersonal networks. But an overcommitment to a particular method, such as the survey, can be self-limiting. Some see only what the instrument to which they are wedded is designed to show. Those who build their case against the concept of mass on research by focusing on individual variation are apt to miss the forest because they see only trees. The more recently "discovered" barriers to communication did not elude the sociologists discussed in our review, whose insightful reflections, however vulnerable to parody, merit our continuing attention. Mass, we repeat, is a valid sociological concept. It denotes a temporary convergence of choices by a geographically dispersed multitude that lacks cohesion. Such a mass — referred to as a diffuse crowd by Tarde and Park — grows, disintegrates, or renews itself with every shift in its attention. The participants are indeed anonymous, but only with regard to their presence in a particular mass. At best, they have a vague awareness of the numerous but nameless others attracted by the same object or media content, who adopt the same fashion, behave in a similar way, or move in a parallel direction, either as individuals or as members of some group to which they belong. The frequency and ease with which masses form is a hallmark of mass society. Other features include the expansion of the universe of discourse, increases in the role of reason, the growth of individualism, and the potential for establishing links between people living in different worlds. Such a conception has nothing to do with social pessimism or nostalgia for a lost world. That the large audiences "assembled" by the media fit this concept of mass is beyond question. Masses do exist, even if only as statistical aggregates and without a distinct will or common goal. Their existence, however, is fully compatible with families gathered around a television set, a group of friends going to the movies together, and exchanges among people in general about what they read or have seen. None of these joint activities detract from the power of the mass, which resides primarily in its numbers. Massive shifts do have serious consequences. The extent to which masses control the issues at hand, instead of being manipulated, is an interesting question for which there is no categorical answer. Nevertheless, the mass as a mere aggregate — of individuals, of households, of circles of friends, of work associates, and what have you — cannot achieve anything, or even discuss and exchange ideas with persons and authorities outside their normal orbit, without some sort of organization. A mass is not synonymous with a public. The consistent and ongoing effect of the media is to expand the range of common experience among the participants in the mass they attract. People have become much more responsive to distant events. Research on the effects of mass communication needs to focus equally on two different levels: that of the individual, and that of the larger polity and society. The two are not always commensurate. What appears on the micro-level of interpersonal discourse as a small movement confined to an already impressionable minority can have significant impact on political culture. To take one example: a national election, where each vote counts the same, and where the outcome is determined by their distribution within a mass. A remarkably small number of swing-voters acting within a short time span can actually reverse an expected outcome. Three conditions predispose the mass of prospective voters to media influence: weak party preference at the outset, issues that emerge during the campaign, and pressure from family and peers. The upset, in short, is caused by voters who deviate only minimally from their original personal and social dispositions. They may not have had a clear preference to begin with; the campaign may have increased the salience of issues already important to them, and whatever their doubts, they may have been swayed by people to whom they normally listen. None of this matters as much as the impact of minimal shifts by a small number of people on the political fate of a country. A similar paradox operates outside elections as well. A mere reinforcement of existing attitudes can sharpen polarization to a point where the compromises necessary for an effective policy are out of reach. Similar phenomena occur in the economic and cultural realms. A major change may represent nothing more than a change in brand preference or between two similar television serials by enough people to cut into the profitability of corporations or, in some circumstances, of industries. Sometimes, behavior consistent with prior attitudes can even become the trigger for an economic downturn. In culture, too, we need to focus as much on changes in fashions and fads as on who follows them for what personal reasons. A final word on mass communication. For a complete assessment of its impact, one needs to look beyond specific outcomes by focusing on the pervasiveness of the media. On some matters, and especially at critical times, they provide vital information. Even the Internet, often considered an alternative to the mass media, takes account of the news and, on occasion, serves as the primary source for a major story. The two are inextricably linked. As Tarde, Lippmann, and many other early writers recognized, the power of media with access to the mass stems less from what they ask of people (prescription and persuasion) than from their portrayal of the world beyond the personal acquaintance of audiences. Unable ever to catch the full diversity of events and situations, the media supply the bits and pieces that, when put together, form the symbolic environment to which active citizens, including bloggers and nerds, are bound to react in one way or other. Hardly anyone — not even those who scorn the media — escapes their reach. In at least one regard, institutional leaders and élites enhance this influence through their concern about likely third-person effects, which makes them forever anticipate, and attempt to forestall, the response of the anonymous multitude to the continuous flow of images over the mass media. The resultant discourse and maneuvering, much of it played out in the public sphere and difficult as it is to map, needs to be moved into sharper focus by researchers in mass communication. How to do so lies beyond the scope of this paper.

REFERENCES

1. Baschwitz, K. (1923). Der Massenwahn, seine Wirkung und seine Beherrschung. Munich: C. H. Beck.
2. Bauer, R. A. (1958). The communicator and the audience. Journal of Conflict Resolution, 2(1), 67-77.
3. Bauer, R. A., & Bauer, A. H. (1960). America, "mass society" and mass media. Journal of Social Issues,10(3), 3-66.
4. Bell, D. (1960, Winter). The end of ideology in the West. Columbia University Forum, 34, 4-7.
5. Bell, D. ([1956] 1959). America as a mass society. In The end of ideology. Glencoe, IL: Free Press.
6. Bernays, E. L. (1928). Propaganda. New York: Horace Liveright.
7. Blau, P. (1955). The dynamics of bureaucracy: A study of interpersonal relations in two government bureaucracies. Chicago: University of Chicago Press.
8. Blumer, H. (1933). Movies and conduct. New York: Macmillan.
9. Blumer, H. (1935, August). Moulding of mass behavior through the motion picture. Publication of the American Sociological Society, 9(3), 115-127.
10. Blumer, H. ([1936] 1951). The field of collective behavior. In A. M. Lee (Ed.), Principles of Sociology (pp. 165-222). New York: Barnes & Noble.
11. Bornecque, H. (1921). La France et la guerre: Formation de l'opinion publique pendant la guerre. Paris: Payot.
12. Burgess, E. W. (1929). Communication. American Journal of Sociology, 34, 1072-1080.
13. Colm, G. (1924). Die Masse: Ein Beitrag zur Systematik der Gruppen. Archiv für Sozialwissenschaft und Sozialpolitik 52, 680-694.
14. Cooley, C. H. ([1909] 1929). Social organization. New York: Scribe's.

15. Davis, J. (1935). Capitalism and its culture. New York: Farrar & Rinehart Fromm, E. (1941). Escape from freedom. New York: Rinehart & Winston.
16. Geiger, T. (1949). Die Legende von der Massengesellschaft. Archiv für Rechts- und Sozialphilosophie, 39, 305-323.
17. Geiger, T. (1926). Die Masse und ihre Aktion: Ein Beitrag zur Soziologie der Revolutionen. Stuttgart: Ferdinand Enke.
18. Geiger, T. (1955). Die Legende von der Massengesellschaft. Acta Sociologic, 1, 75-79.
19. Goldthorpe, J. (1968). The affluent worker. London: Cambridge University Press.
20. Hazlitt, W. ([1816] 1877). Lecture IV: On Beaumont and Fletcher, Ben Johnson, Ford, and Messenger. In Lectures on the dramatic literature of the age of Elizabeth (pp. 85-114). Philadelphia: Lippincott.
21. Hazlitt, W. ([1817] 1930a). Why the arts are not progressive?- a fragment. In P. P. Howe (Ed.), The complete works of William Hazlitt, Vol. 4, pp. 160-164. London: Dent & Sons.
22. Hazlitt, W. ([1818] 1930b). On Thomson and Cowper. In P. P. Howe (Ed.), The complete works of William Hazlitt, Vol. 5, pp. 91-98. London: Dent & Sons.
23. Katz, E., & Lazarsfeld, P. F. (1955). Personal influence: The part played by people in the flow of mass communications. Glencoe, IL: Free Press.
24. Kornhauser, W. (1959). The politics of mass society. Glencoe, IL: Fisher Unwin.
25. Kris, E., & Leites, N. (1947). Trends in twentieth-century propaganda. Psychoanalysis and the Social Sciences, 1, 393-409.
26. Lasswell, H. D. (1927). Propaganda technique in the world war. New York: Knopf.
27. Lasswell, H. D. (1935). The study and practice of propaganda. In H. D. Lasswell, R. W. Casey & B. L.
28. Smith (Eds.), Propaganda and promotional activities: An annotated bibliography, pp. 1-27.
29. Minneapolis, MN : University of Minnesota Press.
30. Lasswell, H. D., & Bienenstock, D. (1939). World revolutionary propaganda. New York: Knopf.
31. Lazarsfeld, P. F., Berelson, B., & Gaudet, H. ([1944] 1948). The people's choice. New York: Columbia University Press.

32. Leavis, F. R. ([1930] 1969). Mass civilisation and minority culture. London: Folcroft Press.
33. LeBon, G. ([1895] 1916). La psychologie des foules. Paris: Alcan.
34. LeBon, G. ([1896] 1926). The crowd: A study of the popular mind. London: Fisher Unwin.
35. Lederer, E. (1940). State of the masses: The threat of the classless society. New York: Norton.
36. Lee, I. (1925). Publicity: Some of the things it is and is not. New York: Industries Pub.
37. Lerner, D. (1957). Communication systems and social systems: A statistical exploration in history and polity. Behavioral Science, 2, 266-275.
38. Lippmann, W. (1922). Public opinion. New York: Harcourt, Brace.
39. Lippmann, W. (1925). The phantom public: A sequel to Public Opinion. New York: Macmillan.
40. Mannheim, K. (1935). Mensch und Gesellschaft in einem Zeitalter des Umbruchs. Leiden: Sijthoff.
41. Michels, R. ([1926] 1987). Die Besinnung zur Politik. In Masse, Führer, Intellektuelle: Politischsoziologische
42. Aufsätze 1906-1933, pp. 81-98. Frankfurt/Main: Campus.
43. Nicolai, W. (1920). Nachrichtendienst, Presse und Volksstimmung im Weltkrieg. Berlin: E.S. Mittler & Sohn.
44. Ortega y Gasset, J. ([1925] 1968). The dehumanization of art. In The dehumanization of art and other essays on art, culture, and literature, pp. 3-54. Princeton, NJ: Princeton University Press.
45. Ortega y Gasset, J. ([1929] 1930). The revolt of the masses. New York: Norton.
46. Park, R. E. ([1902] 1972). The crowd and the public and other essays (D. Levine, Ed.). Chicago: University of Chicago Press.
47. Park, R. E., & Burgess, E. W. ([1921] 1969). Introduction to the science of sociology (3rd ed.). Chicago: University of Chicago Press.
48. Ponsonby, A. (1928). Falsehood in war-time, containing an assortment of lies circulated throughout the nations during the great war. New York: E. P. Dutton.
49. Roethlisberger, F. J., & Dickson, W. J. (1934). Management and the worker. Cambridge, MA: Harvard University Press.

50. Shils, E. (1948). The present state of American sociology. Glencoe, IL: Free Press.
51. Shils, E. (1957). Daydreams and nightmares: Reflections on the criticism of mass culture. Sewanee Review, 65, 587-608.
52. Shils, E. ([1962] 1975). Center and periphery: Essays in macrosociology. Chicago: University of Chicago Press.
53. Shils, E. A., & Janowitz, M. (1948). Cohesion and disintegration in the German Wehrmacht in World War II. Public Opinion Quarterly, 12, 280-315.
54. Simmel, G. (1907). Philosophie des Geldes (2nd ed.). Leipzig: Duncker & Humblot.
55. Simmel, G. (1950). The metropolis and mental life. In The sociology of Georg Simmel, pp. 409-424. New York: Free Press.
56. Simmel, G. (1950). The sociology of Georg Simmel (K. H. Wolff, Trans.). New York: Free Press.
57. Stouffer, S. A., et al. (1949). The American soldier. Princeton, NJ: Princeton University Press.
58. Tarde, G. ([1898] 1969). On communication and social influence (T. N. Clark, Ed.). Chicago: University of Chicago Press.
59. Tarde, G. ([1898] 1904). L'opinion et la foule. Paris: Alcan.
60. Tönnies, F. ([1887] 1922). Gemeinschaft und Gesellschaft: Grundbegriffe der reinen Soziologie (4th ed.).Berlin: Curtius.
61. Vleugels, W. (1926). Der Begriff der Masse: Ein Beitrag zur Entwicklungsgeschichte der Massentheorie. Jahrbuch für Soziologie, 2(176-201r).
62. Wallas, G. ([1914] 1917). The Great Society: A psychological analysis. New York: Macmillan.
63. Whyte, W. F. (1945). Street corner society: The social structure of an Italian slum. Chicago: University of Chicago Press.
64. Willey, M. M. (1935). Communication agencies and the volume propaganda. Annals of the American Academy of Political and Social Science, 179, 194-200.
65. Woodbury, D. O. (1931). Communication. New York: Dodd, Mead.

Chapter 3

THE ROLE OF MASS MEDIA IN BHUTAN: ACCESSIBILITY, INFLUENCE AND ITS IMPACTS

Lhamo T[1] and Oyama T[2]

[1] Public Policy Program, National Graduate Institute for Public Policy, Tokyo 106-0032, Japan

[2] Professor of Public Policy Analysis, National Graduate Institute for Public Policy, Tokyo 106-0032, Japan

INTRODUCTION

In Bhutan, mass media primarily refers to radio, newspapers, cinema, television, and the internet [1]. It comprises a variety of modes by which senders can record information and experiences and transmit them to a large audience fairly rapidly. This definition summarizes those commonly used in writings on the media [2]. The mass media constitute a powerful and infusing force in our lives. We are bombarded by media messages daily. Today, most of the information that we get about our local, national, and international news comes to us through these mass media, which is very different from the situation before 1999 in Bhutan. TV and the internet were introduced in 1999 and mobile phones in 2003. The information and views communicated through these media have a great impact on our attitudes toward people, events, and problems. The media have relayed information to the people about the country's five year plans, development programs, and education systems, and this has motivated people to become partners in the progress of the country. Accessibility of information and communication have improved, and people are constantly consuming information; however, its excessive influence may undermine the traditional culture and value system [1]. Therefore, realizing the important role of mass media and, its impacts on society, and determining its future direction have become very important. Castell in 2007 stated that, throughout the history of information and communication, mass media is considered as a powerful factor that shapes social change. It can construct or deconstruct the norms and values on which the society is built, because the real challenge in society is the battle over the minds of the people [3].

The Ministry of Information and Communication, Bhutan conducted media impact studies in 2003, 2008, and 2013, which studied the trends of media evolution, its impacts, and challenges. These studies have presented thought provoking results. Further attention is required because many historically relevant events have occurred recently in Bhutan, such as, the second democratic elections in 2013, the building of community centers to improve the accessibility of information, and enhanced media and communication technologies. This paper attempts to provide an account of how media accessibility, its influences, and its impact have progressed over the years and provide policy recommendations. The findings presented are based on survey results and interviews.

LITERATURE REVIEW

Wright in 1975 stated the major functions of mass media as the investigation of news, finding correlations, the transmission of culture, entertainment, and mobilization. However, he also stated that, there are underlying functions accompanying each of these. The underlying function of investigation is that the media provides news and data. Correlation means that the media displays the data to us after they have selected, translated, and interpreted it. The social transmission of culture implies that the media portrays our beliefs, norms and values. Media likewise entertain us in our leisure time and provides a respite from our everyday schedules. Mobilization is how the media function to promote societal interest, especially during crises [4]. Subsequently, McQuail in 1979, put forward five functions of the media., First, they can draw attention to problems, solutions, and higher authority;, secondly, they can confer status and rightfulness;, thirdly, they can persuade and influence execution;, fourthly, they can help organize groups and maintain them; and fifth, they are a means of bringing psychic rewards and fulfillment[5]. There is an ongoing attempt to integrate various approaches to understand the effect of the mass media in society, but for Bhutan we have yet to determine the underlying functions of mass media. With economic development, the media have produced a much more networked and horizontally connected society, as opposed to the vertically connected society of a decade ago [6].

Jurgen Habermas in his sociological theory explains that the mass media are controlled by political and economic forces to manipulate the information consumer [7]. He states that this compromises the rightfulness of the communication power exercised by the mass media. However, the German political scientist Peter Klier does not agree with Jurgen's theory [8]. Klier argues that, there is a large amount of information freely available in addition to the mass media, and that people can choose among them. Another researcher, Doyle explains how mass media uses the cultural selection theory to bring about social change [9]. Cross-cultural comparisons indicate that the structure of the mass media may have a strong effect on political developments, and the mass media are influenced by many dynamics such as the overall editorial policy of a medium, and economic and cultural factors [10]. New innovations in technology are further influencing the effect of media. However, media critics argue that mass media are not able to fulfill their role due to many inherent barriers that are prevailing in any society.

According to the Classical Marxist approach, mass media are assumed to follow the ideological interests of the dominant class in society. The Marxist media theory perceives the media as a fusion of the existing economic and political elites and, therefore, reflects their interests. On the other hand, the liberal approach sees the media as facilitating social agreement through the dissemination of information and conflicting opinion. A review of the literature also suggests that although the media have a central role in mediating information and forming public opinion, the initiation of press freedom has created room for unprecedented manipulation via unethical mass communicators and influential people in society [11,12]. Much of this could impact the media consumer in a society.

Mass Media in Bhutan

Bhutan is one of the last countries to introduce these media, and people are enjoying the contents that media has to offer. There are still not many studies on the role that mass media has played in society. However, the few studies done have pointed out that, along with the increasing consumption of mass media, there are positive advancements with great potential in the fields of education and entertainment, and in terms of connecting Bhutan to the modern world. At the same time, it also symbolizes the beginning of the end for Bhutan's unique identity and culture with commercial advertisements [1,13]. The government philosophy requires that the Bhutanese media emphasize public service rather than commercialism, and it is important that mass media fulfill this requirement [14].

Most of us rely on mass media for current news and for information regarding what is important and what we should be aware of. People usually trust mass media as a source of news, information, education, and entertainment. Considering this, we should be aware of how mass media works in all regions of the country. However, it is difficult to make mass media accessible to remote areas because the challenge for any developmental plan in Bhutan remains the mountainous terrain, with more than 60% of the people living in rural areas. According to national statistics, the urban population consists of 196,111 persons, while 438,871 are in the rural areas [15]. The Bhutanese media has a central role in the operationalization of government philosophy, which is not only to inform, educate, and entertain the audience, but to actually empower people so that they enhance their ability to make the right decisions and achieve the freedom to attain happiness [16].

The Bhutanese media have been criticized for aping the global media instead of drawing lessons from them [6]. Unlike developed countries like the US and Japan, where mass media have developed over time, the proliferation in Bhutan has been very fast, and various forms of media are developing at the same time, such as TV, the internet, and mobile phones. As a result, Bhutan is experiencing substantial changes in terms of the structure of the family and society. Bhutan is a small nation and is already witnessing some undesirable impacts of the intensive mass media development such as the weakening of social connections and family bonds, reduced attention to homework as well as increased violence among youth, increased materialism, and other negative effects including the misuse of apps through smart phones. Access to information has become so easy that within a few seconds, anyone can produce and distribute media content. This kind of media usage and consumer behavior calls for a proper understanding of the situation. Many of the media policies such as the social media policy, advertisement policy, and the national media policy are also currently in the draft stage and open for review. It is important to study the role of mass media and provide policy recommendations by understanding what Bhutanese media should be like and what type of content and programs are suitable for a country like Bhutan without succumbing to media imperialism.

Thus, the main objectives of this paper are:

1. Explaining the diffusion and penetration processes of Bhutanese media through various aspects such as accessibility in general, entertainment, education, and participation in democracy and politics.
2. Investigating the influences and impacts of Bhutanese media on Bhutanese society and providing a review, assessment, and evaluation.
3. Looking at the future from the viewpoint of media policy regarding the further utilization and development of Bhutanese media.

This paper aims to assess the impact and influences of mass media as one of the key factors that shapes society, its culture, and values by investigating the growth of the media, its purposes, and the inherent barriers in media coverage and information dissemination. We will discuss the role that mass media currently plays in Bhutanese society and analyze its impact by studying media growth and investigating people's choice of media content, preferences of media type, and its impacts on their work life, personal relations, attitudes and behaviors.

MASS MEDIA IN BHUTAN: PAST AND PRESENT

Media Development

Mass media in Bhutan is at a very early stage and is currently developing. There is consistent growth in all forms of mass media such as print, broadcast, film, music, mobile phones, and the internet [17]. The concept of the media as a player in the growth of modern society began in the mid 1980`s. The first Bhutanese newspaper, called Kuensel and started in 1967, and first radio service, called Bhutan Broadcasting Service (BBS) and launched in 1973, were delinked from the government. They were made independent after His majesty the fourth king issued a royal decree on 18th September 1992, to enable them to be more effective in fulfilling their responsibilities toward society.

With increasing literacy and changing social needs, today Bhutan has twelve newspapers and seven radio stations. Today we can listen to radio in four different languages (Dzongkha, Sharchop, Lhotshamkha and English). Radio in Bhutan was the most effective media, especially for rural areas. These new radio services have created an avenue for people to voice their concerns and are already addressing a series of social issues. There are only two TV stations, both provided by BBS TV.The channels, BBS and BBS 2, are the only channels that broadcast local news and TV programs in Bhutan. BBS TV was launched on 2 June 1999. It is one of the most important events in the history of electronic media in Bhutan. BBS TV is available in 40 Asian countries, from Turkey in the west to Indonesia in South East Asia. BBS TV broadcasts for five hours daily in Dzongkha and English. The same program is rebroadcast the following day. Various entertainment programs, such as live music request shows and children's educational programs, are broadcast on weekend afternoons for about three hours. Cable television services are available in 19 of the 20 dzongkhags, and about 40 different channels are provided by the cable TV operators, out of which only two channels are Bhutanese. As of 2012, there were 58 cable operators, 54,120 cable subscribers, and 16,632 dish TV subscribers. The first cinema hall was started in 1960, and today we have 12 cinema halls. In 1999, Hindi films were the most popular followed by English movies. These films were not censored in Bhutan because the censor board of India had already approved them, and, therefore, cinema hall managers consider the films permissible to be watched in Bhutan [1]. The first Bhutanese film, Gasa Lami Singye, was produced in 1988. While the film industry is still in its early stages, the number of Bhutanese films has been increasing with more people venturing into the industry. As of 2012, Bhutanese produced 241 films. From the same time that TV was introduced, the internet was also launched in Bhutan in 1999. The number of internet subscriber has increased from 2,117 in 2003 to 109,526 in 2008 and 133,289 as of 2013. Most of the internet subscribers are government offices, while internet connections at home are also on the rise. Internet connection is gaining popularity with more electronic devices entering into the Bhutanese market such as personal laptop computers, smart phones, and tablets. In addition, the number of Bhutanese using online forums and social media sites is on the rise. Though mobile phones entered into Bhutanese society very late, i.e. only in 2003, today there are more mobile phone users than users of any other electronic devices. Mobile phones can be considered as a form of mass media because of their accessibility to mass communication, such as advertisements, public announcements, and the internet. Mobile phones are now emerging as the 7th mass media, joining print, recordings, cinema, radio, TV, and the internet [18]. The number of mobile data users has also increased dramatically from 23,000 in March 2013 to 120,000 by the end of 2013. Today there are over 135,000 mobile data users registered using 3G. The growth rate or the demand rate for 3G has increased by six times in just six months. Recently 4G services have also been introduced in the capital.

As shown in Table 1, we have 560,890 mobile phone subscribers as of 2013, and all forms of media such as books and magazines, computers, internet subscribers, and TV sets have increased except for radio sets, which have decreased from 77,800 in 2008 to 49,641 in 2013. This shows the trends in media growth from 2003 to 2013. Looking at the figures, the mobile phone growth rate is the highest, which means that people now have easy access to information through mobile devices. The average growth rates for the various forms of media are as follows: mobile phones, 73.6%; newspapers, 28.2%; television sets, 7.9%; radio stations, 21.5%; and internet subscribers, 51.3%.

ACCESSIBILITY, INFLUENCES AND IMPACTS OF MASS MEDIA

Data and Methodology

In order to measure the influence and impact of Bhutanese media on society, we use data obtained from our original interviews and surveys conducted in September 2014. Regarding the survey, we first selected two districts out of 20 randomly, i.e. Bumthang and Thimphu (the capital city). Questionnaires were distributed to 150 people, and we finally collected responses from 96 people (a 64% response rate). The target population consists of all age levels, from 14 to 57 years old, and consisted of students, unemployed youth, government officers, housewives, and retired civil servants in order to obtain a true picture of the population. The age distribution of the respondents is as follows: 54.17% were 14-19 years old, 18.75% were 20-29 years old, 18.75% were 30-39 years old, and 8.33% were 40 years old or above. In comparison, the national age distribution is 27.3% for teens, 20.1% for those in their twenties, 40.8% for those aged 30 to 55, and 11.8% for those above 55 (index mundi, 2014). Table 2 shows the details of the respondents of the survey.

The survey questionnaire consisted of 17 interview questions as follows.

Q1. How often do you utilize services provided through community resource centers?

1: Never, 2: Almost never, 3: Occasionally/Sometimes, 4: Almost always, 5: Always

Q2. What do you think would be the best way of utilizing community resource centers more efficiently?

Q3. What medium is the best way of engaging people in discussions about democracy and politics?

1: TV, 2: Radio, 3: Newspapers, 4: Mobile Phones, 5: Social media and online forums, 7: Public meetings and Individual communication

Q4. Does mass media influence your opinion? Yes or No

Q5. If yes, does it change your behavior and attitude towards that event or particular subject?

1: Never, 2: Almost never, 3: Occasionally/Sometimes, 4: Almost always, 5: Always

Q6. Do you think your opinion is being reported by the media? Yes or No

Q7. What level of priority is rural and minority news given in news reports?

1: Not a priority, 2: Low priority, 3: Neutral, 5: High priority, 5: Essential priority

Q8. Do you have easy access to national news and public announcements? Yes or No

Please explain

Q9. Are you aware of the media policy in Bhutan?

1: Not at all aware, 2: Slightly aware, 3: Somewhat aware, 4: Moderately aware

5: Extremely aware

Q10. If you are aware of the media policy in Bhutan, provide recommendations on how we can improve the policy.

Q11. Do reality TV shows such as singing competitions have any impact on Bhutanese culture?

Give reasons

Q12. Does the media (e.g. tape recorders, phones, CDs) have any impact on Bhutanese singing and dancing culture? Give reasons

Q13. How often do you buy products advertised in the media? 1: Never, 2: Almost never, 3: Occasionally/Sometimes, 4: Almost always, 5: Always

Q14. To what extent are your buying decisions influenced by commercial advertisements?

1: Never, 2: Almost never, 3: Occasionally/Sometimes, 4: Almost always, 5: Always

Q15. To what extent does the radio, newspapers, phones, and the internet affect your daily lives?

1: No affect, 2: Minor affect, 3: Neutral, 4: Moderate affect, 5: Major affect

Q16. Who do you think decides what becomes news (agenda setters)?

1: Media, 2: Politician, 3: Government, 4; Businessmen, 5: People, 6: Others

Q17. The policy for advertising and content for the broadcast and print media is being finalized in Bhutan-Do you have any recommendations?

Gross National Happiness, the inspiration for change in Bhutan, requires that the kingdom draw on global experience to adopt what is beneficial and relevant. It also emphasizes a pragmatism through which Bhutan does not succumb to global pressure but chooses technology and skills that strengthen rather than dilute the Bhutanese identity. This section will look at the potential impact of mass media on society – people's daily lives, attitudes, and behaviors, and on the process of democratization. In the knowledge century, Bhutan aims to establish a knowledge society and guarantee access to information as a right of every citizen. This is enshrined as a mandate in the constitution of Bhutan-along with the freedom of expression and freedom of the media- and is established as a government policy spearheaded by the Ministry of Information [19].

Mass media is now acknowledged as a potent tool that can be used to inform and educate those who would otherwise remain unaware of issues that directly affect them. Today, the news media, which includes print, radio, and television, and the internet, is playing an increasingly important role, along with the growth of the Bhutanese blogging community and social networking. During the 1930s, communication researchers were convinced that media had tremendous power. In fact, they believed the power of media was so great that it acted like a "magic bullet," instantly penetrating the human mind [20]. Although researchers have altered their view of the impact of media, almost all researchers, media critics, and philosophers believe that media has the power to shape society, at least in some ways.

Using the survey results obtained from the respondents' replies, we attempt to investigate the accessibility, influence, and impact of Bhutanese media. Accessibility is the quality of information being made available when needed. Influence refers to the process of changing behavior towards a particular program or product. Impact refers to change that is brought about as a result of consuming information from advertisements and other programs.

ACCESSIBILITY

We consider that accessibility of mass media includes government initiatives such as the establishment of community centers and people's engagement in democracy and opinion. In the survey questionnaire, Q8 asks whether Bhutanese people have easy access to national news and public announcements. We find that 88.54% of the respondents answered yes to this question. In an attempt to improve the media accessibility and coverage nationwide, the Bhutan government initiated a project to establish community centers. As of 2014, there were 189 community centers [21]. The community centers have facilities such as internet connection, fax and photocopy machines, and passport photo and telephone services. However, many of the community centers are being underutilized as per the people and also the media reports [22]. Therefore, in an attempt to seek a solution to this problem, we asked the frequency of the respondents' visits to the community centers in Q1, and their replies are shown in Figure 1.

From Figure 1, we find that 58.33% of the people use the community centers occasionally. The percentage of men using community centers is lower, with females using the community centers 3.48% more than men. However, through questioning the community center coordinators in remote areas, it was found that they are being effectively utilized especially for photocopying, taking passport pictures, and browsing the internet in such areas. However, in urban areas, people hardly utilize the community centers. The majority of our respondents reported that they used the facility occasionally, followed by never. However, those respondents aged 40 and above never used the community centers, because none of them said they used community centers almost always or always. In response to suggestions for improving the community centers, the respondents reported that such facilities should be situated in better locations, have more functional machines and capable operators, and that greater awareness of such facilities should be promoted.

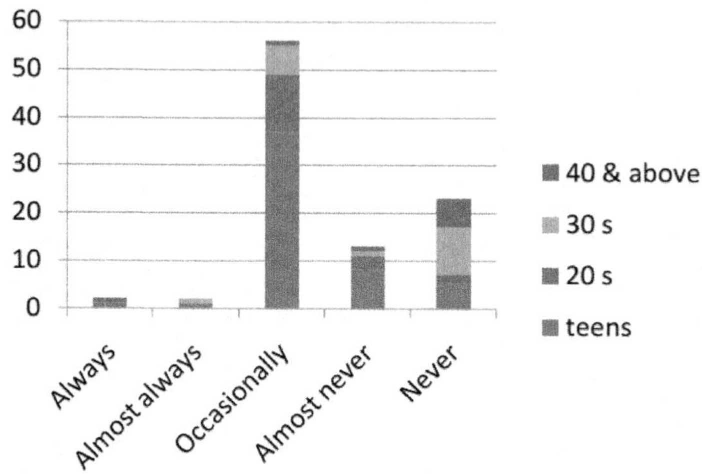

Figure 1: Frequency of respondents' visits to community centers.

Despite the great development in media indicators and the government initiatives to improve information accessibility through various projects, the MIS report 2013 still indicates that, 67% of the respondents did not participate in discussions about democracy and politics. Q3 asks what the best way to engage people in discussions on democracy and politics is. As seen in Figure 2, TV was listed by the respondents as the most effective way to engage the public in discussing political issues. Direct communication was the second most popular way mentioned, followed by the internet. 34 males and 16 female chose TV. As for direct communication, more females chose this option than males (12 females and 5 males). For people in their 30s, the first preference was TV followed by direct communication, but for teens, their first preference was TV followed by the internet. But for those respondents aged 40 and above, newspaper and mobile phones played no role in discussing about politics and democracy

When people feel that their opinions are not being considered, they tend to withdraw from active participation. Q6 asks whether the respondents' opinions are reported by the media or not. In response, 46.8% of them reported positively, saying that their opinions were being reported; however, 42.7%, an almost equal number, say otherwise, and the remaining 10 people did not respond. In both the positive and negative response groups, the proportion of male and female respondents is close, although, comparatively, men tend to have more opportunity to report their opinions in mass media.

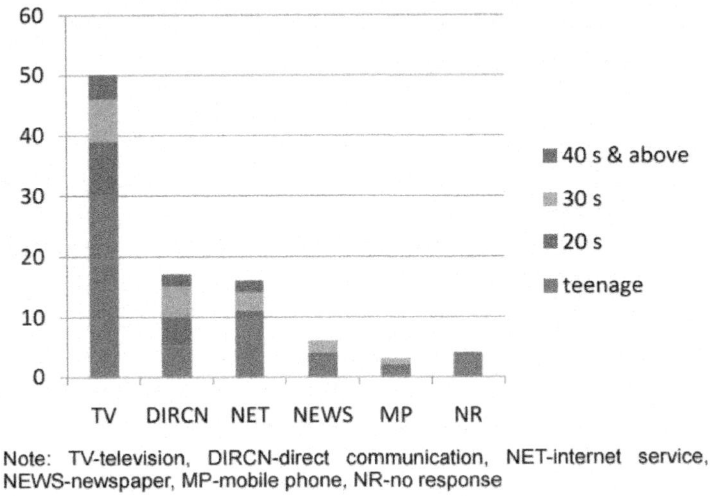

Figure 2: Best way to engage people in discussions about democracy and politics.

Question Q7 asks what priority the respondents think the rural and minority news is given. We find that almost half (48.9%) reported neutral followed by low priority (27%). The positive replies (corresponding to "essential "and "high" priorities) comprise only 6%, respectively. This implies that nearly 90% of the respondents have a rather negative view regarding the equal treatment of rural and minority news currently.

Influences

Responding to question Q4 regarding whether mass media influences the people's opinion, 79.16% respondents replied affirmatively. Even though all the groups have similar tendencies, those who fall in the age 40 and above group are evenly divided regarding affirmative and negative replies. Regarding question Q15 which asks about the extent to which mass media such as radio, newspapers, and the internet has affected their daily lives [13], we found that the largest percentage reported that it affected their lives moderately (32 out of 96 or 33.33%), followed by 23.95% reporting neutral, and 19.79% reporting a major effect, and this result was consistent at all age levels. Females reported a moderate affect followed by neutral and then major effects. However, men reported that, they were affected moderately followed by neutral to minor effects. The effect of mass media on the respondents' daily lives is almost similar at all age levels.

It is clear that Bhutanese lives are now being affected by mass media and the information transmitted. Since a large majority of the people has easy access to certain mass media and is also being affected by the transmitted information, we believe that the mass media must be responsible and play a positive and important role in society.

Figure 3 shows the distribution of respondents' replies to question Q14, which asks to what extent their buying decisions are influenced by commercial advertisements. It is interesting that the largest percentage, 40.63%, reported that they were rarely influenced. They are followed by those who stated occasionally (32.29%), then never (15.63%). People aged in their 30s responded that it influenced them rarely, followed by occasionally, and then a moderate amount. Advertisements here refer to all types of advertisements that people may come across in Bhutan, such as Indian and Bhutanese TV channel advertisements, Bhutanese newspaper advertisements, and internet advertisements.

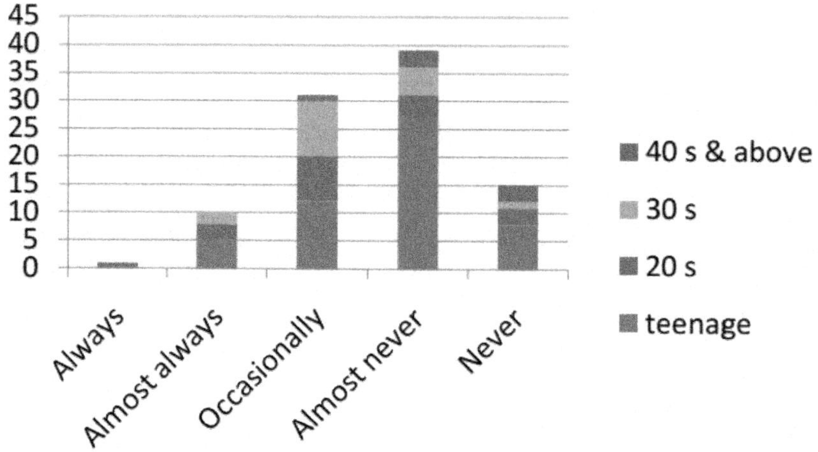

Figure 3: Influence of commercial advertisements on buying decisions.

Impacts

We attempt to investigate the impact of mass media on Bhutanese behavior and attitude. Here we mean by impact the change that is bought in society as a result of consuming information from advertisements and other programs through mass media. The study done by LaPiere found that influencing opinion does not guarantee a change in behavior, which means although people's opinions may be influenced, this influence does not necessarily change their behavior [23]. Thus, the following question asks how mass media changes the respondents' attitude and behavior towards a particular program or event. It is worth noting that men's behavior and attitude is changed more than women by 11.2%. For those who are in their teens and those in their 30s, their behavior is changed almost always, followed by occasionally. Q13 asks whether the respondents bought products after they viewed the product advertisements. We found that people buy products advertised in mass media only occasionally, followed by almost never and never.

Since the advertisement policy is being finalized in Bhutan, it is important for the general public's recommendations to be incorporated in the advertising policy of the country. The respondents said that the policy and content of advertisement should not mislead the public. They also said that the quality mentioned in the advertisement should match the products and services, and thus the advertisement policy should have guidelines for quality checks. In addition, the respondents stated that advertisement time should be less than the time devoted to the main content and announcements, and should not copy Indiantype commercialized advertisements. During the process of drafting the policy, the government should consult the people and involve them. However, some reported that it is no use commenting on policy, and that they had no recommendations because they trusted that the concerned officials are doing their best.

Though there was not much impact of advertisement on people`s buying decisions, many studies point out the impact on culture, which is an important aspect. Bhutan seems to be emerging with a new popular culture of singing and dancing preferences. The traditional culture of dance used to involve dancing along to live singing rather than using tape recorders and other media. It has been a tradition for a long time, and such culture is passed down for generations. Questions Q11 and Q12 ask if Bhutanese reality TV shows, e.g., singing competitions, and various types of music media, such as CDs, have any impact on Bhutanese culture. The respondents replied that children are being influenced by the different culture they are being exposed to, but this exposure also encourages young people to find innovative ways to participate in national and international issues through song and dance, for example advocating drug abstinence. Bhutanese youth are also becoming more interested in Bhutanese songs and dances because of the opportunity to participate in reality shows, so the reality shows are a good way of promoting Bhutanese culture. It seems that through such shows, people are becoming interested in their age old traditions again. Thus, such shows are influential and have a great positive impact on our culture. Although international reality shows also have impacts on society, the respondents feel that some impact and change is inevitable. However, Bhutanese shows help to preserve the culture, and by performing in zhungdra and boedra, it is helpful in making us realize our culture and tradition. We all agree that music media such as tapes and CDs have an impact on Bhutanese singing and dancing culture, which many youth are interested in. However, most of the youth prefer to sing and dance in English. In addition, the communication style has changed among youth; they tend to speak in Dzong-lish (a mixture of Dzongkha and English). Bringing new culture into society by copying neighboring countries' songs and dances is a recent major concern in Bhutan.

Question Q9 asks whether respondents are aware of the media policy in Bhutan. The largest percentage (36.45%) responded that they were not at all aware of the media policy of Bhutan, followed by slightly aware (34.37%). Only those in their 20s reported that they are slightly aware, followed by not at all aware. For those who said they were aware of media policy, Q10 asked how to improve the media policy. To this, they said that those working in the media should investigate the news properly before reporting in mass media. They also said that the media should have the right to publish the news which the people should be aware of and not to enter into the extreme personal issues. They also suggested that the media should take precautions for the viewers if a particular program contains explicit content which is not suitable for children. Finally, they said that the policy should be free of political control or influence.

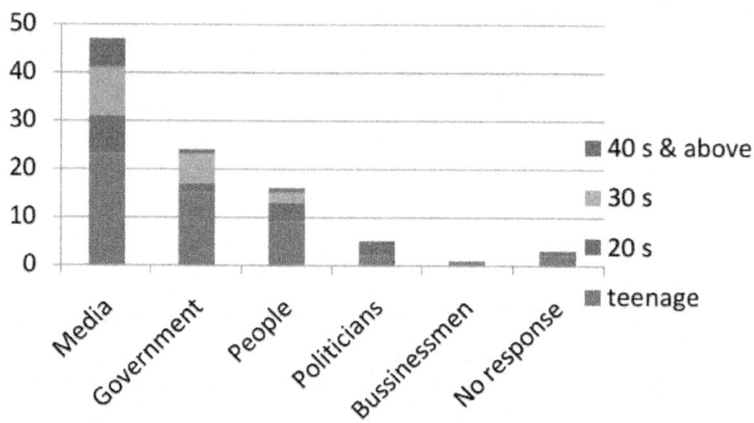

Figure 4: People's perception of agenda setter

Who sets the agenda matters to society. The media must act to spread development messages, and it is their obligation towards society to report events and programs accurately rather than manipulating news to favor an individual or association [24]. As seen in Figure 4, which shows the respondents reply to question Q16, the largest percentage (48.95%) said that the agenda setter is media. This implies that the media decides what become news and sets the agenda for the nation rather than the government. However, when analyzed by age group, people in their 20s reported that it is the media who sets the agenda, followed by the people, and then the politicians. Those in their 30s reported that, after the media, it is the government who sets the agenda, followed by the people. Teens reported that, after the media it is the people, followed by the politicians.

Summary, Conclusion and Policy Implications

Over the decade, the life of the Bhutanese people has changed greatly with the development of the media. Today, almost 80% of the population has access to information through various media. However, Bhutan has its challenges such as the scattered households and rugged terrain which make any development plan difficult. Since the Bhutan Broadcasting Service (BBS) radio, the national public service broadcaster, was started in November 1973 by young volunteers and TV stations provided by BBS TV were launched in June 1999, radio and TV have been the most important electronic media in Bhutan. On the other hand, the internet, also launched in Bhutan in 1999, has seen a drastic increase in the number of subscribers from 2,117 in 2003 to 109,528 in 2008 and 133,289 as of 2013. We know most of the current internet subscribers are government offices, while internet connections at home are also on the rise. Internet connection will become even more popular with more electronic devices entering the Bhutanese market such as personal laptop computers, smart phones, and tablets.

The Bhutanese government has initiated various projects to improve the accessibility of information, for example, by setting up community centers, similar to centers like SARI (Sustainable Access in Rural India) and E-Governance projects in India as described by Choudhary [25]. This would allow peoples to access information and online services; however, there have been critics in the mass media who claim that this is not functioning well. In the attempt to probe this issue, we found that most of our respondents used community centers services only occasionally followed by never. They would prefer that community centers be in better locations, have knowledgeable attendants who can operate the machines, and also provide reliable services. They also suggested promoting better awareness of the community centers. Besides community centers and improvements in media ownership, 67% of the respondents did not engage in discussions about politics. When asked about the best ways to engage the people, they chose TV, followed by direct communication, and then the internet. This could be because of the impact of live debate sessions on TV during election campaigns, and also because people prefer direct communications in the form of social gatherings or visiting each family to explain the parties' manifestos. The internet seems to be experiencing a surge. This could be because the largest group of respondents were teenagers and also because of the increase in subscriptions to 3G. Sometimes, people do not engage in discussions if they feel that their opinions are not being reported, as highlighted by the media development assessment report, which pointed out that bureaucratic barriers and traditional norms hinder the exercise of constitutional rights [14]. Similarly, the survey response also showed this slightly negative trend, and also that the respondents feel that the minority news is not given equal priority in news reports.

It is not surprising that mass media has influenced and affected people's daily lives moderately as well as their opinions. However, it is interesting to note that commercial advertisements, which are available to people via various kinds of mass media, rarely influences their buying decisions.

The behavior and attitude of men are being more affected by programs and events transmitted through mass media than women probably because men watch or read national mass media or sports channels more than women. It is very common to see men discussing sporting events such as archery or football, while women mostly watch Indian soap operas, which have nothing to do with Bhutanese culture and simply provide entertainment. However, people in their 30s are highly influenced, which indicates that this group of people is working in offices and has access to the internet and social media sites such as Facebook. People were occasionally influenced by commercial advertisements, but their behavior remains unchanged. For teenage boys and men in their thirties, the behavior change due to the influence of mass media could have implications. Unlike developed nations, where so much of the impact of commercial advertisements is being reported, Bhutan seems like an exception, where people are not influenced by commercial advertisements. Though their opinions may be influenced at times, their change in opinion does not necessarily influence their behavior or their decisions. This could possibly be because most of the advertisements are provided by foreign channels. The products they advertise are not readily available in the market, and also the content is not relevant in the Bhutanese context. Furthermore, during the interviews, one of the respondents from a rural area of Bhutan said that," if the products are advertised that means that product is not selling well, that's why they are advertising. Good and authentic products always sells out, and they don't need to be advertised". It is interesting to note that, many of the people felt this way. However, considering that Bhutan has a large youth population, it is important to note that of all the age groups, teenagers' opinions are being influenced by mass media the most, especially among boys, which could have policy implications. Regarding men in their thirties, this age group belongs to the working group, and for them, advertisements are not restricted to TV as they have access to all kinds of advertisements through various media, such as smart phones, newspapers, the internet, and social media. Government organizations and businesses have started websites, and Bhutan's draft constitution was launched on the internet. Digital forums, especially kuenselonline.com, and social media sites such as Facebook are now regarded as spaces for discussion, and the public sphere has grown with the internet. Today, media has picked up in vibrancy. For instance, the online edition of the paper provides a public forum for lively discussions on development issues and the policies of the government. Readers post feedback, criticize failed projects and ask the government for accountability. This online feedback system is now joined by social media sites, providing another platform for the people to voice their concerns and raise issues pertaining to national interest. Facebook users have also created groups for buying and selling, and they advertise their products. According to the data obtained from social bakers, 73.3% of Facebook users in Bhutan are in the age group of 18-34 [26]. Social bakers is an online networking analytics that deals with social media administration services.

Thus, in conclusion, we believe that media policy focusing on how to deal with this growing demand for the new "social networking society" based upon the appropriate infrastructure needs to be discussed in the government, mass media, and among academics also. In this sense we emphasize the importance of further investigation of Bhutanese mass media from different viewpoints such as accessibility, influence, and impacts.

ACKNOWLEDGEMENT

I would like to thank Asian Development Bank for providing scholarship funds for this study.

REFERENCES

1. Rapten P (2001) Mass Media: Its consumption and impact on residents of Thimphu and rural areas. Journal of Bhutan Studies 3:172-198.
2. Davison W P, Boylan J R, Frederick T C (1976) Mass media: Systems and effects. Praeger, New York.
3. Castells M (2007) Communication, power and counter-power in the network society. International Journal of Communication 1: 238-266.
4. Wright CR, Page CH (1986) Mass communication: A sociological perspective.Random House, New York

5. McQuail D (1977) The influence and effects of mass media. Mass Communication and Society. Sage Publications, Inc.
6. Royal Government of Bhutan (2008) Bhutan information and media impact study 2008. Ministry of Information and Communication, Thimphu, Bhutan.
7. Habermas J (1989) The structural transformation of the public sphere: An inquiry into a category of bourgeois society. Polity Press, Oxford.
8. Klier P (1990) ImDreieck von Demokratie, Öffentlichkeit und Massenmedien. Duncker&Humblot, Berlin.
9. Doyle G (2002) Understanding media economics. SAGE publications, London.
10. Gunther R, Mughan A (2000) Democracy and the media: a comparative perspective. Cambridge University Press, Cambridge.
11. Cohen J, Weimann G (2000) Cultivation revisited: Some genres have some effects on some viewers. Communication Reports 13: 99-114.
12. Croteau DR, Hoynes WD (2013) Media/society: Industries, images, and audiences. (5th Ed) Sage Publication, London.
13. McDonald R (2004) Television, materialism and culture: An exploration of imported media and its implications for GNH. Journal of Bhutan studies 11: 68.
14. Royal Government of Bhutan (2010) Media development assessment. Ministry of Information and Communication, Thimphu, Bhutan
15. Royal Government of Bhutan (2013) Statistical yearbook of Bhutan 2013. National Statistics Bureau, Thimphu, Bhutan.
16. Dorji K (2006) Media in Bhutan: now and then. Journal of Bhutan Studies 14: 5-23.
17. Royal Government of Bhutan (2013) Bhutan information and media impact study 2013. Ministry of Information and Communication, Thimphu, Bhutan.
18. Ahonen TT (2008) Mobile as 7th of the mass media: cellphone, camera phone, iPhone, smartphone. Futuretext Ltd.
19. Royal Government of Bhutan (2008) The guide to Constitution of the Kingdom of Bhutan, Thimphu.
20. Folkerts J, Lacy S (2005) The media in your life: an introduction to mass communication.(3rd Ed) Allyn and Bacon 08-00, Boston
21. Royal Government of Bhutan (2014) Annual progress report, Ministry of Information and Communication, Thimphu, Bhutan

22. http://www.bbs.bt/news/?p=42237
23. LaPiere RT (1934) Attitudes vs. actions. Social Forces 13: 230-237.
24. Ali A (2015) Media Ownership and Control Versus Press Freedom in Democratic Africa.J Mass Communicat Journalism 5: 239.
25. Choudhary P S (2012) ICT Enabled Community Development in India. J Mass Commun Journalism 2:1-5.
26. Social bakers (2014) Bhutan Facebook Statistics.

Chapter 4

RECONFIGURATION AND EMPIRICAL STUDY ON THE EVALUATION SYSTEM OF WECHAT COMMUNICATION EFFECT OF SCI-TECH PERIODICALS

Feifei Han[1], Zhangzhi Ge[2], Rongting Zhou[1]

[1]Department of Sci-Tech Communication and Policy, University of Science and Technology of China, Hefei, China

[2]School of Public Affairs, University of Science and Technology of China, Hefei, China

ABSTRACT

In the coming Micro-Communication era, many Sci-Tech periodicals have successively registered WeChat Official Accounts and then how to objectively evaluate the communication effects of the WeChat Official Accounts of Sci-Tech periodicals becomes the biggest concern at present. This thesis analyzed the existing communication effect evaluation system of WeChat Official Accounts of Sci-Tech periodicals and its problems, and put forward the following improving strategies: rebuilding a new evaluation system of WeChat communication effect of Sci-Tech periodicals via the selection of evaluation indexes, the division of assessment index weight and the calculation method of evaluation index, then testing the reliability and efficiency of the new evaluation system, and finally putting forward the corresponding policy recommendations.

INTRODUCTION

According to the definition of Sci-Tech periodical in the official document "Science and Technology Periodical Management Regulations", Sci-Tech periodical is a serial publication which holds the fixed publication format and reports science and technology as the main content, and an effective media which is used to publish scientific research achievements for professionals and spread the scientific and technical information. Due to the strong professional of the scientific achievements and technological information, Sci-Tech periodicals were limited in the audience scope and audience structure to a certain extent. In response to this phenomenon, the major Sci-Tech periodicals have opened WeChat Official Accounts to enhance their communication effect. By taking "Qiushi Journal Online" WeChat Official Account for example, it was authenticated since April 18, 2013, and within one week, such as 2015.11.29-2015.12.05, the reading number on its recommended articles had come to 50,140 and showed a trend of increasing day by day. It has got more attention on WeChat than paper periodical, which has greatly improved the communication effect.

With the diversification of WeChat's application functions and the pluralization of information content and form, the previous evaluation system of WeChat communication effect of Sci-Tech periodicals is facing huge challenges. Combined with the audience's growing appetite for quantity and quality of the technological information and the fierce competition for information resources among those major WeChat Official Account platforms of Sci-Tech periodicals, the defects of current evaluation system are more prominent. In order to ensure the comprehensive and objective of the evaluation system of WeChat communication effect of Sci-Tech periodicals, this thesis tried to correct existing evaluation system, reset new indexes and form the index weight by using new calculation method, and then took the empirical test for the effectiveness of the new evaluation system, and finally put forward policy suggestions to promote WeChat communication effect of Sci-Tech periodicals.

CURRENT SITUATION OF WECHAT COMMUNICATION EFFECT EVALUATION OF SCI-TECH PERIODICALS IN CHINA

Academic Research Status

Since the launch of Wechat 1.0 beta on January 21, 2011, the influence of WeChat communication has been continuous expansion and extension, while the academic research on Sci-Tech periodical WeChat communication started in 2013 (Hu Haixia, 2013; Sun Qianjun, 2013) . Through the analysis of WeChat and Weibo transmission effect, Shi Jing and some other scholars summarized four key elements, namely user, graphic, message and interface, which influence the WeChat communication, and gave prospects for the dissemination of new media of Sci-Tech periodicals (Shi Jin et al., 2014) . Zhong Yonggang appealed for great attention on communication of visual language, professional interest of information, and full interaction among users, authors and editors to strengthen the Wechat communication effect of Sci-Tech periodicals (Zhong Yonggang, 2015) . By comparing Chinese and foreign social media application of medical Sci-Tech periodicals, Cheng Qihou pointed out the shortages of Micro-Communication of Chinese Sci-Tech periodicals, and put forward four suggestions for improvement (Cheng Qihou & Zhang Jing, 2015) .

Overall, there are two main directions of this part in current academic research: one is the discussion on WeChat communication model and its influencing factors; the other is the discussion on WeChat communication characteristics and development strategy in various Sci-Tech fields. At present, few research are carried out on evaluation system of WeChat communication effect of Sci-Tech periodicals, besides existing evaluation index still stays at the explicit level and has not yet formed a unified evaluation criterion.

Actual Application Status

After more than four years' development, the total registered users of WeChat (more than 600 million) has exceeded the total amount of Weibo total registered users (more than 500 million)(Zhan Xun and Yan Xing, 2014) , and becomes an important medium for information communication in all areas. So far, many institutions, such as Aiweibang, Public Opinion Monitoring Center of People's Daily Online, New Rank Index, and Index of New Media and so on, have evaluated the Wechat communication effect, carried out the index ranking, and set up corresponding evaluation column for Sci-Tech periodicals. But these independent institutions respectively set up their own evaluation system, which leads to very different results finally. In addition, these evaluation systems mostly tend to select indexes from the aspect of audience while ignore the others (see Table 1), and also not give explicit description of the correlation degree between indexes according to the actual situation of WeChat communication effect in each field (Li Mingde and Gao Ru, 2015) .

It can be seen that there are obviously insufficient of research on evaluation system of WeChat communication effect of Sci-Tech periodicals in both academia and the industry, which also directly affects the credibility of the practical application. To this end, this article will analyze from two perspectives of both audience and

Table 1: Part of evaluation institutions of WeChat communication effect and their evaluation indexes

Name of Evaluation Institution	Evaluation Index
Micro Rank Index of Aiweibang Net	The number of push articles in each day, the total number of "like", the total number of reading, the average reading number of every day
Public Opinion Monitoring Center of People's Daily Online	The number of push articles' frequency in each day, the number of push articles in each day, the highest reading number of one article, the total number of reading, the average reading number of every day, the total number of "like"
New Rank Index	The number of push articles' frequency in each day, the number of push articles in each day, the total number of reading, the average reading number of every day, the highest reading number of one article, the total number of "like"
Index of New Media	the total number of reading, the average reading number of every day, the highest reading number of one article, the total number of "like", the average number of "like" on one day, the highest number of "like" on one article

operator and try to construct a more scientific and authoritative evaluation system by using the Delphi Method, Analytic Hierarchy Process Method and Efficiency Coefficient Method so that to achieve the goal of measuring the WeChat communication effect of Sci-Tech periodicals.

RECONSTITUTION FOR EVALUATION SYSTEM OF WE-CHAT COMMUNICATION EFFECT OF SCI-TECH PERI-ODICALS

To realize objective and accurate evaluation for WeChat communication effect of Sci-Tech periodicals, firstly, we need to clear the evaluation indexes of it. According to the above status analysis in theory and practice, this article added three indicators—originality degree of articles' content (Zhang Haidong and Sun Jihua, 2015) , push rate of articles, abundance degree of information form (Song Qifan, 2015) to existing evaluation indexes and further classified all indexes into two categories—the audience aspect and the operator aspect. However, to build a scientific, authoritative and suitable evaluation system of WeChat communication effect for Chinese Sci-Tech periodicals, we conduct it from the following three processes: 1) select diversified evaluation indexes; 2) set reasonable weight of every index; 3) determine scientific calculation method of the indexes.

The Selection of Evaluation Indexes

Now, the interaction degree between disseminators and recipients is strengthening continuously in "Internet +" era (Sara K. Yeo et al., 2015) . To ensure that the evaluation index data obtained is more targeted, the selection principles of evaluation index should be: 1) give consideration to both operators and audiences (Zhang Yanping, 2015) ; 2) directly related to WeChat communication effect of Sci-Tech periodicals (Ma Yong et al., 2014) ; 3) can be quantified and counted.

Operators, who are the "gatekeeper" of information push, lead the development direction of WeChat. Although WeChat official accounts' operators of Sci-Tech periodicals can't put too much subjective philosophy in the process of information transmission, they can promote the WeChat communication effect of Sci-Tech periodicals by improving relevant indicators. Operators could measure the WeChat communication effect of Sci-Tech periodicals from the following five indicators: originality degree of articles' content, total push frequency of articles, push rate of articles, total number of push articles and abundance degree of information form. The public is final host of WeChat communication of Sci-Tech periodicals, and audience's behavior and its result is an important measurement of WeChat effective communication of Sci-Tech periodicals. The influence from audiences to WeChat communication effect of Sci-Tech periodicals can be quantitative analysis from following six indicators: total number of reading, average reading number every day, highest reading number of one article, total number of "like", average number of "like" on one day, highest number of "like" on one article (see Table 2).

Division of Evaluation Index Weight

Weight setting of primary indexes (A and B in Table 2) comes to the first. Along with the internet permeability to people's daily life constantly, information communication mode is transiting from one-way closed communication

Table 2: Evaluation indexes of WeChat communication effect of Sci-Tech periodicals

Primary Index	Secondary Index	Index Calculation Method
Disseminator (A)	originality degree of articles' content (X1)	number of papers published in this journal/number of papers from all journal
	total push frequency of articles (X2)	push frequency every day * days
	push rate of articles (X3)	number of push articles/number of published papers
	total number of push articles (X4)	push frequency every day * article number in each push
	abundance degree of information form (X5)	number of articles with various forms/total number of push articles
Recipient (B)	total number of reading (X6)	the total number of reading
	average reading number of every day (X7)	the total number of reading/days
	highest reading number of one article (X8)	the highest reading number of one article
	total number of "like" (X9)	the total number of "like"
	average number of "like" on one day (X10)	the total number of "like"/days
	highest number of "like" on one article (X11)	the highest number of "like"

Note: As the strong "closure" in WeChat communication environment, some indexes are difficult to obtain, such as number of forward, number of fans, number of comments, etc. So these indexes haven't put into this evaluation system.

Note: As the strong "closure" in WeChat communication environment, some indexes are difficult to obtain, such as number of forward, number of fans, number of comments, etc. So these indexes haven't put into this evaluation system.

to two-way open communication, and the role of disseminators and recipients transformed from immobilized mode to automatic mode. The interactive structure between the two bodies becomes “decentralization”, and the status of the two parties gradually tends to be equal in the process of information dissemination in network (Wang Guoyan and Han Feifei, 2014) . Based on the current development situation, this article used the Fuzzy Comprehensive Evaluation Method to quantize evaluation index weight of A and B, whose result is that weight coefficient for both A and B is quite approaching, and the weight coefficient of index B is slightly higher than the weight coefficient of index A($W_B - W_A < 0.01$). In view of this, this article set the same weight for index A and index B as 50%.

Next is the weight setting of secondary indexes (11 indexes in Table 2: X1 – X11). To avoid uncertainty and subjectivism in weight setting, this article used a combined method of qualitative and quantitative analysis. Firstly, we used Delphi Method and questionnaire survey to obtain the evaluation of importance degree of each index from experts and audiences, and on the basis of this evaluation, we use the Analytic Hierarchy Process to quantify the importance degree of every two indicators to the number 1 - 9 and its reciprocal as the scale of the quantitative statistics (Zhang Zhaoguo et al., 2011) . By pair wise comparing the sub indexes for operators (A) and the audiences (B), we got the following judgment matrix:

$$B=\begin{bmatrix} 1 & 1/3 & 3 & 2 & 1/2 & 2 \\ 3 & 1 & 3 & 3 & 2 & 3 \\ 1/3 & 1/3 & 1 & 1/2 & 1/2 & 2 \\ 1/2 & 1/3 & 2 & 1 & 1/3 & 2 \\ 2 & 1/2 & 2 & 3 & 1 & 3 \\ 1/2 & 1/3 & 1/2 & 1/2 & 1/3 & 1 \end{bmatrix} \quad A=\begin{bmatrix} 1 & 3 & 2 & 3 & 1/2 \\ 1/3 & 1 & 1 & 1 & 1/3 \\ 1/2 & 1 & 1 & 2 & 1/3 \\ 1/3 & 1 & 1/2 & 1 & 1/2 \\ 2 & 3 & 3 & 2 & 1 \end{bmatrix}$$

Finally, we used Arithmetic Average Method to get the weight coefficient (represented by W_i inTable 3, i = 1 - 9) of the secondary indexes (Deng Xue et al., 2012). As you can see in Table 3, the largest eigenvalue (λ_{max}) of the two matrix are 5.1571 and 6.2853 respectively. Now that the Consistency Ratio of both sides (0.0351 and 0.0453 respectively) is all less than 0.10, it can be concluded that the weighting coefficient of the secondary indexes is reasonable.

Calculation Method of Evaluation Index

Whether the calculation method of evaluation indexes is objective or not will directly affect the final evaluation

Table 3: Weight coefficient of the secondary indexes from judgment matrix A and B

	W_1	W_2	W_3	W_4	W_5	–	λ_{max}	CR
Disseminator	0.2744	0.1140	0.1420	0.1076	0.3621	–	5.1571	0.0351
	W_6	W_7	W_8	W_9	W_{10}	W_{11}	λ_{max}	CR
Recipient	0.1612	0.3353	0.0887	0.1118	0.2325	0.0704	6.2853	0.0453

result. Now that the value emphasis and operation way are very different in different fields of WeChat communication, and the information attribute in Sci-Tech journals has distinct difference compared to other media's, it is not suitable to adopt a unified and absolute evaluation standard, but should take relative evaluation in each field. After selecting different indexes and setting their weight, we used the Efficacy Coefficient Method to calculate the effect of different functions, and built a new evaluation index (Z_i) for measuring WeChat communication effect of Sci-Tech periodicals, whose computational formula is as follows:

$$Z_i=\left[\sum_{i=1}^{5}\left(\frac{X_i-X_{min}}{X_{max}-X_{min}}\times 40+60\right)\times W_i\right]\times 50\%+\left[\sum_{i=6}^{11}\left(\frac{X_i-X_{min}}{X_{max}-X_{min}}\times 40+60\right)\times W_i\right]\times 50\%,$$

$$=\left[\sum_{i=1}^{11}\left(\frac{X_i-X_{min}}{X_{max}-X_{min}}\times 40+60\right)\times W_i\right]\times 50\%, \quad (X_i-X_{min}<X_{max}-X_{min})$$

In this formula, X_i stands for the actual value of each index; X_{min} and X_{max} respectively stand for the minimum value and maximum value in the whole index ranking of each industry; W_i is the weight of each evaluation index. To translate the Efficacy Coefficient into centesimal system, the two constant terms were set to 60 (as benchmark) and 40.

The calculation method of evaluation index of WeChat communication effect of Sci-Tech periodicals should tend to focus on the authenticity and scientificity of information communication, fully assess the impact of every evaluation indexes on the efficiency value, and make full use of empirical research methods to comprehensively evaluate the effect. From the perspective of operators, the effect evaluation is aim to present the operation state comprehensively of each WeChat public platform in Sci-Tech industry, so it is a comprehensive measure of the function application, service efficiency, supervision level of the Sci-Tech periodicals' WeChat platform. But from the perspective of audiences, the effect evaluation is aim to understand the information feedback of various types of audience groups, as well as to adjust the communication model of WeChat timely according to audience's feedback (Gillian Pearson, 2001) .

EMPIRICAL TEST FOR EFFECTIVENESS OF THE NEW EVALUATION SYSTEM

After building a new evaluation system, how to test its effectiveness has become the next problem. To this end, we can make a comparative research between the results of the new evaluation system and the evaluation results of the Index of New Media (it contained 276,337 WeChat official accounts till December 7th, 2015, which is far higher than other evaluation agencies). We selected 10 active WeChat official accounts of Sci-Tech journals, whose Composite Impact Factor ranked top 1000 in Annual Report for Chinese Academic Journals Impact Factors (Social Science) (Vol 12, 2014), as samples for analysis. And then we collected relevant data according to the above 11 index sequence (see Table 4).

Putting the above index data of 10 samples into the new evaluation index formula Z_i, we calculated the new evaluation index of WeChat communication effect for each Sci-Tech periodical, and compared the new ranking in descending order with the original ranking as shown in Table 5. It can be seen that the index value under the new standard are decreased significantly, and the numerical gap between these values also decreased because of the centesimal transformation of quantitative values under Effectiveness Function.

Table 4: Index information of ten WeChat official accounts of Sci-Tech journals (Nov 29, 2015-Dec 5, 2015)

Official Accounts	Originality Degree of Articles' Content	Total Push Frequency of Articles	Push Rate of Articles	Total Number of Push Articles	Abundance Degree of Information Form	Total Number of Reading	Average Reading Number Every Day	Highest Reading Number of One Article	Total Number of "Like"	Average Number of "Like" on One Day	Highest Number of "Like" on One Article
QS Theory	0.356	7	0.021	34	0.018	50140	1475	6556	376	11	58
China University Teaching	0.352	2	0.033	2	0	4718	2359	3854	43	22	40
Journal of Distance Education in China	0.097	7	0.030	30	0.015	8425	281	2380	120	4	67
Urban Plan	0.076	3	0.030	8	0.019	5000	625	1524	23	3	9
Journalism Review	0.619	3	0.013	5	0.013	2959	592	1142	24	5	8
Library and Information Service	0.116	1	0.012	1	0	920	920	920	12	12	12
Economic Research Journal	0	2	0.524	11	0	3444	313	1565	11	1	5
Journal of Studies in Early Childhood Education	0.274	2	0.037	6	0.006	1574	262	386	13	2	5
Science-Technology & Publication	0.439	2	0.012	2	0.012	810	405	509	4	2	4
Studies in Ideological Education	0.760	2	0.080	2	0	482	241	313	12	6	11

The previous top 3 index values of WeChat official account of Sci-Tech journals—QS theory, China University Education, Journal of Chinese Distance Education still retain the original ranking; but the new ranking of Economic research changes greatly because its two values—"originality degree of articles' content" and "abundance degree of information form" are 0 in the form, which dragged down the overall index; other 6 Sci-Tech periodicals' index ranking just appears slight amplitude adjustment. In general, it has new changes in the results of the new evaluation indexes,

Data source: Annual Report for Chinese Academic Journals Impact Factors (Social Science) (Vol 12, 2014).

Table 5: Results from index of new media and new evaluation indexes

Results from Index of New Media with Previous Evaluation Indexes	Communication Index	Results from New Evaluation Indexes	Communication Index
QS Theory	708.78	QS theory	88.48
China University Teaching	584.10	China University Teaching	76.78
Journal of Distance Education in China	483.46	Journal of Distance Education in China	74.69
Urban Plan	462.42	Journalism Review	73.05
Journalism Review	438.53	Urban Plan	71.63
Library and Information Service	412.10	Science-Technology & Publication	69.01
Economic Research Journal	393.06	Studies in Ideological Education	67.62
Journal of Studies in Early Childhood Education	344.26	Library and Information Service	65.85
Science-Technology & Publication	329.06	Journal of Studies in Early Childhood Education	65.57
Studies in Ideological Education	306.75	Economic Research Journal	64.71

but not dramatic changes. From a macro perspective, the new evaluation results can reflect the WeChat communication effect of Sci-Tech periodicals more completely.

CONCLUSIONS AND POLICY RECOMMENDATIONS

WeChat public platform of Sci-Tech periodicals is an integration product of traditional media and new media, and plays an extremely important role in ensuring the continuous and stable development of Sci-Tech periodicals while extends the information transmission chain. Based on the defects of current evaluation system of WeChat communication effect of Sci-Tech journals, this article builds a new evaluation system from two perspectives of the audiences and the operators comprehensively, and also realizes the following innovation: 1) it introduces new indicators, increases the number of ratio indicators which make the index values relatively stable; 2) it distributes indicators into two sides—the operators and the audiences, and reflects the same importance; 3) it changes the way of calculation, uses centesimal system, makes it more acceptable subjectively, and also uses the Efficacy Function to give the benchmark points which manifest the basis value of the Sci-Tech journals who open WeChat official accounts and spread information; 4) the index calculation process needs to refer to cross- reference data of peer industry, and the relative but not absolute results are more conducive to peer comparison. Finally, through the empirical test, we conclude that the new evaluation system is effective.

To those difficult problems that appeared in the process of building the new evaluation system, this article put forward the following two suggestions.

The first is expanding the scope of the evaluation objects, and speeding up informatization operation. According to the survey of above 1000 Sci-Tech periodicals, few of them open their WeChat official accounts and most of them are still in the traditional information communication phase at present. Some of them have opened the WeChat official accounts while there are also lots of "zombie accounts", which makes data collection for evaluation objects become a difficult problem. However, to obtain more accurate evaluation results, we have to expand the scope of evaluation objects and collect data widely, or the final evaluation results could hardly reflect the real communication situation objectively, but also go against the improvement and adjustment of the evaluation index. In addition, in order to optimize the WeChat communication effect of Sci-Tech periodicals, we need to enrich the content and forms of Sci-Tech information to expand the periodicals' brand influence; and meanwhile, we need to strengthen the communication between the operators and the audiences to stabilize target audience. This is not only beneficial to enrich information communication mode for Sci-Tech periodicals but also important to promote the transformation development of Sci-Tech periodicals.

The second is enhancing the credibility of evaluation behavior, and promoting the standardized management. To make the evaluation system of WeChat communication effect of Sci-Tech periodicals more authoritative, we should establish a professional assessment organization, which can be elected from the bottom up, or be operated by a third party authority, or be original established by the common competent department. Besides, the relative staffs in it should have different knowledge background, different identity, different experience and some other factors, and they are the "opinion leaders" in each field, who can make professional and comprehensive evaluation, and provide the most objective evaluation results to the public finally. It can not only reduce the consumption of manpower, material and financial resources in the process of evaluation, but also effectively purify science communication environment and prevent each of them releasing different index evaluation that causes the loss of evaluation credibility, and further promote the sustainable development of information resources from WeChat official accounts of Sci-Tech journals.

It is worth noting that, as the current limitation of the data acquisition and statistical techniques, part of the indicator data such as the number of fans for WeChat official account has been made public, which has certain influence on the comprehensive evaluation. Therefore, in the future research, it is necessary to further improve the evaluation system of WeChat Communication Effect of Sci-Tech periodicals.

ACKNOWLEDGEMENTS

This work was supported by "Study on the Improvement of the Scientific Quality of Citizens and the Environment of Scientific Communication in Anhui Province" (Soft Science Research Project of Anhui Province in 2015), Project Number: 1502052008.

REFERENCES

1. Cheng, Q. H., & Zhang, J. (2015). The Application and Enlightenment of Science and Technology Journal by Micro Media- Use Top 4 International Authoritative Medical Journal as Example. Science-Technology & Publication, 9, 91-94.
2. Hu, H. X. (2013). Discussion on Micro Era of Sci-Tech Periodicals. New Challenges for Chinese Sci-Tech Journals—Proceedings of the 9th Chinese Sci-Tech journals Development Forum, Hangzhou, 26-27 September 2013, 273-275.
3. Li, M. D., & Gao, R. (2015). Communication Capability Assessment of Media WeChat Public Number: A Research Based on 20 Media WeChat Public Numbers in Shanxi. Journal of Information, 7, 141-147.
4. Ma, Y., Zhao, W. Y., & Sun, S. Z. (2014). The Function Selection Analysis of WeChat Official Account by the Academic Journals. Science-Technology & Publication, 9, 77-81.
5. Pearson, G. (2001). The Participation of Scientists in Public Understanding of Science Activities: The Policy and Practice of the U.K. Research Councils. Public Understanding of Science, 10, 121-137. http://dx.doi.org/10.1088/0963-6625/10/1/309
6. Shi, J., Duan, C. B., Zhou, B. Y., Tan, X., Meng, L., & Yu, P. L. (2014). A Look at Science and Technology Journals Used Weibo & WeChat Platform Influence Evaluation. Chinese Journal of Scientific and Technical Periodicals, 5, 655-660.
7. Song, Q. F. (2015). All Media Publishing Practical Applies in the Field of Science and Technology Journals. Science-Technology & Publication, 4, 77-82.

8. Sun, Q. J. (2013). Humble Opinions for the Future Development of Sci-Tech Periodicals in China. New Challenges for Chinese Sci-Tech Journals—Proceedings of the 9th Chinese Sci-Tech journals Development Forum, Hangzhou, 26-27 September 2013, 395-397.
9. Wang, G. Y., & Han, F.F. (2014). Research on Communication Effect of Data Visualization from the Perspective of the Encoding and Decoding. Journal of Information, 11, 169-174.
10. Yeo, S. K., Cacciatore, M. A., & Scheufele, D. A. (2015). News Selectivity and Beyond: Motivated Reasoning in a Changing Media Environment. Publizistik und gesellschaftliche Verantwortung, 3, 83-104.
11. Zhan, X., & Yan, X. (2014). Research on WeChat Continuously Use Intention Influencing Factors and Its Use and Satisfaction. Modern Communication, 11, 130-134.
12. Zhang, H. D., & Sun, J. H. (2015). Study on Micro-Content Spread of the Scientific Journals. Chinese Journal of Scientific and Technical Periodicals, 9, 925-929.
13. Zhang, Y. P. (2015). Sci-Tech Periodical WeChat Official Accounts Operation Mode Research Based on the Quantitative Analysis of Four Kinds of Core Periodicals of Science and Technology. Chinese Journal of Scientific and Technical Periodicals, 5, 524-531.
14. Zhang, Z. G., Zhang, W. F., & Yang, Q. X. (2011). The Construction of Evaluation System of Internal Control Based on the Objective and Empirical Test. Nankai Business Review, 1, 148-155.
15. Zhong, Y. G. (2015). Establishment and Effect Analysis of Sci-Tech Periodical WeChat Platform. Public Communication of Science & Technology, 12, 115-116.

Chapter 5

NORMATIVITY AND THE PROBLEM OF LOOK IN THE EMERGENCE OF CITIZEN JOURNALISM

Célestin Messanga Obama

Department of Advertisement, Advance School of Mass Communication, University of Yaoundé 2, Yaoundé, Cameroon

ABSTRACT

Citizen journalism (in French Journalisme citoyen) is a form of journalism exercised by the public (the readers, the audiences and tele-viewers), specifically on the internet. Theoretically, it could be seen as a kind of revolution within the public getting into a trade long held jealously mainly by conventional journalists. What accounts for the fact that a trade, whose mastery requires training on its techniques and specific norms, gets invaded by untutored minds? That appears to be the central issue we are seeking to resolve in this article. We go from the hypothesis that citizen journalism has developed as a result of the publics' lack of satisfaction, both at quantitative and qualitative levels with the delivery of conventional journalism. In effect, conventional journalism raises myriad issues that require the consumers to proceed to a kind of selection, which itself could be a problem. However, by their nature, issues that constitute news are complex, and this leads to some manipulation in their treatment. These two axes appear to reveal the main sources of discord between conventional journalism and revolted-publics.

INTRODUCTION

The concept of citizen journalism (in French Journalisme citoyen) may be confusing if it is understood in a civic perspective where citizen refers to "inhabitant of a city". People would see it a conventional journalism practiced with responsibility by citizens. Meanwhile, some authors (Jay Rosen, 2008; Merritt, 2015; Meyer, 2015; Dvorkin, 2015) use indifferently the expressions "public radio journalism" or "public journalism" to express the same reality. It rather appears here the idea of a journalism practiced by the public. Citizen journalism is therefore a journalism especially practiced on the internet by the public of traditional media (readers, listeners or television viewers). Meanwhile, it should be noted that any speaking on the internet cannot be assimilated to citizen journalism; thus, reactions of internet users to newspaper articles considered as feedbacks to those articles cannot be considered as citizen journalism, which wants to be a daily activity of publication of social facts. In fact, public's reactions are punctual and focused not on facts but on what is said about them. We shall hereby refer to citizen journalism in the strict aspect of publication on the internet, of newspaper articles, blogs animation of websites. In this sense, even a blog animated by a journalist shall not be part of citizen journalism because that activity goes beyond the conventional frame working of journalism.

At the theoretical level, citizen journalism can be assimilated to a kind of revolution, a taking of power by the basis, in which the public takes the strong positions so far occupied by conventional journalists. What therefore explains that a job whose practice requires learning in order to master its techniques and specific norms, should be taken in charge by the uninitiated? In other words, what explains that the public decides to change the professional order, moving from their position as receivers to get the statute of senders? That is the central question to which we shall attempt to find an answer in this article.

For revolutions draws their resources from the building up of dissatisfactions of the established order, we shall say by hypothesis that citizen journalism results from dissatisfaction at the double quantitative and qualitative level of conventional journalism which is a regulative activity. For citizen journalism is considered as a form of journalism, an alter-journalism, we shall opt for the concept of "conventional journalism" to express the classical and old activity rather than the one of "professional journalism". The concept of "conventional journalism", on the one hand, allows us to stress the normative character of journalism, and on the other hand, avoid non- productive debates on professionalism, as citizen journalism claims to be an emerging profession.

The subject of this study here is not citizen journalism itself, but the conditions of its emergence. To this effect, we shall not address issues relative to its success and shortcomings, as well as we shall not be interested in its functioning and its effects on the public.

The question of dissatisfaction in relation to conventional journalism raised in our hypothesis is also found at the quantitative level, in relation to the selection of news items (where are they from and how are they selected?) as well as at the qualitative level, in relation to logics (points of view) developed in articles published. These two major axes appear as those which are liable to reveal with ease the main sources of contention between conventional journalism and "revolted public" constituted in citizen journalists.

From the methodological point of view, this article is a qualitative analysis that is based on a corpus of 60 reactions to twelve articles from French press about war in Syria, published in Yahoo in March 2014. The newspapers studied are: Le Nouvel Observateur, L'Express, Le Pointand Libération. The choice of these four newspapers is based on their large audience and the recurrence of their publications on Yahoo. Le point and L'Express are seen as liberal oriented while the two others are socialists. The selected corpus (three articles per press organ and five reactions per article) has enabled us to identify the reasons for dissatisfaction raised by internet users. The assumption, of public's dissatisfaction, of our hypothesis locates logically our observation towards reception. These reactions, generally, are considered either as additional information, or as a problematization (calling into question) of the points of view of articles that have been read. We shall end our study by asking questions on the future of conventional journalism in this revolutionary context.

DIVERGENCES RELATED TO THE SELECTION OF FACTS

The problem of the role of journalists is built in the relation between the depicted reality they produce through their articles and the reference factual reality. An intellectual tendency considers news productions (news articles, radio and television programs) as the reflection of factual reality. Analyses, in this perspective, tend to determine the conformity among the basic facts and the reports made by journalists (the truth) or the gap (lie). In this way, media that constitute the publication framework of news productions can be classified in "truthful media" and "untruthful media". This Manichean perspective is at the basis of the problem that the role of journalists in the society poses.

However, the taking in consideration on the one hand, of the complex nature of news facts and on the other hand, the subjectivity of its apprehension, highlights a more complex reality. Jean-Pierre Esquenazi considers as error, the fact of postulating that "the media could only misrepresent or distort facts they report" (Esquenazi, 2002) . He points out an important fact, that is: the discursive character of any media product. Eliseo Véron goes further when he says: "social events are not objects that could be found ready somewhere in the reality and that the medias would make us know the properties and the avatars afterwards with moreorless faithfulness. They only exist insofar as those media make them." (Veron, 1981) . The concept of event used by Véron here is synonymous with fact.

The constructivist approach of these two authors enables to identify better the issue of citizen journalism from the activities of conventional journalists.

According to Jürgen Habermas(Habermas, 1987) the fact is "the state of things that happen". In fact, many things happen in life so that one can say that "everything is a fact". Conventional journalism therefore finds itself opposite two ordeals: the one of abundance of facts and the one of quality of what is said about them.

The Ordeal of Quantity

The Syrian conflict is spreading out whereas old centers such as Côte-d'Ivoire, Libya, Iraq, Afghanistan and even Palestine are not yet put out. Internet users continue to draw parallels between news reports and these old facts. Such mergers bring to light two types of problems: the selection of facts and media agenda. In relation to selection, it should be noted that a priori, any fact is liable to be the subject of media coverage. Only, in their activity, journalists have a limited adequate time (the duration of an audiovisual program) and space (the page in written press or on a television screen or computer). In order to manage these time and space constraints, facing the plurality of facts, journalists must make choices. Meanwhile, on principle, any choice can be suitable for polemic. Conventional journalism has defined a number of criteria, so as to reduce this tendency for polemic, and to give an objective character to the selection of facts. They are:

- Novelty. Novelty lies in unusual fact. The current example used in most training institutions of journalists is the following: "if a dog bites a person, it is not news; news is when a person bites a dog."
- Current events. Because journalism is based on the daily reporting of facts, choice will be on the most recent events. This principle is justified by the idea according to which old facts are liable to have been published and consequently, are no longer of any interest for the public.
- Proximity. Geographical criteria that can be broken down into what professionals call "the law of kilometric death". Proximity can also be perceived at the socio-emotional level. Through this double prism, journalism gives privilege to facts which are the closest at the geographical and emotional level.
- Controversy. Controversy is based on the assumption according to which the human being is more interested in events marked by disagreement and controversy.
- Fame. Fame expresses the fact that journalism gives privilege to facts related to the life or the activity of personalities or institutions which are known (political leaders, religious and scientific authorities, stars, etc.)

- Opportunity. Opportunity refers to suitability or the pertinence of a fact in relation to context.
- Impact. Impact relates to the number of people concerned by a fact. Between two facts, the one that affects the largest number of people will be selected.

Although criteria aim at making the selection of things objective, there are nevertheless some dissatisfaction, facing a public as heterogeneous as the facts themselves and each criteria above-mentioned can be suitable for polemic. The analysis of the reactions of internet users of our corpus shows that the choice of subjects treated is one of the main causes of dissatisfaction of the public for each of the criteria mentioned above open to discussion. The wealth of facts does not only pose the problem of selection, the agenda of media also appears as an important source of dissatisfaction of the public.

The Ordeal of the Agenda

The criteria of selection analyzed above, suppose a free choice among facts happening at the same time. Meanwhile, Maxwell Mc Combs and Donald Shaw (McCombs et al., 1997) in their theory of agenda setting, reveal that, by putting a certain number of information on the agenda, the media dictate to the public what they must think on, even though they don't always succeed in imposing what they have to think about it. The freedom of judgment that shows through in the formula of agenda setting corroborates the problematization of reactions of the internet users analyzed. The programmatic discrepancy between the media agenda and the political agenda brought out by the two American sociologists is partly symptomatic of the quarrel created by media articles. In fact, it appears through the analysis of the corpus of our study that in reporting the constitutive facts of the Syrian crisis, the agenda of the media studied does not correspond with the expectations anti-establishment internet users. The Syrian crisis breaks out in a trouble world and regional climate. The impossibility of the media to satisfy the different expectations paves the way for the problematisation of the agenda, the unsatisfied public being always to explain the registration or the withdrawal from the agenda of issues of their worries. It is in these lines that some people think that the media take advantage of the Syrian conflict to overshadow the "exactions" of Israel in Palestine. The problem of agenda has become worse with the appearance of agency journalism, this "common source" that has become the real prescriber of the agenda of all the media. In fact, the main transnational media, despite the large network of correspondents at their disposal, treat the same subjects at a given moment. The consequence is a kind of a unique media agenda that contributes to the reinforcement of the feeling of dissatisfaction of the public.

DIVERGENCES RELATIVE TO THE PROCESSING OF FACTS

Let's put aside the positivist perspective that suggests an ontological existence of facts and let's consider the constructivist approach that rather seeks the institutional and mental devices that make possible the rhetoric issuing from social actors. This perspective enables to consider the rhetoric of journalists (the news), not as the reflection of any ontological reality (the facts), but as constructs. Thus, in the process of construction their rhetoric, journalists draw inspiration as well from culture (that enables them to understand and interpret facts observed) as from their interactions with their natural and social environment. In fact, in order to understand the events that they report, journalists contact members of the society considered either as those who make facts (political actors, sportsmen in a competition, victims of an accident, etc.) or then, as witnesses who reveal facts. The professional jargon calls them "sources".

Daniel Bougnoux (2001) shows well how journalists and those sources interact in the process of construction of media discourses. The central problem here is the one of consensus between journalists and the receivers of those discourses (the public). The cooperation between journalists and the society, in the production of news is not permanent. It is a matter of punctual association during which journalists get from some members of the society, particles of facts which after transformation (processing) become news or information. Members of society, suppliers of those facts to journalists, find later on, their statute of public (listeners, readers, television viewers or internet users). The two parties remain linked by their culture that enables them to analyze the construct, thanks to the common sense that they share Jürgen Habermas (Op. cit.) talks about "the reality symbolically pre-structured". Journalists' discourse, in order to be accepted, must correspond to the interpretation that the public make of events they account for. That's the term of the consensus without which there is rejection.

The journalistic (media) truth appears when, not as correspondence with a reference ontological reality, but as correspondence with symbolic expectations of the public. The notions of truth and falsehood here take a particular signification. Is therefore true, not the newspaper article that is in accordance with any reference objective reality, but the one that responds to the public expectations. This principle is the one of selective exposure to media brought to the fore by the Americans Paul Lazarsfeld, Bernard Berelson and Hazel Gaudet (1968) , according to which most people only expose themselves, in priority, to communications that agree with their previous opinions.

The problem of interpretation of facts is all the more pertinent as the protesters are not always the witnesses of the facts reported so as to have elements of reference that would enable them to appreciate the similarity or not of the disputed story. Talking about the ethics of discussion, Jürgen Habermas (Op. cit.), mentions among many others, as principle of validation of statements the consistency of arguments. It is that principle that enables interlocutors to understand each other on what makes sense or not. Such understanding supposes common standard of interpretation. Alfred Schultz (Cf. Corcuff, 1995) and many others show that the construction of common sense is done through cultural heritage, what Shultz terms "the taken for granted", that is what is accepted as truth and which, by that fact, is no longer discussed. It is generally accepted in the public opinion that politicians are liars; a newspaper article which accuses a politician of lies will be more credible than the one which pretends the contrary. Nevertheless, the public shall have only rarely reliable elements of appreciation of such allegations. Quite often, the difference of opinion constitutes the bone of contention among journalists and their public, little attention being paid to reference to facts. Thus, journalism finds itself facing the problem of look.

The Problem of Look

An event is empirically perceived through the senses. In this operation, a particular importance is given to the sight and the hearing. But all facts are not seen in the same manner everywhere, by all, with the same acuity. The object seen depends on the point from where it is seen and they talk about point of view (unique position from which they see). The point of view is not simply a geographical point; it is also a mental attitude, or to say it better, a unique cultural device of the person who sees. The look is therefore at the same time physical and cultural. It follows from this that, the fact perceived and the report made of it, are related to subjectivity that is, all that the observer has as personal, and which moreover is related to a particular context. Because the object seen depends on the subjectivity of the person who looks, discourses on facts are subjective and often problematic. This also applies to media discourse. The dissatisfactions due to the difference of points of view can explain the "revolutionary" reaction of internet users, and be the base of the emergence of citizen journalism.

As we mentioned it earlier, the process of production of news, associates journalists and public on the basis of representations of shared values. In this process, journalists try to determine the form of those values and representations. They establish themselves as opinion leaders, a role that grants them a great responsibility in relation to social peace and concord. The question of the responsibility of journalists is set at the ethical level. If it is true that Paul Lazarsfeld, Bernard Berenson and Hazel Gaudet (op. cit.) weaken the influence of the media by saying that most people expose themselves to the media that correspond to their prior opinions, they do not deny the existence of that influence. Their two step flow of communication theory (Katz Elihu & Lazarsfeld, 1955) shows that the media have an influence on the elite who, moreover, influences the masses. Maxwell Mc Combs and Donald Shaw (Op. cit., 1997), in order to develop their theory of agenda-setting, move from the assumption according to which "if one cannot say that the media have an influence on the public, one can neither say they have no influence on the public". Moreover, it is recognized that the redundancy of media messages have an undoubted influence on opinions.

Conventional Journalism in the Sphere of Constraints

Journalism (the media) is generally called the fourth estate. This appellation makes people understand that there are three other powers, placed well ahead and therefore above it. In fact, this naming classifies conventional journalism after the executive, the legislative and the judiciary powers that we can bring together under the concept of "political powers". However, facing the first three which can be independent or aligned according to the systems, journalism stands as anti-establishment. Such an opposition reduces its scope of action. In fact, the first three powers provide their framework of exercise and determine the consequences in case of crossing of riding area. The respect of frame working or normativity places therefore conventional journalism in an environment of political constraints. Number of facts will thus be withdrawn from its agenda as a result of the law or several pressures. Facts which are not processed by conventional journalists because of the law constitute a source of dissatisfaction from the public which want to know about everything. The more the pressure of politicians is visible, the greater is the dissatisfaction (request to know) of the public. Such dissatisfaction could explain the emergence of citizen journalism thanks to the Internet that appears as a space out of control of politicians.

The economic constraints are more discreet but equally heavy as political constraints. An English adage says: "Who pays owns" to say that the tone of the media is given by economico-financial powers. In fact, facing several functioning charges, and even searching material welfare, journalists are subject to the pressure of economic interests. The weight of advertisement in the media economy is well known today. In fact, beyond official contracts, advertisers who are the main sources of financing for the media impose them more or less occult conditions aiming at influencing the contents in their favor.

In the same vein, the media benefit from miscellaneous subsidies. The sources of these subsidies exercise the same type of constraints as advertisers. The articles thus "manipulated" end by creating a break in relation to the public's expectations and instigate reactions aiming at "balancing" the information. Citizen journalism originates in this type of reactions.

Cultural constraints fall within all extra?professional considerations related to the social belonging of the journalist and with which he practices. It regularly happens that journalists feel culturally involved by some media facts and adopt an editorial tone. The report made on it can instigate public dissatisfaction. In the Syrian conflict, the editorial line of the newspapers of our corpus does not stand out from the point of view of political leaders in Western Europe. Such orientations instigate disapproval reactions in the public favorable to Syrian leadership. Such breaks pave the way for what is today called citizen journalism.

NORMATIVITY AND EMERGENCE OF DISSENT

One could also say that the whole problem of journalism is to account for social reality, in a manner consistent with common values and representations, without upsetting the multiple and divergent sensibilities of the interpretative community (the public). Reaching it necessitates a good command of theoretical principles (Sciences) and know-how (techniques). We mean here the problem of training. Talking about the activity of journalists, Jean-Pierre Esquenazi says:

"…but the exercise of this mission is not an easy job. One can even say that any journalist, as soon as he starts working, finds himself immediately placed in a difficult situation. In fact, he must account for all types of differences and complications, in a single voice. For example, he explains at the same time the claims of strikers and the trade union's impossibility to satisfy them." (Op. cit. p.14)

Exceptional oratory skills are needed to reconcile in the same discourse fundamentally opposed positions. Such a talent cannot be naturally given to so many people apart from those known as journalists. This can only be obtained through learning. Training in conventional journalism thus appears as the key to success in the work of journalists. In fact, training presents a double advantage: on the one hand, it provides learners with principles and methodological tools which enable to overcome the difficulty in the practice of the job. Citizen journalism on the contrary is at odds with this training requirement. After an analysis of ten sites of citizen journalism, Tom Grubisich (2014) says that many articles in those sites lack qualities and contents, and this, despite improvements noticed. This revelation shows the importance of training in the work of journalism. Other researches on citizen journalism show that the supervision of the majority of sites of citizen journalism is carried out by conventional journalists. It appears here that you don't just suddenly become a journalist: a prior learning is necessary.

The training of journalists goes beyond the technical aspect of the job, it also touches ethics that is the moral aspect of the job. We have seen that the job of journalists aims at publishing social facts. Some of those facts are at divergent centers of interest. Professional ethics require from the journalist a balanced processing, which does neither damage nor favor a party. It is not simply a matter of reconciling different positions but a moral problem of justice that postulate equality of all before judgment. Training therefore offers journalists not only technical tools but also a moral demarcation line that makes the knife on which the equilibrium of the social balance rests.

On the other hand, training enables standardization in the practice of the job, facing multiculturality that characterizes the world. Meanwhile, such formatting creates other problems because of standardization and normativity that it instigates, in contrast with the perceptual diversity of the public. In fact, the norm, by demarcating space, restricts it and provokes contradictorily the envy to violate it (cf. the biblical myth of the forbidden fruit in the Eden garden). A look on the commentaries of the internet users, on the articles of our corpus, reveals not only a tendency to contradiction in relation to the aspects mentioned above, but also a clear will to break the norms. The different diffraction points here are on the opinions and the choice of facts actually. In short, if training is necessary for the practice of the job of journalist, it is nevertheless of a stumbling block. In fact, training tends to solve the qualitative problem of information, leaving unsatisfied the question of quantity and perceptual diversity of reality; such dissatisfaction paves the way for citizen journalism, which, itself does not escape from it.

CONCLUSIONS

Citizen journalism appears as otherness to conventional journalism. We have postulated that its emergence is caused by dissatisfaction received by conventional journalism. It appears from the preceding analysis that those dissatisfactions are at the same time of quantitative and qualitative order. As far as dissatisfaction of quantitative order is concerned, it appears that the news, subject to media coverage, is not ready made facts that journalists track down in their natural space. They are discourse on facts, that is, constructions. These constructions are achieved on the basis of numerous natural and social phenomena and this imposes a choice. If professional criteria are defined for the choice of facts, it is equally true that the public's expectations, because they are quantitatively greater, are generally unsatisfied. In fact, to each reported case, corresponds a vast number of similar cases not reported, which constitute such a lot of frustration for people involved. Citizen journalism that claims to be popular, tends, in this sense, to fill the quantitative gap of conventional journalism. The wealth of stories does not simply pose the problem of selection: it raises one of perception of facts itself. Conventional journalism functions with blinkers that reduce the visual field for each journalist as well as for each media organ, what professionals call "editorial line". Because that editorial line separates what is visible from what is not visible, it constitutes in fact a source of contention, because many facts cannot be seen and broadcasted. Facts which are not seen represent such a lot of points of dissatisfaction of the public who find an interest in it. In the same sense, the difference between editorial lines, according to media organs, results in variable imaginaries on the same fact.

In the light of above, it appears that by its essence, conventional journalism is at the heart of subjective issues of the society. Societies and cultures that constitute its cement being varied, it becomes difficult to construct a standard journalism with all the different sensitiveness. The deeper these differences are, the more numerous are the dissatisfactions of the public and the public's desire to fill the gaps is strong. The development of new technologies notably the Internet and mobile telephony offers in this context a fertile ground to this insurrectional practice of the public. Meanwhile, the multiplicity of facts and the divergence of points of view constitute a challenge that this insurrectional journalism can only take up. Consequently, instead of acting as a substitute for conventional journalism, citizen journalism can only consider to become a complement.

REFERENCES

1. Bougnoux, D. (2001). Introduction aux sciences de la communication. Paris: La Découverte.
2. Bowman, S., & Willis, C. (2015) We Media: How Audiences Are Shaping the Future of News and Information. In Wikipedia.
3. Cf. Corcuff, P. (1995). Les nouvelles sociologies. Paris: Nathan.
4. Dvorkin, J. A. (2015). Media Matters: Can Public Radio Journalism Be Re-Invented? In Wikipedia.
5. Elihu, K., & Lazarsfeld, P. F. (1955). Personal Influence; The Part Played by People in the Flow of Mass Communications. Glencoe, ILL: Free Press.
6. Esquenazi, J.-P. (2002). L'écriture de l'actualité. Grenoble: PUG.

7. Grubisich, T. (2014). La base du journalisme: contenu reel. Quoted in the French Version of Wikipedia, 21 November 2014.
8. Habermas, J. (1987). Logique des sciences sociales et autres essais. Paris: PUF.
9. Lazarsfeld, P. F., Berelson, B., & Gaudet, H. (1968). The People's Choice: How the Voter Makes up His Mind in a Presidential Campaign. New York: Columbia University Press.
10. McCombs, M., Shaw, D. L., & Weaver, D. H. (1997). Communication and Democracy. Taylor and Francis.
11. Merritt, D. (2015) News Media Must Regain Vigor, Courage. In Wikipedia.
12. Meyer, E. P. (2015) Public Journalism and the Problem of Objectivity. In Wikipedia.
13. Rosen, J. (2008). A Most Useful Definition of Citizen Journalism. In Wikipedia.
14. Veron, E. (1981). Construire l'évènement. Paris: Editions de Minuit, 7-8.

Chapter 6

NEWS CRAWLS IN LOCAL TV NEWS: DO THEY HELP OR HINDER INFORMATION RECALL AND RETENTION

Brittany L. Pavolik[1], Mark J. Piwinsky[1], Lacey A. Fulton[2]

[1]Department of Communications Media, Indiana University of Pennsylvania, Indiana, PA, USA

[2]Department of Communication, Clarion University, Clarion, PA, USA

ABSTRACT

News crawls have become a common element in local television newscasts. Used as a way to provide more information and compete with content rich online news, the question is whether news crawls help or hinder immediate recall and long-term retention of information. Using a quasi-ex- periment, this study examines immediate recall and long-term retention for a local television newscast. A control and two treatment groups, comprised of students at a public, mid-sized university in the USA, saw one of three versions of the same newscast. The control group saw a newscast with no crawls while the treatment groups saw a version with crawls that reinforced the on- screen story or with crawls that were on different topics from the on-screen story. Considering information overload and the dual-coding hypothesis, this study also examines the impact of the textual element of the crawl as an aid or obstacle in information recall and retention. The study lends support to the dual-coding hypothesis and suggests further research is needed on its impact even when the on-screen story and textual crawl are not covering the same news item.

INTRODUCTION

With the availability of numerous digital and traditional news media outlets, Americans remain loyal to local television newscast as major source information. Mitchell et al. (2013) report that in terms of local news, 71%

of viewers are tuning in regularly. Local television news creates a sense of community; a sense of belonging. Woodstock (2014) characterizes this engagement as the news democracy narrative and suggests that news-viewing habits are a key factor in an individual's level of citizenship. This sense of community or belonging remains strong. In fact, Matsa (2015) found that local television news viewership was increasing as stations expanded their time slots into the early morning and late evening dayparts.

While local news has a regular following, heavy viewers of local news watch more cable news than local news; an average of eleven minutes more each day (Mitchell et al., 2013). With restrictive budgets and the need for advertising dollars, local stations have increasingly mimicked cable news production elements including graphics and news crawls, scrolling information at the lower third portion of the television screen to enhance the appeal of their broadcasts.

As the news democracy narrative sees the importance of informed viewers, a key question is whether these added graphic elements help or hinder the retention of information from the newscasts. Little, at present, is known about the effects of news crawls in local televised news. Research shows, however, that the audience does pay attention to the lower third of the television screen (Rodrigues et al., 2012). Further, research focusing on news crawls in national news illustrates that some types of news crawls can have a negative impact on viewer comprehension of the on-screen story.

Focusing on local news, the impact of news crawl presence and the compatibility of the information in the crawl with the on-screen story are examined for their impact on immediate recall and long-term retention. In addition, this study also examines if the presence of news crawl can influence the retention of information that is presented in the on-screen story, but not textually reinforced in the news crawl.

LITERATURE REVIEW

In 1948, WPIX produced the first fifteen-minute local television newscast, in New York City, utilizing the "talking head" format (Klinenberg & Krause, 2005 ; Hinds, 1995). Beginning in the 1960s, stations began to differentiate their newscasts using elements such as identifiable personalities, music, b-roll, and graphics. The first text-on-screen graphic appeared in the 1980's in the form of a stock ticker (Coffrey & Cleary, 2008). It was with the September 11th, 2001 terrorist attacks that crawls became a key element of a newscast. Due to this association, news crawls were initially identified with a sense of urgency and breaking news. Keefe-Feldman (2007) found that, over time, news crawls have evolved to regularly feed additional and often non-urgent information to the audience. In examining news crawl content, his findings were that news crawls are repetitive and typically not synchronized with the on-screen story. Rodrigues et al. (2012) note that the news crawl is more likely to grab audience attention than any other element on the screen. However, the media industry has often questioned its legitimate impact on the audience (Romano, 2002 ;Strauss; 2002 ; Consoli, 2009 ; Poniewozik, 2010).

Theoretical Perspectives

One purpose of the news crawl is to feed additional information to the viewer that is not in the on-screen story. To determine if news crawls are an aid in information recall and retention, it is necessary to begin with a brief overview of two relevant dimensions. The first concerns short- and long-term memory processing while the second examines the information overload and dual-coding perspectives. These form the basis for this study and the hypotheses.

Various scholars have examined short and long-term information processing with varying interpretations and areas of emphasis. Lindsay and Norman (1972) see information processing as a tri-fold experience beginning with initial exposure to a message. From this, the individual chooses to ignore the message, causing information decay, or encode it into the working (short-term) memory (Ruiji, 2012). Information processed to the working memory is then transferred to the long-term memory where it is stored with other accumulated knowledge until cued for recall (Fleming, et al., 2006).

The first dimension to consider is the capacity of short-term (working) and long-term memory. Cognitive load theory (Schweppe & Rummer, 2014 ; Sweller et al., 1998 ; Chandler & Sweller, 1991) suggests that the working memory only has a limited capacity which can be easily exceeded. Mayer (2005) points out that working memory must maintain and integrate multiple information channels, verbal and visual. In contrast, long-term memory is not seen as having the same capacity limitations. Focusing primarily on long-term retention, the Limited Capacity Model for Motivated Mediated Message Processing (LC4MP) sees three dimensions of cognitive processing, encoding, storage and retrieval, which are constant, continuous and simultaneous (Lang, 2006). Of the components of LC4MP, three are most relevant to this study: people have limited processing capacity, mediated messages contain redundancy in format to impact multiple senses, and cognition is a dynamic process (Fulton, 2014 ; Pavolik, 2015). While the limitations of working memory can inhibit what is successfully pro- cessed into long-term memory, the capacity of long-term memory is significantly greater than working memory (Schweppe & Rummer, 2014).

Information overload and dual-coding, the second dimension, focus on what factors help or inhibit processing by the working memory and the transfer of information to long-term memory. One perspective is that an attempt to synchronously process excessive amounts of mediated messages can result in cognitive and information overload (Toffler, 1970 ; Jacoby et al., 1984). According toWeber, Westcott-Baker & Anderson (2013) , a high level of complexity in a message can result in cognitive overload inhibiting future message retrieval due to the high-level of resources needed for encoding, decoding and retrieval. The redundancy effect (Torcasio & Sweller, 2009 ; Kalyuga et al., 1999, 2004) supports this contention arguing that removing superfluous information from a screen (the same information in different mediated forms) helps the individual to process and retain the smaller amount of information presented.

In contrast to information overload, the dual-coding hypothesis sees additional information as supportive of recall and retention. Dual-coding argues that when exposed to multimedia information, it is encoded both visually and aurally so that it is double-learned (Paivio, 1969, 1971, 1986). With multiple channels, the task of information reception can be partitioned between visual and audio channels freeing more re-sources for cognitive processing (Brunye et al., 2008 ; Mayer, 1997). The research of van der Molen and van der Voort (1997, 1998) support the dual-coding hypothesis. Essentially, the verbal and visual components of television newscasts provide dual channels to support information storage and enhance recall (van der Molen & van der Voort, 2000). This is also seen in LC4MP (Lang, 2000 ; Lang et al., 2004), which sees mediated messages as comprised of redundant information presented via various channels and formats that are dynamically processed as a part of continuous interactive communication.

News Crawls, Recall and Retention

Studies on news crawls address both the information overload and dual-coding perspectives. News crawls, and other on-screen graphics, are production elements that newscasts use to present information, entertain the audience, and distinguish themselves from other stations (Pavolik, 2015). However, when newscasts attempt to address all three of these functions using larger amounts of stimuli, the audience can easily become overwhelmed (Grabe et al., 2000, 2003 ; Lang et al., 1999). As a result, viewers may be unable to correctly comprehend, store, and retrieve the presented news.

Research concerning on-screen graphics, including news crawls, shows that graphics can affect information processing but the findings are variable. Grimes (1990) found that ancillary visuals can cause an audience to misinterpret an intended message because they assume the visuals are meant to reinforce the aural messages. Joesphson and Holmes (2006) found that audience members became particularly overwhelmed when confronted with crawls on topics other than what is being presented in the on-screen story. Matsukawa et al. (2009) used reinforcing crawls to test this perspective. In a post-test only experiment, audience members produced higher immediate recall scores when exposed to crawls that reinforced the on-screen story than when exposed to a newscast with no crawls at all. Keefe-Feldman (2007) found that most crawls do not reinforce the on-screen story and that individuals exposed to these incompatible crawls were less likely to recall information presented in the newscast. A natural corollary is that news crawls containing irrelevant or unstructured information could have a negative impact on retention of the on-screen story (Hargittai et al., 2012). Bergen et al. (2005) used dual-coding to find that when confronted with media embedded with graphics, an individual will focus on the auditory elements more so than the visuals. With regard to the amount of non-reinforcing, extraneous information, Coffey and Cleary (2009) found that news networks also use crawls for self-promotion.

Demographics can also play a part in information overload (Williamson & Eaker, 2012). A consistent pattern in the literature shows that younger audiences, regardless of their news-viewing habits, tend to be more successful than older generations at processing cluttered newscasts (Keefe-Feldman, 2007 ; Bergen et al., 2005). In contrast, Qihao et al. (2014) found that women under the age of 30 were more likely to become overwhelmed with information than any other demographic. Pavolik (2015) , using a sample comprised of college students, found some interaction effects between the compatibility of news crawls with gender and year in school, but not with other demographic factors including age, academic performance (GPA) and interest in news.

Ardac & Unal (2008) point out that the length and characteristics of on-screen text play a less significant role than the memory capacities of the individual. Those with high memory capabilities were more likely to recall information than those with lower memory capacities, regardless of the features of the stimulus. Audience preferences and viewing habits are another factor. Bracken (2005, 2006) found that audience members who prefer high-definition formats retrieved more information from that format than they did from standard definition. Overall news interest is another factor. Ellis (2012) refers to the term "news junkie," a person who regularly seeks out news. A "news junkie" may not be as susceptible to information overload as someone who is rarely exposed to news because they are comfortable with processing large amounts of information on a consistent basis and have the organizational categories to facilitate memory storage.

Attention, and where it is directed, is a related factor. Bradley (2007) uses the "negativity bias" to explain the correlation between arousing information and attention explaining that viewers tend to retain negative information over positive information. However, Lecheler et al. (2015) argue that the specific content of a message, regardless of its positive or negative connotation, is what elicits high emotional responses, which can in turn, dictate retention. Wise et al. (2008) consider both producer and viewer cuts and channel changes during a news program to have a significant effect on cognitive processing. Moments leading up to a change in stimulus, as controlled by the viewer, were found to produce less cognitive processing, while effort, arousal and encoding were increased when presented with the new stimulus (Lang et al., 2005). Lang's study found that memory was better for information between cuts that were related, rather than unrelated.

Focus of the Study

The focus of this study is to examine how crawls in local television newscasts impact the immediate recall and long-term retention of information. There are two perspectives to consider. The first is information overload and cognitive theory that contend additional and/or redundant information negatively impact information recall and retention. In contrast, the second perspective, the dual-coding hypotheses, argues that multiple forms of the message presented through synchronous channelsimproves recall and retention of information. News crawls add a compounding factor for both approaches as they can cover the same topic as the on-screen story (a reinforcing or compatible crawl) or they can pertain to a different news item (an incompatible crawl).

METHODOLOGY AND ANALYSIS

While news crawls have become increasingly common in local TV newscasts, the question of their effectiveness for immediate recall and long-term information retention remains largely unexplored. The news crawl is another level of information that must be perceived and stored to memory. According to information overload and the redundancy effect, adding the news crawl to the story increases the possibility of overload and reduced retention (Toffler, 1970, Mayer et al., 2008). In contrast, dual-coding argues that when exposed to multimedia information, it is encoded both visually and aurally (Paivio, 1971, 1986). Thus, the textual crawls would be an aid in retention. The content of a news crawl is another dimension. The crawl can reinforce the on-screen story being presented (reinforcing crawl) or it can be on a different topic (incompatible crawl). In this research, the focus is on whether the presence and content compatibility of the news crawl (reinforcing or incompatible) helps or hinders retention. In addition, crawl content is examined in the short and long-term to see if there are differences in retention. To explore these issues, six hypotheses were developed with three focusing on immediate recall and three on long-term information retention.

Research Questions and Hypotheses

The first set of hypotheses compares the impact of no crawls, reinforcing crawls and incompatible crawls on immediate and long-term retention. If the content of the crawl reinforces the on-screen story, will this improve retention or add to information overload and an inability to effectively store the information in both short-term and long-term memory? If the news crawl is about a different story and is incompatible with what is being presented on-screen, will this reduce retention? As longer-term memory benefits from dual-coding, will the added textual element of crawls, whether reinforcing or incompatible, still result in greater retention than having no crawls?

RQ1: Does the compatibility of a news crawl with the on-screen story impact short-term and long-term information recall?

H1: There is a difference in immediate recall based on crawl compatibility - no crawls, rein-forcing crawls or incompatible crawls.

H2: There is a difference in long-term retention based on crawl compatibility—no crawls, reinforcing crawls or incompatible crawls.

A related question is whether the information in a news crawl reinforces the retention and recall of other information that is in the on-screen story but not in the crawl itself. The presence of some elements of a story in textual form in the crawl might provide context and reduce the extent of information overload or it could add unnecessary redundancy that might hinder retention. For the long-term, will the added textual in-formation presented improve effective storing and recall of information from a story that is not reinforced in the text of the crawl?

To begin addressing this question, the next two hypotheses focus only on whether the information is in or not in the crawl regardless of whether the crawl supports or is incompatible with the on-screen story. Thus, it examines whether the presence of the textual element of the crawl itself is an aid in retention regard-less of what the on-screen story is presenting.

RQ2: Does the content of a news crawl, regardless of compatibility, reinforce the retention and recall of other information from a story that is not contained in the crawl?

H3: Regardless of crawl compatibility, immediate recall will be greater for information that is contained in both the on-screen story and the news crawl than only in the on-screen story.

H4: Regardless of crawl compatibility, long-term retention will be greater for information that is contained in both the on-screen story and the news crawl than only in the on-screen story.

For the final set of hypotheses, the focus is on the interaction of crawl compatibility and whether or not information in the on-screen story is also included in the crawl. The concept of "dual-coding" would suggest that information presented in the on-screen story and a reinforcing crawl would have the highest level of retention. In contrast, the redundancy effect indicates the added information of the crawls would impede retention. Incompatible crawls create a special issue. Information overload would suggest incompatible crawls would result in lower retention as the amount and diversity of information being presented simultaneously increases. For dual-coding, a question is whether retention is still enhanced if visual and textual information are not presented simultaneously. RQ3, focusing on crawl compatibility and whether the information is in the story only or in the story and crawl, will provide insights on this issue.

RQ3: Is there an interaction effect between crawl compatibility and whether information in the on-screen story is also included in the crawl?

H5: For immediate recall, there is an interaction effect between crawl compatibility and whether the on-screen information is also in the news crawl.

H6: For long-term retention, there is an interaction effect between crawl compatibility and whether the on-screen information is also in the news crawl.

Experimental Method

To investigate the impact of news crawls on the retention of information, a post hoc experimental design was used. Three groups of subject saw the same newscast with no crawls, reinforcing crawls or incompatible crawls. The study was conducted in spring of 2015 at a mid-sized public university in the Eastern United States. The university enrolls approximately 14,300 students with 85% being undergraduates.

For the stimulus, a 30-minute newscast with a strong local focus and no news crawls was used. The newscast was obtained from a station in a medium size television market, near the national median market size (The Nielsen Company, 2013). The station's location is outside the university's traditional recruitment and catchment area. As a result, the risk of prior exposure by the subjects to the geographic area, issues or local personalities was minimal.

Three versions of the newscast were used. The control group saw the basic newscast without crawls. Treatment Group A saw the same newscast with crawls added that reinforced elements of the story currently being presented on-screen. Treatment Group B saw the same newscast and crawls but the crawls were rearranged so that the crawls were from a different story than the one on-screen (i.e., incompatible crawls). The news crawls used a headline approach (Tuggle, Carr, & Huffman, 2004) focusing on the key information in the story. Print size, font and speed were set to reflect typical broadcast practice (Keefe-Feldman, 2007).

Subjects were recruited from a selection of introductory general education classes in Political Science, Geosciences and Communications. Of the 60 subjects, there were 29 females (48%) and 31 males (52%). Most of the participants were seniors (38%) and juniors (28%) with 20-years old (30%) being the modal response. On a 4.00-scale, 42% had a GPA in the 3.00 - 3.49 range and 38% in the 3.50 - 4.00 range. Of the subjects, 32% said they did not watch local TV news and 35% responded they watched it less than once a week. Only 7% watched local TV news four or more times per week. Finally, when asked about their interest in local news, 78% said they were somewhat interested, 17% said they were not interested and only 5% responded very interested. Applicable statistical tests were conducted on each of these six variables (gender, college rank, age, GPA, frequency of watching local news and interest in local news). The tests showed there were no statistically significant differences in the composition of the three groups on any of these demographic variables.

Students who volunteered to participate received an online survey to collect demographic information and schedule their experimental session. Based on the demographics, subjects were assigned to the control or treatment groups to maintain a relatively even balance based on age, gender, and GPA. Upon reporting for the experiment, students watched their assigned version of the newscast then responded to a printed 18-question quiz on the content of the newscast. To test long-term retention, subjects received an email two weeks later asking them to respond to an online survey consisting of the same questions. The dependent variable of information retention was measured by the number of correct answers on the 18-question quiz. Each multiple choice question had four possible answers. There were two questions on the quiz for each on-screen story. One addressed information that was included in the text of the news crawl and the second question covered information in the on-screen story but not in the crawl.

In total, 60 students participated in the immediate recall portion of the experiment with 20 per group and 58 of the students completed the delayed retention portion two weeks later. In the long-term recall portion, one subject was lost from each of the treatment groups (reinforcing and incompatible crawls). All 20 subjects in the control group completed the entire study.

Crawl Compatibility

The first and second hypotheses focus on the impact of crawl compatibility (none, reinforcing or incompatible) on information retention. The scores for all 18 questions were examined across the three groups. For hypotheses H1 and H2, the Levene's test for homogeneity of variances was not significant and a one-way ANOVA was used for the analysis.

H1: There is a difference in immediate recall based on crawl compatibility - no crawls, reinforcing crawls or incompatible crawls.

The first hypothesis examines the impact of crawl compatibility on immediate recall (see Table 1). A one-way ANOVA showed there was a significance difference in the level of immediate recall across the three groups (F = 3.455, df = 2.57, p = 0.038). The group seeing the reinforcing crawls performed the best (M = 12.600) with the no crawl, control group second (M = 11.200) and the group seeing the incompatible crawls scoring the lowest (M = 10.450). A Tukey's HSD was run to see which differences between the three groups was significant. Tukey's HSD showed only a significant difference between the reinforcing and the incompatible crawl groups (Mdiff = 2.150, p = 0.032).

H2: There is a difference in long-term retention based on crawl compatibility - no crawls, reinforcing crawls or incompatible crawls.

The second hypothesis focused on crawl compatibility and long-term recall. In this case, the dependent variable was the number of correct responses when the quiz was re-taken two weeks after seeing the newscasts. Two subjects, one in the reinforcing crawls and one in the incompatible crawls group, did not complete the long-term recall portion. The differences here were not significant (F = 1.761, df = 2.55, p = 0.181).

Table 1: Comparison of groups on immediate recall and long-term retention

Group	Recall and Retention Levels		
	Immediate Recall	Long-Term Retention	Change
Control – No Crawls	M = 11.200, SD = 2.462	M = 9.000, SD = 1.938	−2.200
Reinforcing Crawls	M = 12.600, SD = 2.458	M = 10.263, SD = 1.727	−2.337
Incompatible Crawls	M = 10.450, SD = 2.929	M = 9.789, SD = 2.594	−0.661

Again, the group seeing the reinforcing crawls scored highest (M = 10.263, SD = 1.727). However, the group viewing the incompatible crawls (M = 9.789,

SD = 2.594) scored ahead of the no crawl group (M = 9.000, SD = 1.938).

Of note is that the reinforcing crawls group (diff = −2.337) saw the largest drop in retention from the immediate to the long-term while the incompatible crawl group (diff = −0.661) saw the smallest decline (see Table 1). While the differences were not significant (F = 2.169, df = 2.55, p = 0.124), a similar pattern is also seen with H5 and H6.

Information Included in Crawl or in On-Screen Story Only

The third and fourth hypotheses focus on differences in retention based on whether the on-screen information was also contained in the news crawl. For this portion of the study, the focus was only on the two treatments groups as the control group did not see the news crawls. The comparison is between scores on the nine questions that were addressed in the crawls and the nine questions that were only in the stories. An independent samples t-test was used for H3 and H4.

H3: Regardless of crawl compatibility, immediate recall will be greater for information that is contained in both the on-screen story and the news crawl than only in the on-screen story.

In the case of immediate recall, the differences were significant between the two groups (t = 3.779, df = 78, p < 0.001). The scores for the questions included in the news crawls (M = 6.48, SD = 1.519) were higher than for the questions that were only included in the on-screen stories (M = 5.05, SD = 1.839). A related question is whether this difference holds when we look only at the group receiving the incompatible crawls or if the stronger performance of the reinforcing crawls group, as seen in H1, influenced the overall pattern. To test this, an independent samples t-test was run on the two sets of questions for the group seeing the incompatible crawls. In this case, the same significant pattern emerged (t = 2.160, df = 38, p = 0.037). Even though the news crawls were incompatible with the on-screen story, the subjects scored higher on information contained in both the on-screen story and the crawl (M = 5.80, SD = 1.436) than on information in the on-screen story only (M = 4.65, SD = 1.899). Despite the crawl being incompatible, it appears that it still aided in immediate recall.

H4: Regardless of crawl compatibility, long-term retention will be greater for information that is contained in both the on-screen story and the news crawl than only in the on-screen story.

This portion of the study explores the same issue as with H3 but the focus is on the two-week retention scores. As the Levene's test (F = 4.871, p = 0.030) for homogeneity of variances was significant, equal variances were not assumed. Again, we find a significant difference ($t = 3.865$, $df = 67.549$, $p < 0.001$) with subjects scoring better on questions that were included in the crawls ($M = 6.05$, $SD = 1.184$) than on questions from the on-screen story only ($M = 4.79$, $SD = 1.630$). As with H3, a second analysis was done focusing only on the incompatible crawls group. Again, a significant difference was found ($t = 2.038$, $df = 36$, $p = 0.049$) with the questions covering information in the crawls and on-screen ($M = 5.79$, $SD = 1.398$) showing a higher score than the on-screen only items ($M = 4.79$, 1.619). Thus, it appears the incompatible crawls did aid in retention.

Interaction Effects

Does the combination of crawl compatibility and whether information is in the on-screen story only or also included in the crawl, impact retention? To address this question, the focus is on the two treatment groups. The dependent variable is their retention of information between the questions for the on-screen only story and the questions that were also addressed in the crawls. Hypotheses H5 and H6 used the Univariate General Linear Model in SPSS 22 that adjusts for any problems with homogeneity of variances (Leech, et al., 2011; Norusis, 2008).

H5: For immediate recall, there is an interaction effect between crawl compatibility and whether the on-screen information is also in the news crawl.

The analysis indicated there was no significant interaction effect between crawl compatibility and the inclusion of information in the crawl on immediate recall ($F = 0.583$, $df = 1.76$, $p = 0.448$). As seen in Table 2, the highest scores occur with the reinforcing crawls group for the information contained in the crawls ($M = 7.15$). It is also interesting to note that, while not significant, the incompatible crawl group had better recall on questions relating to information contained in the crawl ($M = 5.80$) than did the reinforcing group on questions not in the crawl ($M = 5.45$). This suggests that some degree of dual-coding or double-learning may be occurring even with incompatible crawls.

H6: For long-term retention, there is an interaction effect between crawl compatibility and whether the on-screen information is also in the news crawl.

As with H5, no significant interaction effects were found across the compatibility groups and question types for long-term recall ($F = 0.642$, $df = 1.72$, $p = 0.426$). The differences on the questions contained in the crawls between the reinforcing ($M = 6.32$) and the incompatible crawls ($M = 5.79$) were much less for the long-term recall (diff = 0.53) than for immediate recall (diff = 1.35). Table 2 also shows that for information not included in the crawl, there was no difference between the reinforcing crawls (M = 4.79) and the incompatible crawls (M = 4.79) groups in long-term retention.

While not statistically significant, H5 and H6 show that in both immediate recall (diff = 1.70) and long-term retention (diff = 1.53), the reinforcing crawls group saw the greatest difference between story information in or not in the crawls (see Table 2). At the same time, the reinforcing crawl group also saw the largest drop between immediate recall and long-term retention for both information in the crawls (diff = −0.83) and not in the crawls (diff = −0.66). In contrast, there was almost no drop between immediate and long-term scores for the incompatible crawls group for information contained in the crawls (diff = −0.01) and for information not in the crawls, the scores actually increased slightly (diff = +0.14).

DISCUSSION

This study examined the issue of news crawl compatibility and its impact on immediate recall and long-term retention of information. One perspective, from information overload and cognitive theory, is that the increased volume of information being presented would hinder recall and retention. In contrast, the dual-coding hypothesis suggests that the additional information assists with recall and improves long-term storage and retention. As with any experimental study, important caveats are the limitations of the sample and methodology. However, the results of this study suggest several interesting possibilities and areas for future research.

Findings and Implications

The findings from H1 suggest that for immediate recall, the addition of textual news crawls that reinforce the on-screen story was an aid. This supports the dual-coding hypothesis and double-learning elements (Paivio, 1969, 1971, 1986), the benefit of multiple channels (Brunye et al., 2008) and reflects the findings of Matsukawa et al. (2009) on reinforcing crawls. It also suggests that, at least at the level of content in the news crawls, the redundancy effect does not come into play. In contrast, the incompatible crawl group scored the lowest suggesting that incompatible crawls were a hindrance to immediate information retention. This is consistent with the observations of Keefe-Feldman (2007) and Hargittai et al. (2012) . It also suggests that the incompatibility of information between the crawl and on-screen story may cross the threshold of information processing creating overload and inhibiting immediate recall (Joesphson & Holmes 2006).

While the differences were not statistically significant for H2, the results are interesting and suggest an area for future study. While the reinforcing group scored the highest in long-term retention, the incompatible crawl group did better than the no crawl group. Unlike the negative impact on immediate recall, the textual element of the incompatible crawls may have facilitated the processing and encoding of information into long-term memory. Other studies have focused on concurrent processing and immediate recall (Matsukawa et al., 2009 ; Bruyne et al., 2008 ; van der Molen & van der Voort, 2000). The findings for H1 and H2 suggest that the impact of incompatible crawls may differ for short-term recall compared to long-term retention. For the long-term, it may be

Table 2: Crawl compatibility and information in or not in the crawls

Recall and Retention Type	Crawl Compatibility	Story Information: Included In Crawl	Story Information: Not Included In Crawl	Story Information: Difference In or Not In Crawl
Immediate	Reinforcing	M = 7.15, SD = 1.309	M = 5.45, SD = 1.731	−1.70
	Incompatible	M = 5.80, SD = 1.436	M = 4.65, SD = 1.899	−1.15
	Difference Reinforcing and Incompatible	1.35	0.80	
Long-Term	Reinforcing	M = 6.32, SD = 0.885	M = 4.79, SD = 1.686	−1.53
	Incompatible	M = 5.79, SD = 1.398	M = 4.79, SD = 1.619	−1.00
	Difference Reinforcing and Incompatible	0.53	0.00	
Difference in Immediate to Long-Term	Reinforcing	−0.83	−0.66	
	Incompatible	−0.01	0.14	

that the additional information of the crawl, even if not presented concurrently with the story, is an aid in retention.

H3 and H4 provide additional support for the concepts of dual-coding and double-learning within the scope of this study. When the news crawl contained information from the on-screen story, immediate recall and long- term retention were both greater than for information presented in the on-screen story only. This held even for the incompatible crawl group. For these two hypotheses, a follow-up comparison was done focusing only on the incompatible crawl group to be certain the stronger performance by the reinforcing crawl group was not influencing the overall results. The significant findings suggest that even when the visual/aural and textual information are not presented simultaneously, the textual information still contributes to enhanced immediate recall and long-term retention. One reason behind this phenomenon could be related to active learning theories. A person is more likely to recall information they cognitively process. The act of reading the information requires active viewing rather than passive viewing, causing the viewer to cognitively process and organize the text-based information (Clark & Mayer, 2011). Similar to H2, this suggests that some form of dual-coding is occurring even when the multiple formats of the information are not presented simultaneously (Brunye et al, 2008 ; Mayer, 1997 ; Van der Molen & Van der Voort, 1997, 1998, 2000).

The results for H5 and H6, while not statistically significant, suggest some interesting possibilities for future study. For the reinforcing crawls group, both immediate recall and long-term retention were higher for information contained in both the crawl and the on-screen story. However, the reinforcing crawl group saw the largest drop in information retention from the immediate to the long-term for both on-screen only items and on-screen plus the crawl. In contrast, the incompatible crawl group saw minimal decline for information in the crawl and the on-screen story and even a slight increase from immediate to long-term for information not in the crawl. This raises the possibility that simultaneous dual-coding achieves higher levels of immediate recall but a greater decline in long-term retention.

From Table 1, we can see a similar pattern of decline overall whether or not the on-screen story information is reinforced in the crawl. Overall, the incompatible crawls group started with a lower-level of immediate recall (M = 10.450) compared to the reinforcing crawls (M = 12.600) and the no crawls group (M = 11.200). However, the smallest decline from immediate to long-term occurred for the incompatible crawls group (diff = −0.661) with reinforcing (diff = −2.337) and no crawls (diff = −2.200) showing much larger declines. As existing studies focus primarily on immediate retention of information from news crawls, the issue of long-term retention is worthy of future study. LC4MP (Lang, 2000, 2004), with its focus on memory processing for long-term retention, provides some insights and possible factors for consideration in such a study.

CONCLUSION

This study offers some interesting initial conclusions as well as areas for future study. H3 and H4 provide support for the dual-coding hypothesis as the immediate recall and long-term retention of information is greater for items included in the crawls. This suggests that while synchronous presentation produces higher levels, the presence of incompatible crawls also does improve recall and retention. However, reinforcing crawls show higher recall, as seen in H1, indicating that synchronous presentation has an advantage in immediate recall. Focusing on longer-term retention, H2, H5 and H6, while not statistically significant, provide some items for future study. These suggest that the impact of reinforcing crawls produces higher initial recall but faster decline over time than incompatible crawls. Future studies focusing on reinforcing and incompatible crawls would help provide added insight into this issue and the possibility dual-coding that is not simultaneous is actually occurring and supporting long-term retention.

ACKNOWLEDGEMENTS

The authors would like to thank the Center for Media Production and Research at Indiana University of Pennsylvania for their assistance with this research project.

REFERENCES

1. Ardac, D., & Unal, S. (2008). Does the Amount of On-Screen Text Influence Student Learning from a Multimedia-Based Instructional Unit? Instructional Science, 36, 75-88.http://dx.doi.org/10.1007/s11251-007-9035-4
2. Bergen, L., Grimes, T., & Potter, D. (2005). How Attention Partitions Itself during Simultaneous Message Presentations. Human Communication Research, 31, 311-336.http://dx.doi.org/10.1111/j.1468-2958.2005.tb00874.x
3. Bracken, C. C. (2006). Perceived Source Credibility of Local Television News: The Impact of Television Form and Presence. Journal of Broadcasting & Electronic Media, 50, 723-741.http://dx.doi.org/10.1207/s15506878jobem5004_9
4. Bracken, C. C. (2005). Presence and Image Quality: The Case of High Definition Television. Media Psychology, 7, 191-205.http://dx.doi.org/10.1207/S1532785XMEP0702_4
5. Bradley, S. (2007). Dynamic, Embodied, Limited-Capacity Attention and Memory: Modeling Cognitive Processing of Mediated Stimuli. Media Psychology, 9, 211-239.http://dx.doi.org/10.1080/15213260709336810
6. Brunye, T., Taylor, H., & Rapp, D. (2008). Repetition and Dual Coding in Procedural Multimedia Presentations. Applied Cognitive Psychology, 22, 877-895.http://dx.doi.org/10.1002/acp.1396
7. Chandler, P., & Sweller, J. (1991). Cognitive Load Theory and the Format of Instruction. Cognitive and Instruction, 8, 293-332.http://dx.doi.org/10.1207/s1532690xci0804_2
8. Clark, R. C., & Mayer, R. E. (2011). E-Learning and the Science of Instruction: Proven Guidelines for Consumers and Designers of Multimedia Learning. San Fransisco, CA: Pfeiffer. http://dx.doi.org/10.1002/9781118255971
9. Consoli, J. (2009). Keeping the News Crawl Running during Ad Breaks. The New York Times. http://www.nytimes.com/2009/04/30/business/media/30adco.html?_r=0

10. Ellis, J. (2012). How We Read, Not What We Read, May Be Contributing to Our Information Overload. Neiman Lab. http://www.niemanlab.org/2012/11/how-we-read-not-what-we-read-may-be-contributing-to-our-information-overload/

11. Fulton, L. (2014). Information Retention of Audio Based Public Service Announcements: The Impact of Messages Created Using Different Production Methods. Doctoral Dissertation. Indiana, PA: Indiana University of Pennsylvania.

12. Grabe, M. E., Zhou, S., & Bolls, P. D. (2000). Packaging Television News: The Effects of Tabloid on Information Processing and Evaluative Responses. Journal of Broadcasting and Electronic Media, 44, 581-598. http://dx.doi.org/10.1207/s15506878jobem4404_4

13. Grabe, M. E., Lang, A., & Zhao, X. (2003). News Content and Form. Implications for Memory and Audience Evaluations. Communication Research, 30, 387-413.http://dx.doi.org/10.1177/0093650203253368

14. Grimes, T. (1990). Encoding TV News Messages into Memory. Journalism Quarterly, 67, 757-766. http://dx.doi.org/10.1177/107769909006700430

15. Hargittai, E., Neuman, W. R., & Curry, O. (2012). Taming the Information Tide: Perceptions of Information Overload in the American Home. The Information Society, 28, 161-173. http://dx.doi.org/10.1080/01972243.2012.669450

16. Hinds, L. (1995). Broadcasting the Local News: The Early Years of Pittsburgh's KDAK-TV. University Park, PA: Pennsylvania State University Press.http://dx.doi.org/10.1086/208981

17. Jacoby, J. (1984). Perspectives on Information Overload. Journal of Consumer Research, 10, 432-435. http://dx.doi.org/10.1086/208981

18. Joesphson, S., & Holmes, M. (2006). Clutter or Content? How On-Screen Enhancements Affect How TV Viewers Scan and What They Learn. Proceedings of the 2006 Symposium on Eye Tracking Research & Applications, San Diego, 27-29 March 2006, 155-162. http://dx.doi.org/10.1145/1117309.1117361

19. Kalyuga, S., Chandler, P., & Sweller, J. (1999). Managing Split-Attention and Redundancy in Multimedia Instruction. Applied Cognitive Psychology, 13, 351-371.http://dx.doi.org/10.1002/(SICI)1099-0720(199908)13:4<351::AID-ACP589>3.0.CO;2-6

20. Kalyuga, S., Chandler, P., & Sweller, J. (2004). When Redundant On-Screen Text in Multimedia Technical Instruction Can Interfere with Learning. Human Factors: The Journal of the Human Factors

and Ergonomics Society, 46, 567-581.http://dx.doi.org/10.1518/hfes.46.3.567.50405

21. Keefe-Feldman, M. (2007). The Cable News Ticker, View Comprehension, and Information Overload: Less Is More. Master's Thesis, Washington DC: Georgetown University.
22. Klinenberg, E., & Krause, M. (2005). Public Service and the Transformations of the Journalistic Field: Local Reporting in US News Media 1890-2000. Philadelphia, PA: The American Sociological Association. http://dx.doi.org/10.1177/0163443710385502
23. Lang, A., Bolls, P. D., Potter, R., & Kawahara, K. (1999). The Effects of Production Pacing and Arousing Content on the Information Processing of Television Messages. Journal of Broadcasting & Electronic Media, 43, 451-457.http://dx.doi.org/10.1080/08838159909364504
24. Lang, A. (2000). The Limited Capacity Model of Mediated Message Processing. Journal of Communication, 50, 46-70. http://dx.doi.org/10.1111/j.1460-2466.2000.tb02833.x
25. Lang, A., Schwartz, N., Yongkuk, C., & Seungwhan, L. (2004). Processing Substance Abuse Messages: Production Pacing, Arousing Content, and Age. Journal of Broadcasting & Electronic Media, 48, 61-88. http://dx.doi.org/10.1207/s15506878jobem4801_4
26. Lang, A. (2006). Using the Limited Capacity Model of Motivated Mediated Message Processing to Design Effective Cancer Communication Messages. Journal of Communication, 56, 57-80. http://dx.doi.org/10.1111/j.1460-2466.2006.00283.x
27. Lang, A., Shin, M., Bradley, S. D., Wang, Z., Lee, S., & Potter, D. (2005). Wait! Don't Turn That Dial! More Exciting to Come! The Effects of Story Length and Production Pacing in Local Television News on Channel Changing Behaviour and Information Processing in a Free Choice Environment. Journal of Broadcasting & Electronic Media, 40, 460-477. http://dx.doi.org/10.1080/08838159609364369
28. Lindsay, P., & Norman, D. (1977). Human Information Processing: An Introduction to Psychology (2nd ed.). New York: Academic Press.http://www.phon.ucl.ac.uk/courses/spsci/audper/SDT%20Lindsay%20&%20Norman%20App%20B.pdf
29. Lecheler, S., Bos, L., & Vliegenthart, R. (2015). The Mediating Role of Emotions: News Framing Effects on Opinions about Immigration. Journalism and Mass Communication Quarterly, 92, 812-838. http://dx.doi.org/10.1177/1077699015596338

30. Matsukawa, R., Miyata, Y., & Ueda, S. (2009). Information Redundancy Effect on Watching TV News: Analysis of Eye Tracking Data and Examination of the Contents. Library and Information Science, 62, 193-205.

31. Mayer, R. E. (1997). Multimedia Learning: Are We Asking the Right Questions? Educational Psychologist, 32, 1-19. http://dx.doi.org/10.1207/s15326985ep3201_1

32. Mayer, R. E., Heiser, J., & Lonn, S. (2001). Cognitive Constraints on Multimedia Learning: When Presenting More Material Results in Less Understanding. Journal of Educational Psychology, 93, 187-198. http://dx.doi.org/10.1037/0022-0663.93.1.187

33. Mayer, R. E. (2005). Cognitive Theory of Multimedia Learning. In R. E. Mayer (Ed.), The Cambridge Handbook of Multimedia Learning (pp. 31-48). New York: Cambridge University Press. http://dx.doi.org/10.1017/cbo9780511816819.004

34. Mayer, R. E., Griffith, E., Jurkowitz, I. T. N., & Rothman, D. (2008). Increased Interestingness of Extraneous Details in a Multimedia Science Presentation Leads to Decreased Learning. Journal of Experimental Psychology: Applied, 14, 329-339.http://dx.doi.org/10.1037/a0013835

35. Mitchell, A., Olmstead, K., Jurkowitz, M., & Enda, J. (2013). How Americans Get TV News at Home. Washington DC: Pew Research Center.

36. Paivio, A. (1969). Mental Imagery in Associative Learning and Memory. Psychological Review, 61, 179-211. http://dx.doi.org/10.1037/h0027272

37. Paivio, A. (1971). Imagery and Verbal Processes. New York: Holt.

38. Paivio, A. (1986, 1990). Mental Representations: A Dual Coding Approach. New York: Oxford University Press. http://dx.doi.org/10.1093/acprof:oso/9780195066661.001.0001

39. Pavolik, B. (2015). News Crawls and Audience Retention: A Test of Information Overload in Local Television News Programming. Doctoral Dissertation, Indiana, PA: Indiana University of Pennsylvania.

40. Poniewozik, J. (2010). The Tick, Tick, Tick of the Times. Time Magazine Online.http://content.time.com/time/specials/packages/article/0,28804,2032304_2032745_2032850,00.html

41. Qihao, J., Sypher, U., & Ha, L. (2014). The Role of News Media Use and Demographic Characteristics in the Prediction of Information Overload. International Journal of Communication, 8, 699-714.

42. Rodrigues, R., Veloso, A., & Mealha, O. (2012). A Television News Graphic Layout Analysis Method Using Eye Tracking. Proceedings of the 16th International Conference on Information Visualisation, Montpellier, 11-13 July 2012, 357-362.
43. Romano, A. (2002). Ticker Embedded in News. Broadcasting & Cable, 132, 26.
44. Ruiji, L. (2012). The Development on Multimedia Teaching Resources Based on Information Processing Theory. International Journal of Advancements in Computing Technology, 4, 58-64. http://dx.doi.org/10.4156/ijact.vol4.issue2.8
45. Schweppe, J., & Rummber, R. (2014). Attention, Working Memory, and Long-Term Memory in Multimedia Learning: An Integrated Perspective Based on Process Models of Working Memory. Educational Psychology Review, 26, 285-306.http://dx.doi.org/10.1007/s10648-013-9242-2
46. Strauss, R. (2002). Crawls Speed News to Antsy TV Viewers. Orlando Sentinel.http://articles.orlandosentinel.com/2002-01-04/lifestyle/0201030384_1_crawls-huang-viewers/2
47. Sweller, J., van Merrienboerm, J., & Paas, F. (1998). Cognitive Architecture and Instructional Design. Educational Psychology Review, 10, 251-296.http://dx.doi.org/10.1023/A:1022193728205
48. The Nielsen Company (2013). Local Television Market Universe Estimates Comparisons of 2012-13 and 2013-14 Market Ranks.http://www.nielsen.com/content/dam/corporate/us/en/public%20factsheets/tv/2012-2013%20DMA%20Ranks.pdf
49. Toffler, A. (1970). Future Shock. New York: Random House.
50. Torcasio, S., & Sweller, J. (2009). The Use of Illustrations When Learning to Read: A Cognitive Load Theory Approach. Applied Cognitive Psychology, 24, 659-672.http://dx.doi.org/10.1002/acp.1577
51. Van der Molen, W., & Van der Voort, T. (2000). The Impact of Television, Print, and Audio on Children's Recall of the News: A Study of Three Alternative Explanations for the Dual-Coding Hypothesis. Human Communication Research, 26, 3-26.http://dx.doi.org/10.1111/j.1468-2958.2000.tb00747.x
52. Weber, R., Westcott-Baker, A., & Anderson, G. (2013). A Multilevel Analysis of Anti-Marijuana Public Service Announcement Effectiveness. Communication Monographs, 80, 302-330. http://dx.doi.org/10.1080/03637751.2013.788254
53. Williamson, J., & Eaker, P. E. (2012). The Information Overload Scale. Proceedings of the 75th Annual Conference of the American Society for

Information Science & Technology, Baltimore, 26-30 October 2012, Page.

54. Wise, K., Lee, S., Lang, A., Fox, J., & Grabe, M. (2008). Responding to Change on TV: How Viewer-Controlled Changes in Content Differ from Programmed Changes in Content. Journal of Broadcasting & Electronic Media, 52, 182-199.http://dx.doi.org/10.1080/08838150801991773

55. Woodstock,L.(2014).TheNews-DemocracyNarrativeandtheUnexpected Benefits of Limited News Consumption: The Case of News Resisters. Journalism, 15, 834-849.http://dx.doi.org/10.1177/1464884913504260

Chapter 7

SOCIAL MEDIA AND ON-LINE POLITICAL CAMPAIGNING IN MALAYSIA

Sara Chinnasamy, Izyan Roslan

University Technology Mara, Selangor, Malaysia

ABSTRACT

Since the controversies surrounding the 2008 and 2013 Malaysian general elections due to the rising popularity of Opposition, social media networks have played a vital role in conveying political messages and debates. The social media continues to report significantly in the 2014's state by-elections on the political unrest issues especially an allegation on the Malaysian famous Opposition leader, Anwar Ibrahim. The Kuala Lumpur Court of Appeal found him guilty of sodomy and sentenced him to five years jail, which disqualified him from contesting the Selangor State Assembly seat of Kajang on 23 March 2014. He was expected to win this election and further had opportunity to be elected as the chief minister of Selangor state, the country's main economic hub surrounding Kuala Lumpur. In another tragic event, which was spotted on the social media coverage was the death of another well known Opposition politician, Karpal Singh, "the Tiger of Jelutong", following a motor vehicle accident. This has caused another by-election taken placed at the Bukit Gelugor, Penang. Yet, this paper takes a closer lens, on Kajang by-election and analyzes how the Facebook had been utilized for the Opposition leader, Dr. Wan Azizah Wan Ismail's (Anwar Ibrahim's wife) victory in the election. Using compliance gaining theory, this paper presents strategies used by the two major political parties, Barisan Nasional (BN) and Pakatan Rakyat (PR) to achieve their electoral goals. Though online political campaigning is not new from a Western perspective, it is for a semi-democracy country like Malaysia. To understand how the compliance gaining approach works in practice, selected political parties' Facebook advertisements are examined within two weeks after nomination day and election observers from diverse backgrounds are interviewed. It can be concluded that since 2008 political messages have been heavily debated through blogs. Independent Internet Media, Facebook and Twitter are very popular among Malaysian political candidates and voters.

INTRODUCTION

An election can be defined as the contest for the highest stakes in national politics. The electoral system is a set of predetermined rules for conducting elections and determining their outcome. In Malaysia, elections were held before it achieved its independence in 1957. Malaysia conducts general elections every five years, and its democracy has been described by scholars in terms such as "quasi democracy" (Zakaria, 1989), "semi-democracy" (Case, 1993), "modified democracy" (Crouch, 1993), "Democracy a la Malaysia" (Muzaffar, 1989), "democracy according to our own mould" (Hassan, 1997) and "pseudo-democracy" or as "flawed democracy" (Tan & Ibrahim, 2008). Chinnasamy (2013) argues these terms, denoting gaps or flaws, in themselves, and demonstrates that democracy in Malaysia strains the usual categorisation procedures. Intelligence Unit's Democracy Index (2011) indicates that Malaysia is in the 71st place among "flawed democracies".

The conduct of elections in Malaysia continues to attract global and local attention. At present, Malaysia has two types of elections. Firstly, general elections are held once every five years, and secondly, by-elections are held locally. The latter do not involve the dissolution of any assembly, and do not follow a fixed schedule, because they occur on the sudden death of a Member of Parliament or a particular political candidate changing from one political party to another. Thus, elections are considered democratic practices that forge the link between the people and political candidates or party to form a government.

The BN is a government party, a coalition of fourteen primarily ethnically-based political parties that have ruled the country since independence in 1957. The 2008 general elections result portrayed the public's partial rejection to the BN government. It was perceived as forceful and unexpected, and described as a "political tsunami" (Asli, 2008 ; The Star, 9 March 2008a). It was the BN's worst performance in Malaysia's electoral history (Oorjitham, 2008 ; Sani, 2005 ; Welsh, 2004). The rising popularity of the Opposition, namely Pakatan Rakyat/People's Alliance (PR) in the 2008 and 2013 elections had much to do with the success of former Deputy Prime Minister (DPM) Anwar Ibrahim, who unified the three Opposition parties (the People's Justice Party (PKR), the Democratic Action Party (DAP) and the Pan-Malaysian Islamic Party (PAS)) under one umbrella. This was known as PR after GE2008. In the GE2013 the BN won a bitter election, taking 133 out of 222 parliamentary seats. In contrast, in the GE2008 the BN had 140 seats (Chinnasamy, 2013).

In Malaysia's election whether it is general elections or by-elections, political advertisements have played a vital role even though advertisements remained traditional tools in the GE2008. Networking sites and political advertisements were not so developed during this time. The BN and its candidates employed traditional methods such as posters, political rallies, small group discussions (ceramah) and door-to-door efforts; a "sledgehammer" approach focused on the BN's achievements with the slogan "Security, Peace and Prosperity" (Moten, 2009). Moten stated that in the GE2008, the BN had bought 1100 pages of full colour advertisements in the print mainstream media to attract voters. Yet, the Opposition parties used the Internet skillfully to highlight BN government's poor performance and weakness. Before the election, most of the Opposition parties' leaders had their own social networks such as Lim Kit Siang (www.limkitsiang.com) and Anwar Ibrahim (www.anwaribrahim.com), which discussed their political activities, the government's malpractices and its failure to develop certain projects.

Political advertising consists of political campaigns putting out political messages to the public. Any communication process has involved communication channels and the media (Shireen, 2008). Political messages that have to be conveyed using advertisements or campaigns must be appropriate to make voters get the information and then trust whoever provides it. Campaign advertisements strong in sophisticated content and advertising bring information in a systematic way. Like product advertising, political advertisements are methodically tested and professionally produced. Freedman et al. (2004) argue that text, image and music work to strengthen each other. An advertisement's primary message is to recognize easily. By using advertising as a medium of political campaign will make voters influence to vote for their choices. Using text or images helps them to vote for a certain politician. Nevertheless, political advertisements work differently at various campaign moments. Because they are different and complicated in their structure, it is difficult to classify them into groups either by class of text such as announcements, declarations, exhortations or information (Guy, 2001). Political advertisements wield much influence and they are the only way to show abilities of candidates as leaders who communicate with the voters.

Advertising now leads campaigns and new media technologies have provided them with new ways to influence media messages. Journalists recognized the importance of voters needing to be supplied with independent information such as advertising messages (Kaid, 2009). Parliamentary activities generally change all the time (Andrew, 1992). In order to comprehend how democratic politics supply this social end, we must understand that the social role is achieved, as it were, incidentally; in the same sense as production is incidental to the creation of profit. This influences political candidates to start their political campaigns and change voters' perceptions. Contemporary voters use the mass media for most of their information about political candidates and issues. Sometimes, the political candidates provide information that can be controlled openly and usually it is in the form of televised political advertising.

This paper focuses on a by-election held for the Selangor State Assembly seat of Kajang on 23 March 2014, due to the resignation of the incumbent assemblyman, Lee Chin Cheh on 27 January 2014 (Themalayianinsider.com, 2014). Cheh was contested under the ticket of PKR, PR coalition. He won by a majority of 6824 votes against 5 other candidates in the GE2013 (Channel News Asia, 2014).

From the nomination day, 11 March 2014 until the polling day, both BN and PR candidates (mainly Dr. Wan Azizah-PKR and Chew Mei Fun-BN) were actively engaged on social media networks and especially Facebook. Facebook has become the most used social media website globally and replaced printed media or broadcast media. This was proved after Dr. Wan Azizah won the election. The Internet changed communication patterns and increased communication channels for people. In the election campaign Facebook provide awareness to people, helping promote candidates and display election results.

Social networking sites have proved successful in gaining voters' trust and at the same time spread the political beliefs and policies of candidates better than the broadcast media or print media. In the US, the Internet was used to raise huge amounts of money through personal websites, such as my.BarackObama.com, and Facebook and Twitter (Chinnasamy, 2013). Pew (2008) reported that one in ten Internet users donated money to a candidate. Howard Dean, former Vermont Governor, claimed that the Internet was a promoter and reviver of democracy due to his large online fundraising in the 2004 campaign (Williams & Tedesco, 2006). Although his presidential campaign was unsuccessful, Dean was regarded as a pioneer in raising the profile of Internet-based fundraising and grassroots organising (Center for Public Integrity, 2005). In the US presidential election of 2008, Barack Obama created a record by fundraising $532,946,511 in a few months from individual small donors (Hitwise, 2008), while Ron Paul, Representative from the Texas 14thdistrict, raised a record $6 million dollars in one day via the Internet (Vogel, 2007). Thus, the Internet proved extremely useful in electoral gains and it became an important tool for political communication.

RESEARCH AIMS

This paper aims to investigate the impact of political advertising on the Kajang by-election through Facebook; the extent it influenced the voters in the decision-making process. Furthermore, the inclusion and exclusion of Facebook's political advertisements by both political parties (the BN and the PR) and political candidates will be explored. Every political candidate has his or her own strategies in conducting political campaigns. The paper will assess how people were aware of those advertisements and how they impacted on them. Using Kajang's by-election as a case study, this paper also discovers if Facebook was important in political campaigning. The difference between the mainstream media news and social networks news, which been posted by some of the independent news portals (INP) will determine the electoral outcome, and which medium of popular news consumption influenced voters. This argument will be further strengthened with important key informant interviews.

COMPLIANCE GAINING SOCIAL MEDIA ADVERTISEMENTS

Scholarly work on compliance research has analyzed how various techniques process information and target or influence people. Most analyses attempt to recreate an accurate construction of the situation and respond accordingly to it. Compliance-gaining theory aims to comprehend the strategies we use when we want to dominate others (Dallinger, 2003). Shelly (2003) suggested compliance is used by people in different ways. The individual will specify which strategies are necessarily and/or ethically adequate. In the social media campaign for elections, political candidates had to work hard to gain people's trust in order to be seen as credible.

Compliance-gaining is made up of "persuasion" which highlights beliefs, attitudes, attention and behaviors while the term "compliance" typically refers to a transformation in a person's overt behavior (Michelle, 2002). Existing research claimed compliance-gaining strategies influence people and get attention from others in discrete ways. The theory was constructed to explain build interpersonal communication (Schmitt, 1967). O'Keefe (1988) sees it as aiming to achieve multiple if conflicting goals while to Deborah (2000) it an attempt to change another person's attitudes. In political advertisements the politicians have their own targets to influence and convey messages that articulate specific goals. The compliance-gaining approach can be applied to this study on how political candidates use social media advertisements to get people's votes. Social media is an electoral medium that links political candidates and targeted voters. Campaigning activities will be announced and updated on Facebook that the public can access. Thus, compliance gaining explores how political candidates utilized Facebook to gain people's trust in this particular by-election. These include how the candidates structured their messages and complied with people's wishes for leaders to follow the rules.

Political Advertising

Political advertising is an important element when a political party wants to attract voters during an election. The major function of political advertisements is to convey messages from candidates to their voters. While Christina et al. (2006) agree that political advertising is a medium that candidates use to promote themselves, Kates (1998) claims politicians engage with media in different contexts. They use it to build their images, clarify their platforms and convey messages to the public. Political advertising has to be effective under certain conditions for different types of voters, image development, agenda setting or attacking opponents. Valentino et al. (2004) highlighted that information in political ads may replace other kinds of information. These findings confirm the view that citizens are cognitive misers who retain some general and limited, request for political information.

Furthermore, looking for information requires effort, and even the most aware will not apply that effort unnecessarily according to Vincent (2004), who states that one probably unique benefit of exposure to political advertisements is that benefits citizens who are uninterested or uninformed about politics. Advertising seems to influence the least aware most powerfully, apparently because those citizens are looking for simple decisions upon which to base their electoral choice. The definition of political knowledge according to Charles (2010) is an individual's ability to recall candidates' names, personal characteristics, and qualifications; to recognize election issues and current campaign developments and to recognize connections between candidates and issue positions. Furthermore, the collision of general mass media campaign communications on gains in knowledge has been contingent in numerous voting studies, based on finding in a moderate association between media exposure and campaign-related knowledge. Recent research evidence indicates that television advertising supplies voters' knowledge levels. McClure and Patterson report that about three-quarters of the voters who recalled seeing a political advertisement in the 1972 presidential campaign could correctly identify the ad's message. The effect of political messages was straightforward like a hypodermic needle (Franz & Ridou 2007). It can be said that political advertisements impact on voters who will be persuaded by what they see. Ernest et al. (2013)argue such intense uses of political advertisements have many problems in politics.

Moten (2009) stated that the use of political advertisements in Malaysia has widened over the past years particularly as elections beckon and they are the main communication tool for a party. They have been widely used by various political parties and electoral candidates over the past two decades. Studies have found that political campaigns are not only using traditional ways but also using new media. In a developing country like Malaysia, this improvement makes political campaigning an interactive process. Previous research has helped to explore the Kajang by-election in the context of examining how social media networking helps candidates win.

Facebook Approach

Social networking platforms like Facebook and Twitter are a form of two-way communication (Thomas 2012). The study found that some social media platforms, such as websites and the blogosphere, embody two-way communication with asymmetric responses, allowing for site visitors to leave comments, but without removing the host's voice. Social networking provides people with indirect communication experiences. Twitter is a medium of political campaigning, and recent studies by scholars have found that Facebook is now a main medium for political campaigning.Christine and Girish (2008) argue that the arrival of social networks had signified a further major divergence in elections since 2008. Facebook appeals to a youthful demographic that has unexpectedly increased participation levels. Facebook facilitates candidates' supporters to develop interpersonal links regarding his/her activities. The social media is able to organize members according to where they live, manage their profiles, networks and organize offline meetings.

Westling (2007) highlights the importance of social media as the only method of campaigning that get an effective response from the public. Since the Howard Dean campaign in 2004, political strategists perceived that the Internet can measure the interest of the public as well as connect community members to the political process. Thus, Facebook is able to arrange and interact with supporters in a very efficient way. At the same time, it provides members of the public with the ability to voice their thoughts and organize autonomously (Westling, 2007). Facebook is also a platform where candidates and voters can communicate and acknowledge the democratic process (Christine & Girish, 2007, 2012). The social network formed a matching section within a main site called Election Pulse in the US. This feature provides much information about the candidates and their profiles in states and districts. Scholars recognized Facebook's victory in the 2008 US presidential election. Political candidates were given online pages for profile placement that were parallel with personal profiles. Candidates are able to post online various kinds of campaigning materials, for example campaign activity announcements, links to other pages such as video sharing YouTube, candidate notes, photo albums, and events that allow voters to post their own comments. This was evident in Canada where Tamara (2008) asserted that Facebook was just one part of the complicated on-line strategy of the Canadian political parties. Though several parties had utilized other political websites that had a narrower focus, the impact of Facebook on electoral politics still needs to be assessed. It can be concluded that Facebook does have an impact on political campaigns in and these include events in Malaysia.

METHODOLOGY

The qualitative method is used to measure the effectiveness of Facebook's political campaign in the Kajang by-election. Elizabeth and Kate (2009) explain that qualitative research focuses on the details of social phenomena and help in understanding the real social world. This method is effective and produces good results because it explores the topic and objectives of the research. This argument is also supported by Patton and Cochran (2002) who state that qualitative research generates more and better data than numbers through use of study informants. Such an interpretation can be applied to the case of the Kajang by-election. This study examines how BN and PR (PKR) political candidates promote their abilities and political messages to Kajang people using advertising in social online networking websites. Furthermore, of the variety qualitative research methods, I selected textual analysis, in-depth interviews and an online research strategy, after establishing the political context of the period studied. There is potential for researcher bias, which has been suggested as a limitation of this method (Lester, 1999). Purposive sampling was necessary to establish two categories of research respondents, i.e. media practitioners as one group and journalists and observers constituting the other.

Textual analysis is used to portray and clarify the characteristics of an evidence or visual message that expresses the content, structure and roles of messages contained in media texts (Frey et al., 1999). The main deliberation in textual analysis is to choose the types of texts to be studied, obtaining proper texts, and then analyze them. If versen (2003) argues that this type of analysis is linked to the linguistic form that associates memory with testimony and testimony with writing. Textual analysis is also known as discourse analysis, and it is a significant way in which to observe cultural artifacts or texts to ascertain their meaning (Matthew, 2008). By connecting the circumstances of production to the review of content this will help to see how institutional and professional control of the text is maintained.

Facebook is the unit of analysis. The sample of this study is drawn from Facebook starting from the nomination day on 11 March 2014 until polling day on 23rd March 2014. The focus will be on how political candidates advertised their political campaigns during the Kajang by-election. Facebook's text will be analyzed and findings will be explained. The connection between media text and the social message will be examined in terms of determining the framework that politicians use to attract voters. The findings will be interpreted from textual analysis and in-depth interview. The results will reflect how effective social media advertisements were during the 12-day campaigning period. Below are examples of screen shots from Facebook (Figure 1 and Figure 2). Graphics, text and all information will be analyzed from the collected data to produce explanations on what they mean.

In analyzing the text the emphasis is on the political advertising in terms of news coverage on Facebook. Thus, the focus is only on candidates in the Kajang by-election. This analysis will examine the meaning of the text in advertisements and visuals that persuade voters to make their choice. The graphics that appear in advertisements present an opportunity to study candidates' stands during their political campaigns.

Figure 1: Screenshot of the BN candidate, Chew mei fun facebook (12 March 2014).

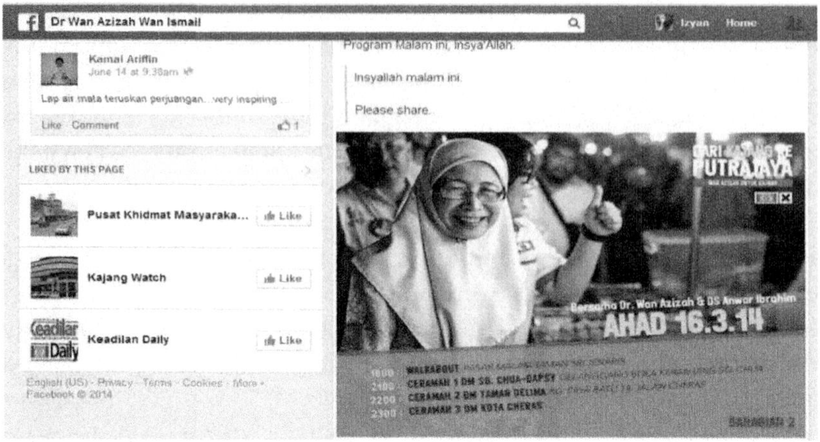

Figure 2: Screenshot of PKR candidate, Dr.wan azizah facebook (16 March 2014).

In-depth interviews constitute another way to collect data by interviewing knowledgeable and experienced people. Informants include nine respondents such as scholars, non-governmental organizations (NGOs), and advertisers who will be referred to as R1 - R9 (i.e. respondent 1 to respondent 9). These respondents were selected based on their experience in political discourses and also their role as political observers. The interviews conducted in Kuala Lumpur to discover their perspectives on a particular idea, program or situation. Information-rich feedback and opinions on the Kajang by-election will be obtained from the in-depth interviews. Known as an unstructured interview, this method helps to acquire information from the interviewee's point of view or situation (Patton 1987). This type of interview involves asking informants open-ended questions to obtain data, specifically relating to the Kajang by-election.

RESULTS

Political Advertising

Thematic analysis is used to analyse the themes or messages that appear in Facebook political advertisements. The research question focuses on the effect, influence and perceptions of voters regarding political campaigns, and will generate descriptive answers from respondents. Thematic analysis is an expressive way to present qualitative data (Rosemarie, 1997). Braun and Clarke (2006) argue that thematic analysis does not require detailed theoretical and technological knowledge of approaches such as grounded theory. It can offer a more accessible form of analysis. For instance, thematic analysis was used by Sindane (2010) to analyse South African political parties' advertisements on television. The answers from the textual analysis and interviews done will lead to focused and specific conclusions. In the Kajang by-election, BN had two candidates who used social media: Chew Mei Fun and Fauzi Zahari. For the PR, Dr. Wan Azizah and Azmin Ali (PKR) used Facebook (Figure 3).

Figure 3: BN candidates.

1) Promoting Leadership

The advertisements produced by BN promote the concept of leadership, which emphasizes a candidate's credibility and how they attract voters. Most BN advertisements covered the important themes in one advertisement in order to get the message across simply to voters. Both BN's statements promote BN leadership, but these did not lead to the expected results in the 2008 and 2013 elections. In contrast, the PKR advertisement promoted leadership better than BN and this change people's ideas and their voting decisions. Below are some samples (Figure 4).

In PR candidates' advertisements, certain elements attracted voters to get them to participate. On Azmin Ali news coverage on his Facebook page, he claimed to solve problems in his area by becoming involved with people's activities; this helped to cement his relationship with voters. The activities undertaken by PR will con-

Figure 4: PKR Candidates.

vince voters and at the same time improve their election results, which occurred in 2008 when they won 5 seats unexpectedly. The advertisements reveal that promoting leadership was the priority for the political parties. The main difference between BN and PR were the extent to which they accepted into voters' lives and sense of trust. In every election both parties tried to improve their campaigns through their own social media by promising better leadership and improved lifestyles.

2) Promoting Benefits

Using the examples below (Figure 5 and Figure 6), it can be seen that both political advertisements focus on the benefits of choosing the candidates of a particular party. BN has used social media more than television or radio for political advertising purposes. This is because it is focusing on promising what it can and will do for people who vote for it. PR did the same thing in its political advertisements but there are some differences their approach to promoting their message.

The sample advertisements above are from the Facebook pages of PR candidates (Figure 7). Their campaigns highlight the benefits of choosing them to govern. As can be seen from the results in the Kajang by-election, PR candidates attracted more voters better than the BN because their method of messaging and the themes they covered were more effective in fulfilling voters' hopes.

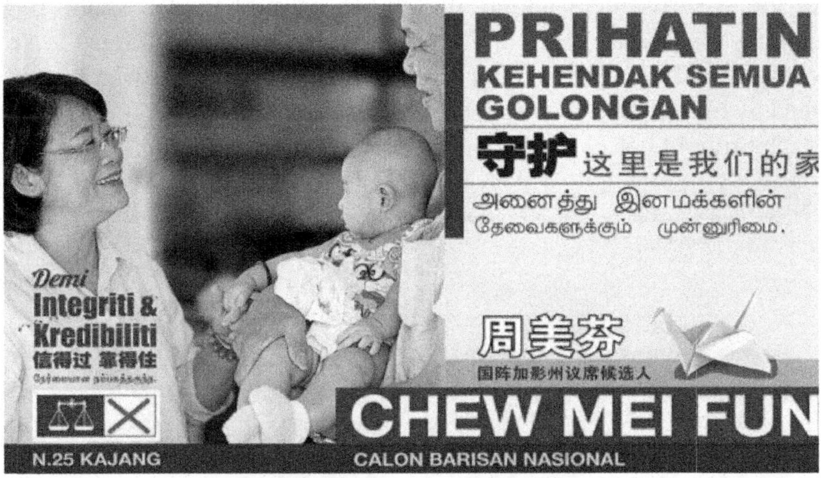

Figure 5: Advertisement on the benefits of voting for the BN.

Figure 6: Advertisement of raising sympathy by PR candidate.

3) Promoting Honesty

In the Kajang by-election campaign, personality elements were promoted by both parties' candidates. Issues that personally affect a politician will lead to a damaged image or reputation. The BN candidate Chew Mei Fun faced a controversy in that it was rumored she employed and abused a maid, which she denied on her Facebook page (Figure 8). While her reputation was damaged she gained the respect of voters when she finally admitted her fault. In contrast the PKR candidate, Dr. Wan Azizah, is seeking sympathy from voters (Figure 9).

In the advertisement above, the slogan used "Lap Air Mata, Teruskan Perjuangan/Wipe your Tears and continues your struggle" shows is seeking sympathy from Kajang voters. As Malaysians were aware Anwar Ibrahim was replaced by his wife Dr. Wan Azizah who contested the election. The sympathy approach brought her

Figure 7: Advertisement of promoting the candidate himself and his activities.

Figure 8: BN's chew mei fun's statement on maid abuse case (2014).

Figure 9: Advertisement by PKR, Dr. Wan azizah for voters' sympathy (repetitive).

victory because people did actually support her husband and his ideals. The way she approached people with the slogan "Lap air mata, teruskan perjuangn" was to emphasize the sadness of being without her husband during the campaign. However:

Although there are some political analysts who opine that PKR puts Dr Wan Azizah Wan Ismail as the candidate to obtain sympathy votes, this columnist's PKR friend revealed that sympathy votes will not be forthcoming for her as the voters will vote based on who can be the better problem-solver (Tay, 2014).

This analysis from a political commentator recognized the strategy by Dr. Wan Azizah to get the sympathy vote. This is how PR influences its voters through psychology and appeals to emotion. A comparison is made between Chew Mei Fun who is single, and Dr. Wan Azizah who is missing hers and has been perceived as being treated unfairly. Basically all the elements of humaneness are employed to attract voters and get their attention.

Findings of In-Depth Interviews

1) Confirming the effectiveness of political advertisements on Facebook

The in-depth interviews confirmed that Facebook advertisements regarding the Kajang by-election had a great impact on voters. For instance R1 said,

Yes, in certain ways they did. Kajang's election is too much of a rumours and facebook did its job by spreading it and making an issue viral. That has helped in making the society always aware of the upcoming election although it was only a small one.

It is evident that Facebook is succesfully being used as the medium for political candidates to convey their political messages and benefits. As mention earlier, Facebook advertisements have the potential to promote the benefits of voting for certain political candidates. R1's response is supported by Messing and Westwood (2012) who states that social networks represent a fundamental break from traditional news modes and are templates for new forms of news discussion. Websites and mobile applications display content from many sources and users no longer have to select one news source when they have a wide-ranging discussion template.

2) Facebook advertisements' strong influence during the campaining period

From the textual analysis discussed earlier, some advertisements portray candidates' real concerns on political events. R2 stated that:

In my opinion, I will choose to look for more information of the campaign.

R2 is convinced that political campaigns through online medium do influence voters. Moten (2009)argues that online political advertising in Malaysia has increased in recent years because it is the key communication tool for a party. The purpose of political campaigning through social networks is to win an election. Doing this means using online media to share photos, opinions, etc. that are important to voters. The European Parliamentary Research Service by Davies (2014) contends that social media can be used in election campaigns in various ways, to organize a candidate's supporters and to persuade the as yet unconvinced. Social media encourages candidates to change their traditional reliance on mediators such as traditionally trained journalists.

R3 stated that,

Facebook is one of the effective medium used to attract the society. So, by posting a status, activities that they have done for the society or using nice words when communicate with the Facebook user, it will surely give a good impact to those candidates.

The answer from R3 confirms previous research findings on the uses of social networks in our daily lives. People are using social networks to gain access to political candidates. In the Kajang by-election, not so much exposure is needed because Kajang is just a small "adun" but the key point is the effectiveness of Facebook advertisements. R3 said by posting their status and activities the political candidates revealed their concerns for society, not just in Kajang but for Malaysia as well. In contrast, R4 related the impact of the Kajang by-election to the case of Anwar Ibrahim and the recent MH370 tragedy. These incidents made the Kajang by-election more widely relevant and received much positive or negative comment. R4 explained this:

Facebook have a high impact on the elections in Kajang and at the same time Anwar Ibrahim was sentenced by the court and it started to spread in social media, then apply a bit of anger by supporters and it cause crowd gathered at kajang stadium to express dissatisfaction but it cannot be seen the ending because of mh370 tragedy happen on the same night.

A lot of speculation about the MH370 tragedy occurred and an effort was made to connect it with Anwar Ibrahim. However, this backfired when Dr. Wan Azizah, Anwar Ibrahim's wife, won the election. The effect of the campaign in social networking also can be seen through the comments that were posted on Facebook where certain people accused Anwar Ibrahim for the MH370 tragedy. This campaign tactic did not stop people voting for PR and it went on to win the election.

3) Mixed feelings of voters towards online political campaigning

Advertisements provided both negative and positive perceptions from voters. R5 stated that:

Yes, it gives a negative perception but in other ways it can be positive for people who have taken it as a political culture. Political candidates have their own way to promote their benefits and to attract voters to choose them.

Online political campaigns do attract voters. However, it is the content of advertisements that persuades people to vote or not to vote for a political candidate. The content of political advertisement has its own rules and aims not to be negative. Williamson, Miller and Fallon (2010) argue that political leaders accept the need to control the communication setting, and they will sense what the public desires and wants from online campaigns. Political parties also recognized that online campaigns depend on what happens during offline campaigns. The content of political advertising must suit the environment and target the right voter audiences. Politicians must monitor the content to control or negate any negative perceptions about them during a campaign.

4) Reputation of the Malaysian Political system

Online political advertisements must connect with voters directly. Social media networks are global in character and in this context; social media advertisements during an election campaign can be accessed by both Malaysians and non-Malaysians. For instance R4 said:

It affects the people who are hiding something, but for those who revealed will gain support. In the old days just rely on the traditional media means that elections are not as defection as now because voters need to know everything before voting.

It is evident that online political advertisements affect the political system in Malaysia in both positive and negative ways. In a positive way it will give a good impression to voters in that political candidates maintain relationships with citizens. In a negative way political activities can create racial or ethnic unrest, which is characteristic of Malaysia. For example, the Bersih Assembly increased many people's participation in street rallies for electoral reforms. R6 also supported this by stating:

Actually, online political campaign do affects Malaysian image in both ways, positive and negative way. Social media became a bridge to outsiders, allowed them to get a picture on political landscape in Malaysia. The negative way is our Malaysians are too obsessed about certain party politics and they didn't encouraged any discussion in public about others party politics. Even it happened, but end up the comments are full of insulted.

According to research by the European Parliamentary Research Service (2014) the influence of social media during elections varies according to countries' political and electoral systems. Nevertheless even a small percentage of the population can (at least in some electoral systems) make a significant difference to the results of a party or an individual candidate. The answers from respondents prove that online political advertisements have impacted on the Malaysian political system in both positive and negative ways. Furthermore, according to R3:

Yes. Because online political campaign can be like a viral, as everyone and anybody in the world could view and access the campaign in Facebook. It does give the negative effect if it reflects the negative sides of the Malaysian political party.

R3 contends that online political advertisements have influenced Malaysia's image in that globally used social networks can promote a bad image when negative comments are made or reported during an election campaign. Advertisements and information can be manipulated by a third party or outsiders.

In contrast to this R1 remarked:

Universally, we are still under controlled compared to the developed country that practiced a full freedom of speech. We in Malaysia still bounded to law and for me, our country is still being viewed in positive ways.

Certain people abuse freedom of speech for political ends. From the statement above it can be concluded, however, that online political advertisements and campaigns create more positive perceptions rather than negative.

5) The difference between online and mainstream media during political campaigns

Online media are increasingly popular in election campaigns. As explained earlier, in the US Barack Obama use Facebook and Twitter to spread his political message and at the same time connect to citizens. This was replicated in Malaysia where people prefer to communicate online with their leaders. R4 commented on the differences between traditional and online political campaigning:

Cost, and target audience, if they target teenagers they will invest in social media campaign but they are candidate outside from urban area, usually they will use traditional media for campaign.

The main differences between traditional and online media political campaigning are cost and target audience. The traditional media campaign is more expensive but internet networks can be accessed everywhere. Social media users are mostly early adults and adult citizens that politicians want to reach in their campaigns. Rajaratnam (2009) highlighted that during the 2008 election the role played by the online media increased dramatically and especially during the recent 2013 election. R2 also the views concerning the importance of online media:

In my view, the social media political is worldwide but compare to traditional media campaign is just focus on certain location only.

The traditional media campaign as stated by R2 answer focused on certain regions only. The mainstream media focused on outside urban areas while online media covered both areas. This was typical of the Kajang by-election where the online media was more popular than traditional media developed technologies were part and parcel of urban life. The effectiveness of using online media is much greater than the traditional media because it covers a larger audience. R3 supported this contention:

For me, I would say that social media is the most effective way to influence the society is social media. Social media have the capability to attract the mass audience. Hence, the young adults like me might easily influence with the advertisement on social media.

The statement above has seen the effect of online political campaigning where it can retain a large target audience and particularly young adults who have voted for the first time. Social media is a place for communication for all ages, and in this context political candidates can persuade people through social online networks. In contrast R2 argues traditional media is still popular but people also are exposed to online media:

I will prefer social media as it's accessible and convenient to get the information about political campaign but using traditional media you can able to meet the political candidates face to face and we can report all the difficulties towards them. It depends on the availability of the individual and their preferences.

The option whether to choose online media or mainstream media depends on individual preferences.

DISCUSSION

1) The role of political advertisements in social media networks

The major finding is the power of using political advertisements on Facebook. Malaysiakini.com website on 8th March 2014 reveals the promotion of leadership by emphasizing political candidates' activities with the public. It is evident that online political campaigning is effective because political advertisements are read by people online every day, so they connect with people. Political parties have to increase online campaigns because voters are increasingly online themselves and communicate in that way. Christopoulos (2013) states that influential politicians are noticeable through directed media (print, radio, television) but the structures of such media means they are not immediately accessible. Compliance-gaining theory can show how politicians attract voters and access their ideas of leaders or what they expect of them.

The Kajang by-election campaign witnessed online political advertising campaigns to attract voters in order to spread both parties' propaganda. Based on the screenshot using the BN candidate Chew Mei Fun, Facebook emphasized the role of BN's leadership. This was similar for the Opposition party candidate Dr Wan Azizah. The screenshot taken from her Facebook page reveals elements of leadership, as indicated in R1's statement. Other respondents are also influenced by the advertisements and what politicians did such as make donations to the poor and appeal to their emotions. According to Westling (2007) the media should be fair and objective when conveying information to the public. It should also hold the government to account by examining and authenticating the information it provides. So Facebook in political advertising has the same function as the traditional media in producing the messages that political parties want.

2) The impact of online political advertising during the campaign period

The next major finding is that the results of the Kajang by-election reflect online political advertising that voters see. Malaysiakini.com proved this on 24th March 2014 immediately after the election results were announced. Malaysiakini.com is evidence that people are more attracted to what is published on Facebook and the way it persuades voters. R3 supported Malaysiakini.com's statement that Kajang will be ruled by the PR party. The interviews indicated that Facebook encouraged people in Kajang to vote for their preferred political candidate and updated events and politicians' opinions in order to attract social support.

3) The content of online political campaigns

Based on the major findings, it can be concluded that online political advertisements omit negative content and seek not to humiliate political rivals. The screenshots of Chew Mei Fun and Dr. Wan Azizah's Facebook pages are evidence of this. This was supported by respondents who stated that negative content came from a third party that sort to manipulate content. An online political campaign should be monitored because there are many people who could manipulate the objectives of the campaign. This finding answered whether online political advertisements impacts on voters. It can be seen from the results and feedback given on the day of the Kajang by-election. PR had a good political campaign when Dr. Wan Azizah won.

4) Effects on the Malaysian Political System

The major findings do not mean that the Malaysian political system is unaffected. The online social media represent a worldwide view and can impact on the Malaysian political system where voters believe what is online but not in newspapers. It is supported by the statement from R4 that the days of relying on traditional media to get information about elections are gradually ending as online media assert their influence. Christine and Girish (2012) argue that candidates control and manipulate their profiles, discussion topics, posting of comments, videos and photographs. Facebook users who are "friended" by a candidate can also post material and comments. In practice this means that negative comments can be traced and isolated, which is a problem for the Malaysian political system.

5) The manipulation of online political advertisements

During the Kajang by-election candidates promoted notions of sympathy and honesty, as evident in the screenshot for 10th March 2014 during the election campaign. It can be seen that PR advertisement promoted sympathy of Dr. Wan Azizah when she has replaced her husband. The interview session noted opinions that tallied with this observation. R4 answered that during the election campaign period Dr. Wan Azizah gained much support when her husband was charged in ambiguous circumstances. A slogan demonstrated the sadness of Dr. Wan Azizah in order to get the sympathy vote. The screenshot from Chew Mei Fun's Facebook page espouses her honesty in handling the crisis about her maid. R1 remarked that such crises strengthen a political candidate's power to win many voters.

Political advertisements that are online are presented differently from those in traditional media. The manipulation of advertisements will be greater because certain things happened before the Kajang by-election. According to Christopoulos (2013) social media's efficiency depends on the power of a personal connection. For example Dr. Wan Azizah had powerful connections with the Kajang people and got their vote due to support for her husband. The manipulation of online political advertisement occurs like it does in traditional media so that politicians get more votes. This finding emphasizes the compliance-gaining approach where Dr. Wan Azizah and Chew Mei Fun got voters' attention by having widespread political campaigns.

CONCLUSION

Using Facebook in political campaigns to attract voters is a good strategy due to the speed of information that audiences receive and respond to, regardless of age, gender and ethnicity. The utilization of both traditional media and online media needs to be balanced in order to reach targeted audiences and reduce the problem of the "digital divide". Negative elements that may harm the country's image through online political advertisement are unavoidable. Facebook cannot be censored in Malaysia and this allows outside people to witness the political and social changes occurring in the country. Online political campaigns will not damage Malaysia's political system and are in fact symbolic of healthy competition between the government (BN) and Opposition (PR) parties. At the same time, the media needs to be fair when covering news and political campaigns. The mainstream media is still important because previous elections have used them to target the non-developed areas like Sabah and Sarawak. In Kajang's by-election, it can be concluded that the usage of Facebook in conveying political messages was well received. However, political parties should be careful when using online social media because it can be manipulated by a third party or unknown person.

REFERENCES

1. Andrew, W. (1992). Promotional Culture. Thousand Oaks, CA: Sage Publications Ltd.
2. ASLI (2008). An Analysis on 2008 General Elections. Report. Kuala Lumpur: Asian Strategy and Leadership Institute.
3. Braun, V., & Clarke, V. (2006). Using Thematic Analysis in Psychology. Qualitative Research in Psychology, 3, 77-101.
4. Case, W. (1993). Semi-Democracy in Malaysia: Withstanding the Pressures for Regime Change. Pacific Affairs, 66, 183-205.
5. Center for Public Integrity (2005). Democrats Likely to Choose Howard Dean as Leader. 8 February, Washington DC.

6. Channel News Asia (2014). Kajang By-Election Set for March 23. Channel News Asia, 5 February.
7. Charles, A., & Gary, H. (2010). Effects of Political Advertising. The Public Opinion Quarterly, 40, 216-228.
8. Chinnasamy, S. (2013). A Study of the Impact of the Internet, Malaysiakini.com and Democratizing Forces on the Malaysian General Election. Adelaide: The University of Adelaide.
9. Christina, H.B., & Lynda, L.K. (2006). Political Advertising in International Comparison. Thousand Oaks, CA: Sage Publications, 2-12.
10. Christine, B. W., & Girish, J. G. (2007). Social Networks in Political Campaigns: Facebook and the 2006 Midterm Elections. Thousand Oaks, CA: Sage Publications, 1-23.
11. Christine, B. W., & Girish, J. G. (2008). What Is Social Network Worth? Facebook and Vote Share in the 2008 Presidential Primaries (pp. 1-25). Thousand Oaks, CA: Sage Publications.
12. Christine, B. W., & Girish, J. G. (2012). Social Network in Political Campaigns: Facebook and the Congressional Elections of 2006 and 2008 (pp. 51-71). Thousand Oaks, CA: Sage Publications.
13. Crouch, H. (1993). Malaysia: Neither Authoritarian nor Democratic. In K. Hewison, R. Robison, & G. Rodan (Eds.), Southeast Asia in the 1990s: Authoritarianism, Democracy and Capitalism (pp. 135-158). St. Leonards: Allen & Unwin.
14. Davies, R. (2014). Social Media in Election Campaigning. European Parliamentary Research Service 2014, 1-8.
15. Ernest, C. R., Jee, T. W., & Lau, W. M. (2013). Negative Political Advertising: It's Impact on Voters. Asian Journal of Business Research, 3.
16. Franz, M. M., & Ridou, T. N. (2007). Does Political Advertising Persuade?https://www.google.com.my/does+political+advertising+persuade
17. Freedman, P., Franz, M., & Goldstein, K. (2004). Campaign Advertising and Democratic Citizenship. American Journal of Political Science, 48, 723-741.http://dx.doi.org/10.1111/j.0092-5853.2004.00098.x
18. Frey, L., Botan, C., & Kreps, G. (1999). Investigating Communication: An Introduction to Research Methods. Cambridge: Pearson.
19. Guy, C. (2001). The Language of Advertising. New York: Taylor and Francis Group.

20. Hassan, S. (1997). Asian Values and Democracy: Islamic Oriented Non-Governmental Organisations in Malaysia. Paper Presented at the 3rd International Workshop on Discourses and Practices of Democracy in Southeast Asia, Copenhagen.
21. Hitwise, E. (2008). Top Presidential Candidate 2008 Websites. United States.
22. Intelligence Unit's Democracy Index (2011). Democracy Index 2011: Democracy under Stress: A Report from the Economist Intelligence Unit. The Economist, 4 December.
23. Kates, S. (1998). A Qualitative Exploration into Voters' Ethical Perceptions of Political Advertising: Discourse, Disinformation, and Moral Boundarie. Journal of Business Ethics, 17, 1871-1885. http://dx.doi.org/10.1023/A:1005796113389
24. Lester, S. (1999). An Introduction to Phenomenological Research.www.sld.demon.co.uk/resmethy.pdf
25. Matthew, W. F. (2008). Left behind: A Textual Analysis of Media Frames from National TV Journalists Covering Hurricane Katrina's Evacuation Centers (pp. 1-75). Master's Thesis, Columbia, MO: University of Missouri-Columbia.
26. Messing, S., & Westwood, S. (2012). Selecting Exposure in the Age of Social Media: Endorsements Trump Partisan Source Affiliation When Selecting News Online.http://crx.sagepub.com
27. Moten, A. R. (2009). 2004 and 2008 General Elections in Malaysia: Towards a Multicultural, Bi-Party Political System? Asian Journal of Political Science, 17, 173-194.http://dx.doi.org/10.1080/02185370903077469
28. Muzaffar, C. (1989). Challenges and Choices in Malaysian Politics and Society. Penang: Aliran Kesedaran Negara.
29. Oorjitham, S. (2008). New Media Spurring the Wind of Change. New Straits Times, 8 March 2008, 20-21.
30. Pew Internet & American Life Project (2008). The Internet and the 2008 Election. Washington DC: Pew Research Centre.
31. Rajaratnam, U. D. (2009). Role of Traditional and Online Media in the 12th General Election, Malaysia. South East Asia Research Centre, 1, 33-58.
32. Rosemarie, A. (1997). Thematic Content Analysis (TCA) Descriptive Presentation of Qualitative Data.
33. Sani, M. A. M. (2005). Media Freedom in Malaysia. Journal of Contemporary Asia, 35, 341-367. http://dx.doi.org/10.1080/00472330580000201

34. Sindane, S. (2010). The Rise of Political Advertising on Television in South Africa and Its Implications for Democracy. Master's Thesis, Johannesburg: University of the Witwatersrand.

35. Tamara, A. S. (2008). The Facebook Effect? On-Line Campaigning in the 2008 Canadian and US Elections. http://archive.irpp.org/po/archive/nov08/small.pdf

36. Tan, E., & Ibrahim, N. (2008). Blogging and Democratization in Malaysia: A New Civil Society in the Making. Kuala Lumpur: Sage Publications.

37. Themalayianinsider.com (2014). Kajang Rep Quits for By-Election, Anwar or Rafizi Slated to Stand. The Malaysian Insider, 27 January.

38. Valentino, N. A., Hutchings, V. L., & Williams, D. (2004). The Impact of Political Advertising on Knowledge, Internet Information Seeking, and Candidate Preference. Journal of Communication, 54, 337-354. http://dx.doi.org/10.1111/j.1460-2466.2004.tb02632.x

39. Vogel, K. (2007). Money Bomb: Ron Paul Raises $ 6 Million in 24-Hour Period. USA Today (The Politico), 17 December.

40. Welsh, B. (2004). Real Change? Elections in the Reformasi Era. In E. T. Gomez (Ed.), The State of Malaysia: Ethnicity, Equity and Reform (pp. 131-156). New York: Routledge Curzon.

41. Westling, M. (2007). Expanding the Public Sphere: The Impact of Facebook on Political Communication (pp. 1-13).

42. Williams, P. A., & Tedesco, J. C. (2006). The Internet Election: Perspectives on the Web in Campaign 2004. Lanham, MD: Rowman & Littlefield.

43. Zakaria, H. A. (1989). Malaysia: Quasi Democracy in a Divided Society. In L. Diamond, J. J. Linz, & S. M. Lipset (Eds.), Democracy in Developing Countries: Asia (Vol. 3, pp. 347-381). Boulder, CO: Lynne Rienner.

Chapter 8

AN ETHNOMETHODOLOGICAL PERSPECTIVE ON THE CONFLICT BETWEEN MAGISTRATES AND JOURNALISTS IN CAMEROON

Jean-François Nguegan, Thomas Essono

University of Yaoundé II, Advance School of Mass Communication (ASMAC), Yaoundé, Cameroon

ABSTRACT

The report of the magistrate profession to that of a journalist in Cameroon can be studied from the perspective both of the sociology of professions and sociology of the conflict; the actors, who belong to different territories, are usually against the quality, legitimacy and competence required to deal with media information, and judicial control, individual freedom. This relationship is mainly studied in this research in terms of symbolic interactionism, to emphasize first of all on the importance that judges and journalists themselves give to their profession and secondly on the rationality of their game in the construction and the demarcation of their respective territories. This article is a contribution to the study of the discourse of these two groups of professionals who compete with each other.

INTRODUCTION

The opposition between magistrates and journalists in Cameroon can be seen in the mobilization of these actors that protect their respective interests, maximizing their strategic gains while minimizing their losses when wearing blows with their opponents, reciprocally (Ebert, 1993). Relations between the actors of these two professions are included within the explanation of the concept gives by Lester (1980) and Cabin (2000) who drew their inspiration from George Herbert Mead (1934) , the socio-psychologist. Namely, the social fact is not a given but a process that is built through concrete situations. Social fact, they say, is the dynamics of exchange, and it is through the meaning that individuals give to their action, that the essence of the social game can be captured.

Socio-political life is a behavioral system which is different from the environment in which it is located and is open to its influences (Mattelart & Mattelart, 2010). And the ability of the system to master social tension depends, they say, on the presence and nature of the information that is returned to the actors and decision makers. Freund (2003) meanwhile clearly raises the conflict as the most relevant analyst of modern societies.

We consider studying these relationships in the ethno methodological perspective then we will return to analyze how actors of both professions come into contact, inaugurate, maintain and finally conclude exchange sequences and the consequences of these exchanges on social change as it could be considered in the long term. It is a relationship combining a reaffirmation of identity and mobilization of strategic allies, bilateral or crossed, structured around the political game.

We assume, in view of these premises, the existence of a conflict between judges and journalists, and, in this article, the first in a series of two, we indicate the scope of the study (I); proceed to the construction of the object of study (II); state the research methodology (III); and briefly discuss hypotheses and partial conclusions, which in this article, are still only programmatic (IV).

RESEARCH OBJECTIVE

A study of the relationship between judges and journalists in Cameroon tends to prove that the media, in Africa, too, become like in the West, where previous studies have revealed, and even resolved most social conflicts; and, therefore, over determine the game of the actors in the political public sphere. It addresses the dynamics of exchange between the actors and questions the social representations over the meaning of these exchanges (Boyomo, 1996, 1999). It intends to check and establish the fact that the public media space provides a relevant frame of reference for social change.

The Scope of the Study

The scope of this research is linked both to its theoretical framework and its trans-disciplinary anchorage.

The Theoretical Framework

The public space is a production device of choice for social actors in the sense of Habermas (1981) , Foucault (1975) or Bourdieu (1980) . It postulates inter-subjectivity. Individuals, out of their private sphere, come into relationship with each other and express on a daily basis, usually divergent views on all sorts of subjects, because unanimity is rare, and consensus is built on tensions and interests defined, quantified and traded.

The inclusion of social representations makes this research more complex and juridicist. The bonds of social representation are programmatic and preparatory (Moscovici & Vignaux, 2000) in their psycho sociological approach:

"If a social representation is a 'preparation for action', it is not only insofar as it guides the behavior, but especially in so far as it reshapes and constitutes the elements of the environment where it is to take place".

For these authors, social representations thus determine the possible communications field, and the values or ideas present in the visions shared by the groups. The socio-professional conflicts between the magistrates and the journalists in Cameroon, has been rendered more complex by an almost infinite perspective of identical profiles difficult to analyze, because this country has 275 languages. For some pending court cases, the socio-po- litical environment leaves us to subsume that a bamileke journalist would out rightly criticize the instructions or proceedings of a journalist or bulu magistrate if his judgement condemns a bamileke defendant like Yves Michel Fotso. These professionals are the elites that can rank among the dominant players and who according to Guy Rocher, affect social change:

"The elite includes individuals and groups who, because of the power they hold, or their influence, contribute to the historic action of a community".

In the public space, in fact, four major types of speech claim, to hold the dominant discourse on specific issues: they are the speeches of politicians, journalists, intellectuals, and those of socio-professional actors. This is the discourse on professional practices of the judiciary and those of journalists, practices on civil liberties, justice and political governance.

The Legal and Sociological Basis

This research is transcendental because it is situated at the edge of sociology of law and political science. In their relations with journalists, magistrates act in the political public sphere, through government and public action, based on the monopoly of legitimate violence of the State from which they proceed constitutionally; and anticipate from journalists, a predominance of the latter, actors of power that was simply instituted, they argue them and even challenge them.

The study of urban dynamics has shown that ethnicity has gradually given way to corporatism, but has not totally disappeared. So the conflict between judges and journalists is not totally devoid of tribalistic threats when the sociology of the actor's name is used, in a cyclical manner in the judicial investigation and consequently on how journalists report judicial decisions.

This research which addresses the concepts of public space, the state, professions; and paradigms of mediation, conflict, and information; therefore, has as base a strong sociological and legal anchorage before being focused on the specific field of information and communication.

Journalists, meanwhile, have camped their action in the public media space of which they have the monopoly of expertise and control. The magistrates are forced to join them in an attempt to regain the initiative of organized action around the crystallization of public opinion. The latter has become a major challenge for the society in the 21st century whose most significant determinants are information and communication.

The Universal Declaration of Human Rights explicitly proclaims two great truths:

- Men are born equal.
- Men have the right to freedom of speech, conscience and worship, information and communication.

The preamble to the Universal Declaration of Human Rights emphasizes the ideal of equal inalienable rights of freedom and of justice based on the dignity of the members of the human family. It emphasizes at the same time, on the urgent need that human rights should be protected by the rule of law, a democratic regime, so that man is not forced, as a last resort, to rebellion against tyranny and oppression.

The African Charter of Human Rights exists. It supervises and organizes the freedom of individuals and peoples, modeled on European or universal instruments in this area.

National texts also exist. The law 90/052 of 19 December 1990 on freedom of social communication, the decree of 1996, which formally abolished censorship on the one hand and on the other, that of 3 April 2000 on the liberalization of the audiovisual sector in Cameroon have increased the symbolic and strategic capital of a profession, that of journalists, actors in the social representations here are seen as fearless and unrepentant whistleblowers. The unveiling of hidden facts or phenomena, combines with their tribune of functions and role is universally recognized to contribute to research and to the manifestation of the truth.

It is with regards to these principles that journalists and judges, both fully exercise their functions with the understanding that only the magistrate has the prerogative to evaluate breaches of criminal law and obtain eventual imprisonment to all citizens including journalists.

Information and Communication

Relations between judges and journalists are built on the basis of this unavoidable fact, the entire society, like any organization, is a group of people living together in a space, having a goal or a common destiny and empowering themselves to achieve it. It is an association between individuals who must overcome the individual interests. No society can function without this organic link that connects individuals into a greater whole. Somehow, communication refers to how each social actor relates with the other.

Information Communication Sciences is interested in the identities and profiles of the actors, as it analyses the names, languages, status, territories and the search for meaning in these actors. The role and challenges of journalism and the media can be found in international texts, those of UNESCO, the African region, and those of national laws regulating the practice of this profession and therefore reflecting the interest that the creation and use of the media have for States and the international community.

Freedom of communication is, according to UNESCO, the essential means of disseminating knowledge and values. Its main function in democratic societies is to enable citizens to express themselves and be heard, and therefore hope to influence social policy. These texts, especially those of the years 1989 to 1995, were aimed at the promotion of independent and pluralistic media in particular, and cooperation between private African newspapers, with the idea to help them exchange their publications and information.

The action of UNESCO for the promotion of press freedom in the world is clearly expressed in Resolution 4.3 adopted by the General Conference at its 26th session in 1991.

Construction of the Research Objective

Construction of the Objective

Reports and commentaries from journalists on pending cases before the courts are governed by a strict legal and regulatory framework that journalists regard as a humiliation, a restriction that empties the essence of their profession: freedom of information. The facts sought by the two categories of the stakeholders for their information, are in themselves external to magistrates and journalists. Legal information and media information are productions, constructions, whose sequences can be manipulated, from data collection or during processing.

The claims of this article are to contribute to the admissibility of the conflict paradigm in the study of relations between judges and journalists. The strategies of the actors are analyzed from the information and communication science field where research allows the consideration of another paradigm, that of mediation.

Historically, the predominance of the law over political institutions conferred to magistrates, in the collective imagination, such an ascendancy over other social body that judges use as replicas than from a consolidated executive power by the security apparatus of the military, or those from the legislature. The essence of the magistrate's profession is to ensure compliance by all to the rules of law enacted under the ideological premise in a democratic regime, only the law should stop the law. For journalists and the media, to emerge in the face of constituted powers, it must overcome political inertia. The magistrates, who by conservation reflex fight them with legal arguments, do not seem to be devoid of ulterior motives or strategic interests.

The National School of Administration and Magistracy (ENAM) was established on 1 July 1959, and the School of Journalism was established in 1970. But the question being debated here is not that of training to acquire a skill that one would like to apply and evaluate. This allows us to relativize the question of whether committing offenses is limited or not to the category of so-called journalists trained on the job or that of magistrates put under scrutiny by the Chancellery.

To the mockery of journalists, magistrates brandish a rigorous application of the law, even when it is proven that journalists are accountable for their acts twice as many times as judges. We are in the presence of two major players in institutions with very strong social inclusion and having both, a claim to act only for the universal ideal of truth and justice.

But truth and justice are not transcendental here. In these sub-groups of the judiciary and media information, they are built by the presentation of facts in the court. Between prosecution and defense, the most equipped, organized and skillful party wins, after the judge has assessed the evidence presented by the protagonists. The empirical observation of these relations is corroborated by the sociology of media in Cameroon and the mobilization of peripheral players, allies and each other's opponents.

Journalists of CRTV and Cameroon Tribune which are public service corporations and state organs, however, benefit a priori of a presumption of competence before the judges which is justified on first sight by the fact that these journalists a priori of a presumption of competence before the judges which is justified on first sight by the fact that these journalists lean on the position power against the decriminalization of press offenses. Magistrates and journalists clash, under the arbitration of a third pole, that of the Executive. This triadic game, par excellence, of social interaction, offers the ground for a triple and reversible manipulation.

There exists a discourse of judges on journalists within doctrine, in jurisprudence and through public speaking. And there is also a discourse of journalists on the judiciary, mainly used in the media and supported by activists from the civil society.

This demonstrates the existence of direct or deferred exchanges that permits the study of the content of their proclamations and alternately perception of their relations with each other—the epistemological relationship between information and communication (science of the study of the meaning of discourse) and mobilization of actors, which necessarily exists prior to information (Bougnoux, 1998). The actors' strategies reveal their intentions and ultimately the ideology of their respective professions. Discourses are a set of socially or ideologically marked statements historically dated and have a value for established communities.

Cultural anthropology and social psychology certainly throws move light on the hatred of the local actors' vis-à-vis those who dare reveal their turpitude. But we grasp them at the interstices of law, communication science and sociology, political science where territory and concepts are explicitly defined and codified.

Problematization

The social problem of this relationship is that of a double disrespect, first, the apparent harassment by the judges of journalists, who are innocent victims persecuted by an essentially repressive judiciary; then that of irascible journalists who challenge the magistrates that no one dares to attack. The strategies used by these actors include open and hidden aspects that disturb the readability of the social game.

The scientific problem is that of the demarcation of the territories without fully distinct borders. The concept of territory retains the original idea of physical geographical space, territorial or air, as element of determining the state in international public law. The nation-state designates indeed a human community; and the territory bounded by borders, is one of its hardware components and at the same time a dispatcher of skills.

According to this metaphor, a territory, psychologically speaking, means a domain of definition of intellectual competence, a sphere reserved for the personal and intimate radiation of individual or collective actors. It refers to organizations where agents or actors interact to build a given social reality. The territory is finally as area of interest, a field of defined specific interest to the generality. It is a place of express transversal problematic issues, scientifically, in the sociology of territories or urban sociology, for example.

The relationship between journalists and judges show, as in states where problematic border flows are the sign of identity crises, the conflicting tensions that exist (Lewis, 1956, 1984). What is at stake here is a conflict. That is to say clashes between collective actors on values, status, power or scarce resources and in which the objective is to neutralize each protagonist, weaken or eliminate their rivals. It is first of all a social interaction revealing the antagonistic interests, and therefore, the hostile behavior of actors against each other.

The second problem is that of the discourse on the independence of judges or of the judiciary in the democratic ideal of balance of powers. This issue will be the subject of a particular study in the subsequent articles. We shall develop more hereon the first problem, that of border demarcation. Why, is it that magistrates and journalists who do not have the same occupations, compete with such determination?

If we accept that this is just a conflict for the monopoly of the dissemination of judicial information, so, who between the journalist and the magistrate in the exercise of his profession, can determine in advance the use of the facts that later will return to a judicial investigation, and therefore, proscribe or permit the partial or total distribution of information relating to these facts?

Research questions

1. In what way can one of the camps, by itself, establish and impose non-consensual operating rules on the other?
2. This conflict, is it only an allocation conflict or a conflict of jurisdiction and what are its implications?
3. How can the overall game be interpreted and explained?

The research hypotheses

1. Conflict zones appear to be those where there is interference or trespassing. Socio-professional boundaries therefore have no formal bounded areas, as magistrates and journalists feel they have a right to claim.

2. The magistrates have, in relation to journalists, the advantage of constituted power over institutionalized power.
3. Executive power is the determinant instance around which a triadic game is played, and in which we see just judges and journalists.
4. The actors sometimes have encrypted strategies, and sometimes have open strategies whish, indicate that the conflict has an alibi at the origin. The ultimate challenge is concealed by socio-political elite unwilling to strengthen the power of the media and journalists, which dominates social cadet in an exacerbated system of patrimonialism.

From these hypotheses, the first one is verified in this introductory article that establishes the general framework of the study objective and presents the problem. The other two hypotheses are verified and eventually validated in the second article, on a fully operational and decrypting all data collected from the field where the game between judges and journalists is observed.

Research Methodology

Our methodology shows the means, techniques and tools for the collection of field data, paradigms convened in demonstrations or the administration of evidence and the process of validating our assumptions.

Methodological Tools

We use a partial and transversal method to enlarge a part of the reality studied, in order to observe the phenomenon better. Less salient aspects are mentioned and temporarily excluded. They will be considered in a later study. Thomas ESSONO and I (Nguegan, 1996) are using participatory observation and knowledge inherited from professional practice as political analysts at the State Radio and Television, in a cumulative period between 1984 and 2008, during which we have observed the game from within, even live some friction with magistrates. We question the upstream logic.

Paradigms Used

Four main paradigms are used in this section of methodology. These are: actionalism, mediation and structuring power of media discourse; ethnomethodology and French discourse analysis. The symbolic interactionism and ethno methodological analysis are used because they enable us to show the exchanges between actors considered in their relationship to the executive power.

To understand and explain the activity, cohesion and social balance, interactionists propose paradigms and theories which are different from these functionalists. The reasons why individuals let others decide in their stead, and that despite explicit crises, there will be no explosion or social implosion are due the paradigms of exchanges, hence "interactionism", the inevitable contact among individuals, and the meaning that these individuals themselves place in these exchanges hence qualifier "symbolic" (Boudon, 1977 ; Touraine, 1965).

The social fact is a constructed process that the researcher captures and restores through direct observation (Mead, 1934).

Social life is thus a kind of theater where everyone plays roles, and pretends to take seriously the role of other actors (Goffman, 1959).

In the basic principles, it is always necessary to combine overt forms and covert forms of behavior: interactions and symbols (Gagnon & Hebert, 2000). The researcher must, each time, highlight the views of stakeholders and bring symbols to the particular context of the actor; uphold the direct observation taking into account the conditions of the interaction. The re-visitation of these principles shows that they define ethnomethodology and allows us to consider both the theoretical and methodological framework.

Indexicality, reflexivity and practical common knowledge are then used to highlight the agonal character of the conflict.

Verification of Hypotheses

Ethnomethodology is the description of semantic fields as it occurs in a specific social context (Garfinkel, 2007). It favors the views of those involved in the construction of a social reality and the historical or psychological social contexts in which these actors are taken, following the example of the conflict between magistrates and journalists. The members of each society and therefore give meaning to the social order.

We should be attentive to the actions observed on the surface and distinguish the logic that guides these actions in depth (Gumperz, 1989 ; Schegloff, 2007). This model designed in linguistics to analyze verbal interactions, is applicable in communication when added to the model of mediation.

In the interpretative and explanatory framework we use, by resonance, explanations and writings of academics, communication specialists and those of the Law. This mechanism shows the players in their structural opposition, not grouped, as in focus groups. Since we are not working on opinions, we do not do samplings. We work on representations. Interviews are more appropriate. The study is qualitative. The actors are presented in a way those maps out the two main camps in conflict.

It implies thenceforth to demonstrate that the conflict here has an alibi origin and that at the second degree, behind the duality between the primacy of law and the established power of the media, (organized power) there is actually, the conflict of interest, a clash for the control of resources that only the Executive provides.

Findings

The construction of the scientific objective of the study permits, at the same time to present and analyze environmental data and the structuring of the actors involved, and to establish that the relationships between judges and journalists can be eligible for an ethnomethodological approach in Cameroon.

Indexicality is stated, in its principle, to express the dimension of self-identification which determines the speech of each group of actors on itself. Reflexivity, in its principle, expresses the hetero identification dimension, what others think or say about opponents. These elements of the socio professional profiling of the actors involved will be formally documented in the next article to support the evidence of the existence of the conflict. But they are already considered here in the construction of the objective, and they allow us to verify and validate the first research hypothesis. The socio-professional boundaries present areas which are not formally demarcated between magistrates and journalists.

Each territory is therefore trying to uphold its legitimacy, not on all the skills of the competitor but on this pivotal platform or segment of human rights. In this confrontation for marking territories, judicial information meets media information in the search for facts, their sequencing, their interpretation, the release of some information which is judged premature by some magistrates, the effective judgement of detainers justice done or not, on behalf of the people (Eyike & Youssoufa, 2004). It is the untraced part of the delimitations of the socio-profes- sional territories between journalists and magistrates.

By including in the Constitutional provisions the important work of journalists in the flow of information and respect for human rights, the State of Cameroon would formally confine the territories of journalists and that of the judges, territories in which each side feels entitled to claim a monopoly of jurisdiction.

The ideal society of freedom and justice is traditionally thought by installing, in the States, the judiciary as the guarantor of the rights and duties of citizens. This power is embodied by judges and lawyers who act under habeas corpus. Article 10 of the Universal Declaration of Human Rights proclaims the supremacy of the courts in these terms:

"Everyone is entitled in full equality to a fair and public hearing by an independent and impartial tribunal, in the determination of his rights and obligations or the truths of any criminal charge against him".

It does not give the media and their journalists an article with equal strength to that of Article 10 of the Declaration text. The paradigm of conflict is therefore an interpretative register which permits us to use the theory of untraced territories for modelling.

It is a conflict felt by intuition at the beginning like a conflict of allocation or a conflict of competence of which the alibi origin offers a variety of reading material for modern and post modern societies.

CONCLUSIONS

If the regulatory instruments of international life that are contained in these texts constitute the source from which the magistrates and journalists draw their philosophy of action, it is the States' responsibility in their national laws to give substance facilities consequences of arbitration that harmonize wanting to live together.

This study assumes, at the same time, the notion of the interactionist and that of the system agent, used by systemists, because the parties to the conflict bring together alternate identities for themselves and for the others (Dubar, Tripier, & Boussard, 2011). These positions emphasize at the same time the significance of individual characteristics with the methods of creating one's self-psychology, and collective characteristics better expressed by sociology. It ultimately allows us to express social symbolism:

"A form of language, a substitute activity or compensation, a medium of exchange of values, a system of relationships between individuals, attributing the same meaning to things, to constitute a community..." (Riviere, 1988).

Our research, organized in a series of articles, brought to completion, through the interpretative model, is expected to verify whether we are, in Cameroon, in the presence or absence of an open society, the dominant discourse society.

REFERENCES

1. Boudon, R. (1977). Perverse Effects and Social Order. Paris: Presses Universitaires de France.
2. Bourdieu, P. (1980). The Distinction: A Social Critique of the Judgement. Paris: Minuit.

3. Boyomo, A. L. C. (1996). The Construction of the Identity of the Journalist. Polis, Cameroon Political Science Review, Political Identity and Democratization in Cameroon, 1, 111-128.
4. Boyomo, A. L. C. (1999). Media and Democracy in Cameroon: An Ethno Methodological Approach. Paris: Karthala.
5. Cabin, P. (2000). The Rise of Interactionist Sociology. Auxerre: Editions Sciences Humaines.
6. Dubar, C., Tripier, P., & Boussard, V. (2011). Sociology of Professions (3rd ed.). Paris: Armand Colin.
7. Ebert, F. F. (1993). The Role of Media in the Democratic Process in Cameroon. Yaoundé: Friedrich Ebert Fondation.
8. Eyike, V., & Youssoufa, B. (2004). The Criminal Litigation of Press and Audiovisual Communication in Cameroon. Yaoundé: Editions St Paul.
9. Freund, J. (2003). The Essence of Politics. Dalloz.
10. Gagnon, M., & Hebert, D. (2000). Seeking Sciences: Introduction to Epistemology. Montréal: Fides.
11. Garfinkel, H. (2007). Research in Ethnomethodology. Paris: PUF
12. Goffman, E. (1959). The Presentation of Self in Everyday Life. Edinburg: Anchor Books
13. Gumperz, J. (1989). Start a Conversation. Introduction to Interactional Sociolinguistics. Paris: Les Editions de Minuit.
14. Habermas, J. (1981). The Theory of Communication Action. Paris: Fayard
15. Lester, K. (1980). A Primer in Ethno Methodology. New York: Oxford University Press.
16. Mattelart, A., & Mattelart, M. (2010). History of Communication Theories. Paris: Ed. La Découverte
17. Mead, G. H. (1934). Mind, Self and Society. Chicago, IL: University of Chicago Press.
18. Moscovici, S., & Vignaux, G. (2000). Social Representations: Explorations in Social Psychology. Cambridge, UK: Polity Press
19. Nguegan, J. F. (1996). Professional Journalists and Institutional Communicators in Cameroon: Conflict of Competence or Conflict of Interest. Dissertation of Specialization in Political Analysis and Public Relations. Yaoundé: DSSTIC.
20. Riviere, C. (1988). The Political Liturgies. Paris: PUF.

21. Schegloff, E. A. (2007). Sequence Organization in Interaction: A Primer Conversation Analysis Volume 1. Cambridge, UK and New York: Cambridge University Press.
22. Tourain, A. (1965). Sociology of Action. Paris: Seuil.

Chapter 9

ANALYSIS ON THE INTERNATIONAL SITUATION AND EVOLUTION OF RESEARCH: QUANTITATIVE ANALYSIS ON THE SSCI THESES FROM 2005 TO 2014

Jingqian Tang
Library of Jinan University, Guangzhou, China

ABSTRACT

Bibliometrics and descriptive statistical analysis on the research papers published on the 74 kinds of journals of journalism and communication included in SSCI from 2005 to 2014 will be conducted through key variables, like annual distribution, regional distribution, research institutional distribution, authors distribution, frontier of research, knowledge base and its evolution, subject impact index, etc. From the qualitative and quantitative perspective, we will reveal the international posture of journalism research and the international prestige and potential problems in studies of journalism and communication in Mainland China to promote the internationalization process of domestic journalism and communication research.

INTRODUCTION

Journalism and communication is one of the most popular research directions in the humanities and social sciences and the internationalization of the research results is a major problem. In recent years, concerning China's journalism and communication studies, the vision, and the scope of it has expanded, but the depth is insufficient and the academic level is not high enough. Some scholars believe that strengthening method training and grasping the international theory research is the key to improving the academic level of China's journalism and communication studies (Liao et al., 2014). Therefore, it is urgent to establish the international awareness of the research on journalism and communication, to understand and master the research orientation, the research trends and the development trend of the international mainstream academic journals and representative results. However, the wave of big data is coming, mastering and using correctly the empirical research methods to deal with the mass of information is a challenge for the journalism and communication researchers. Science Citation Index Social (SSCI) is generally considered to be an important tool for collecting data from various fields of social science. The number and level of the papers published in the journals included in the SSCI can reflect the degree of internationalization (Liu & Liu, 2009). Journalism and communication science is an important subject of SSCI, which is helpful to promote the development of domestic journalism and communication, and to promote the international progress of the academic achievements and academic journals. Some scholars had carried on the analysis of the study of journalism and communication in China on the basis of SSCI. For example, Li Wu, Huang Pei and other scholars take the research papers of journalism and communication included in the SSCI, A&HCI and CPCI-SSH as the study subject, to dissert on the foreign new media research progress from several perspectives by using mapping knowledge domain (Li, Huang, & Li, 2013 ; Liu et al. 2013 ; Li, 2013). The analysis and discussion undoubtedly have given us great help to understand some part of the present international situation of the research on journalism and communication science. However, there are still shortcomings on the aspects such as the holistic overview of journalism and communication studies, especially the study of the frontier, knowledge base and the whole evolution characteristics, and the effect of journalism and communication research on other disciplines, etc. In view of this, this paper takes research papers published on 74 kinds of journal of journalism and communication studies included in SSCI from 2005 to 2014 as research object. We try to answer the following questions: 1) what kinds of form features do journalism and communication study papers included in SSCI take on? What are the evolution characteristics of them? 2) What major issues do journalism and communication study papers included in SSCI concern? What is the frontier area, the knowledge base and the evolution of the research? 3) What are the implications of these papers on the research field of social science?

DATA SOURCES AND ANALYSIS METHODS

Data Sources

JCR data show that there are 74 kinds of journal of journalism and communication included in the SSCI (38 in Britain, 25 in the United States, 4 in Holland, 3 in Germany, 1 in Spain, 1 in Switzerland, 1 in Australia, 1 in Slovenia). Concerning the research field they are involved, in addition to the research of journalism and communication, these journals are also involved in psychology, business, linguistics, library and information science, political science and other fields (Table 1). Retrieve simultaneously in the two fields of Publication Name and Published Year in SSCI. The preliminary retrieval results include 30,100 records and there are 20,647 of re-

Table 1: Journals of journalism and communication included in SSCI (IF > 1.5)

Publication source	Publication cycle	Country	IF(2013)	Other subjects
Communication Research	Bimonthly	America	2.444	No
Research on Language and Social Interaction	Quarterly	Britain	2.421	Psychology, Linguistics
Journal of Communication	Bimonthly	America	2.076	No
New Media Society	Monthly	Britain	2.052	No
Public Opinion Quarterly	Bimonthly	Britain	2.033	Political Science、Social Sciences
Journal of Computer-Mediated Communication	Quarterly	America	2.019	Library and Information Science
Public Understanding of Science	Bimonthly	Britain	1.932	Philosophy of history
Human Communication Research	Quarterly	America	1.886	No
Journal of Health Communication	Monthly	America	1.869	Library and Information Science
Political Communication	Quarterly	America	1.825	Political Science
International Journal of Press-Politics	Quarterly	America	1.761	Political Science
International Journal of Advertising	Bimonthly	Britain	1.754	Business
Journal of Advertising Research	Quarterly	America	1.651	Business
Interaction Studies	3 Issues/year	Holland	1.564	Linguistics

search papers, 6878 of book reviews, others are conference abstracts, editorial material, communication and news, etc. After above retrieval, 20,647 of sample papers are obtained excluding editorials, news, biographies, book reviews, conference abstracts and other types of documents.

Methods and Tools

This paper will carry on analysis of the basic characteristics, research frontier, knowledge base, discipline influence and other aspects of the papers in journalism and communication included in SSCI in order to answer the above questions. 1) For the basic characteristics of the papers, we select the annual distribution, national/re- gional distribution, research institutions, the authors distribution and other variables of sample papers to carry on statistical analysis by using Online Analyzer of SSCI database; 2) For the research frontier of the papers, we select the author key words of sample papers (Author Keyword field in SSCI database) to carry on data processing and statistical analysis by using Endnote, Excel and Citespace. 3) For the knowledge base of the papers, we select the reference literature (References Cited field in SSCI database) of sample papers and use Citespace software to carry on the visual analysis, and use Excel and Endnote to carry out data processing and statistical analysis; 4) For the discipline influence of the papers, we select literature from sample papers(Citing Articles field in SSCI database) to carry on citation analysis to reveal the impact of journalism and communication studies included in SSCI on other social sciences field.

DATA ANALYSIS

Basic Features of Journalism and Communication Research Papers

The total number of journalism research papers published on 74 kinds of journals during 2005-2014 is 20,647 and the annual distribution and change trend is shown in Figure 1. The data shows that the annual output of the research papers in the field of journalism and communication studies is stable and the average output is about 192 every year in the 10 years. These papers are from 115 countries/regions respectively, showing a trend of focus on a small number of countries/regions. The total number of papers of the top 10 countries is 18,317 which accounts for 88.72% of the total. Among them, a total of 10,903 papers of the United States accounted for 52.81% of the total (see Table 2), which is the most. It is worth noting that, although the data inTable 2 shows that China (not including Taiwan) ranks ninth place with 586 papers, but there are only 183 published papers, of which the first author or the corresponding author are from mainland China. The number of papers published by the author from Hong Kong is 259 and from Macao District is 20. There are 124 papers for cooperation. This indicates that the international visibility and influence level of the research achievement of journalism and communication in the Mainland China is very low and the research level is not only significantly behind the western developed countries, such as the United States and other western countries, but also there is a big gap behind Hong Kong. One of the important obstacles may be the language problem: English in the SSCI papers accounted for the absolute advantage. In the sample papers there are 20,245 ones are written in English, accounting for 98.05% of the total. In addition, China has not yet any kind of periodical of journalism and communication studies to be collected by SSCI, which also greatly restricted the pace of the research results of China's journalism and communication studies to the world.

The research status of representative writers group in a certain subject field reflects the trend of the research in this field. We can grasp the depth and breadth of the research field of journalism and communication by analyzing those representative writers group. From the ranking of the number of papers published by the Research Institute (see Table 3), we can see there are 9 American universities published more than 200 papers, which indicates that the United States occupies the leading place in the research field of the international journalism and communication. From the number of papers published by the author (see Table 4), we can see there are 16 people published more than 25 papers, among whom 10 are from the United States, 3 from Holland, 1 each from Hong Kong, Taiwan and Belgium. There is no doubt that these scholars, especially from the United States, are the leading figures in the study of journalism and communication, and have an immeasurable effect on the promotion of its research.

Frontier and Knowledge Base of Journalism and Communication Research Papers

The research area normally can be defined as a series of related issues and concepts, which are concerned by the

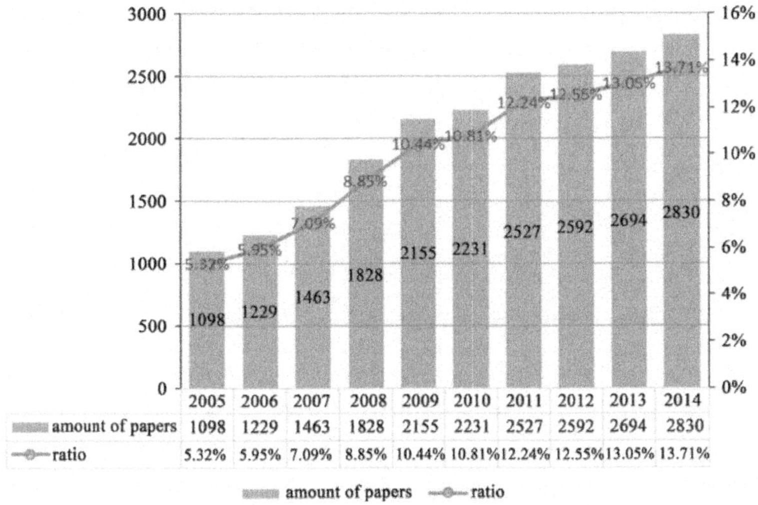

Figure 1: Annual distribution of the journalism and communication papers.

Table 2: Countries/regions distribution of the journalism and communication papers (Top 10)

Countries/Regions	Number of papers	Proportion	Cumulative ratio
America	10,903	52.81%	52.81%
Britain	1694	8.21%	61.01%
Australia	1384	6.70%	67.72%
Holland	925	4.48%	72.20%
Canada	730	3.54%	75.73%
Germany	631	3.06%	78.79%
Spain	598	2.90%	81.68%
China (including Hong Kong, Macao)	586	2.84%	84.52%
Korea	490	2.37%	86.89%
Belgium	376	1.82%	88.72%

Table 3: Research Institute distribution of the journalism and communication papers (number of papers > 200)

Organization name	Country	Number of papers	Proportion
Wisconsin University	America	400	1.94%
University of Illinois	America	361	1.75%
Michigan State University	America	358	1.73%
University of Amsterdam	Holland	336	1.63%
University of Texas at Austin	America	323	1.56%
Ohio State University-Columbus	America	320	1.55%
Pennsylvania State University	America	312	1.51%
University of Pennsylvania	America	266	1.29%
University of Georgia	America	232	1.12%
Indiana University	America	227	1.10%
Purdue University	America	223	1.08%
University of North Carolina	America	222	1.08%
University of Michigan	America	216	1.05%
University of Missouri	America	210	1.02%
University of Calif Santa Barbara	America	202	0.98%

Table 4: Authors distribution of the journalism and communication papers (number of papers > 25)

Author's name	Research institution	Number of papers
Valkenburg, Patti M.	University of Amsterdam (Holland)	33
Scheufele, Dietram A.	Wisconsin University (America)	33
Knobloch-Westerwick, Silvia	Ohio State University-Columbus (America)	33
de Vreese, Claes H.	Leiden University (Holland)	33
Lee, Francis L. F.	The Chinese University of Hong Kong (China)	32
Chang ChingChing	National Chengchi University (Taiwan)	32
d'Haenens, Leen	The University of Leuven (Belgium)	30
Paek, Hye-Jin	Michigan State University (America)	28
Walther, Joseph B.	Michigan State University (America)	28
Niederdeppe, Jeff	Cornell University (America)	27
Shah, Dhavan V.	Wisconsin University (America)	27
Peter, Jochen	University of Amsterdam (Holland)	26
Dutta, Mohan J.	Purdue University (America)	26
Brossard, Dominique	Wisconsin University (America)	26
Tamborini, Ron	Michigan State University (America)	25
Levine, Timothy R.	Michigan State University (America)	25

academic community. The key words and their frequency distributions are often used to reveal the subject areas of their research (Chen, 2006). If we take a series of related issues and concepts concerned by the highly cited papers lately published in the last several years as the latest developments in the field, then the references of the frontier study form their knowledge base (Persson, 1994). Therefore, through statistics and analysis of the highly cited papers and keywords of the references of these papers published during 2005-2014, we reveal the frontiers, knowledge base and the evolution process of the journalism and communication research

Analysis of the Frontier Areas of Journalism and Communication Research Papers

Statistics indicates that during 2005-2014 there are 14,389 SSCI papers quoted more than once in journalism and communication research, which accounted for 69.69% of the total number of the sample papers. The highest cited times of a single paper was 659. The total number of keywords in these 14,389 papers was 36,038 (the average number of keywords in each paper is 2.5). After classification, summarization and eliminating numbers, symbols and words that means nothing substantive to the journalism and communication study area, the results of using Citespace software to do visualization analysis are shown as Figure 2. In particular, the keywords with frequency more than 600 times are in Table 5. After using Citespace to further analyze the link between high frequency keywords, we found that (Figure 2): communication, media, Internet, information, has been the research hotspots of journalism and communication in recent ten years. In recent years, the main focus of the frontier areas of journalism and communication research is on the following areas: 1) the study mainly on news reports. The study mainly concerns the application of mass-media in the news reports, the media of the news reports, press and the news reports of journalism and communication in the field of natural science, such as climate change, etc.; 2) in social support area, the study mainly concerns stress, adjustment of personality and quality, physical and mental health of family, children, adolescents and women, etc., such as depression, breast- cancer, et al.; 3) The study on interpersonal relationship including close relationship and romantic relationship, etc.; 4) through analysis of the sharp changes of key words We can find the new research areas of journalism and communication , such as the application of Twitter, Facebook and other social media and computer media on journalism and communication.

Analysis of the Knowledge Base of Journalism and Communication Research

As mentioned above, the references of these 20,647 sample papers constitute the knowledge basis of journalism and communication research. Therefore, we can reveal the knowledge basis of the journalism and communication research though analyzing these references, especially the highly cited ones. We got the following results as

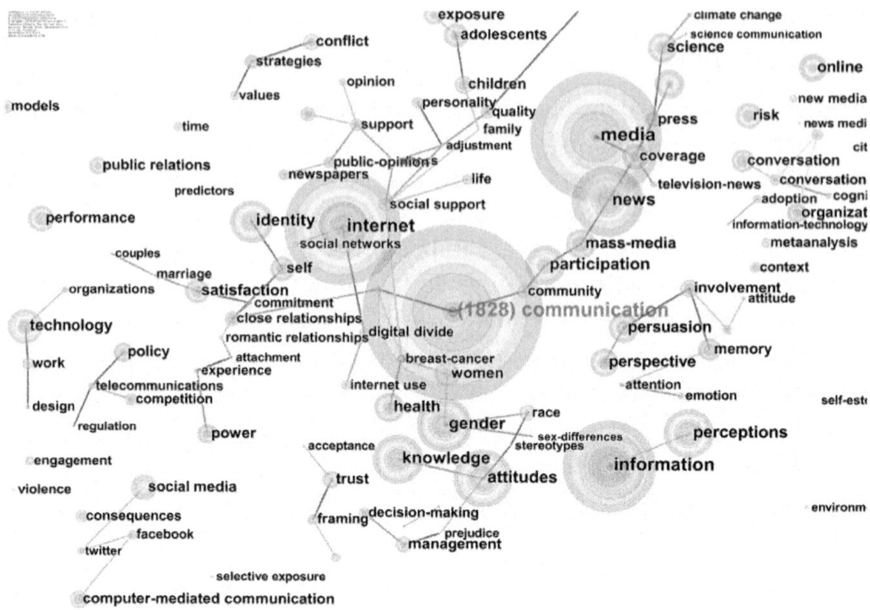

Figure 2: Relation map of high frequency keywords from high cited papers.

Table 5: High frequency keywords from high cited papers (frequency > 600)

Keywords	Frequency	Keywords	Frequency
Business	2048	Television	822
Linguistic	1854	Language & Linguistic	820
Information Science & Library Science	1842	Culture Studies	810
Media	1595	Model	805
Film, Radio, Television	1418	Impact	710
Psychology, Social	1344	Gender	669
Internet	1256	Health Policy & Services	647
Sociology	1210	Discourse	642
Information	1084	Management	640
Political Science	998	Telecommunications	623
Behavior	914	Knowledge	619
News	902	Perceptions	603

shown in Figure 3 and Figure 4 by using Citespace software to visualize all the references analysis. In particular, the top 20 researchers whose papers are cited most frequently and their representative references are in Table 6. After further analysis we found the following characteristics: 1) Concerning the representative researchers, the research achievement of Scheufele, D.A., Iyengar, S., Eveland, W.P., Bandura, A., Entman, R.M. constitute the core references of the journalism and communication studies included in SSCI

(Table 6). 2) Concerning the area and content of the research, these knowledge basis are related to the role of Communication theory and television news in social life, and the contrast of the influence of publication, broadcasting and internet in communication,

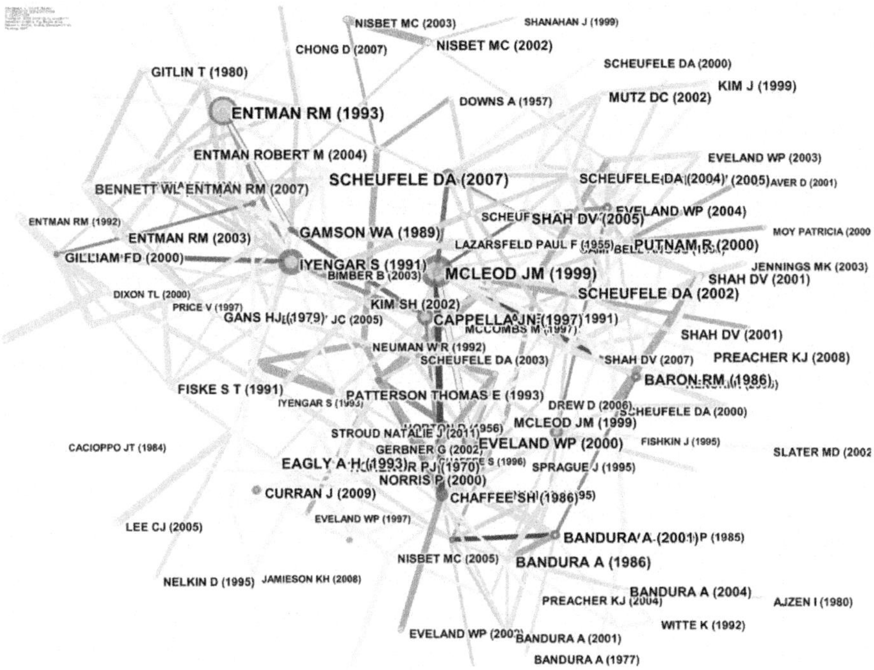

Figure 3: Relation map of high frequency documents of the journalism and communication papers.

context and community. For example, Scheufele, D.A. discusses the evolution of the following three models: framework, agenda setting and prediction (Scheufele & Tewksbury, 2007). Another example, Iyengar, S. studies the impact of television news on the citizen cognition of international affairs (Iyengar, 1987). 3) Concerning the relationship between the reference and the cited (seeFigure 3 and Figure 4), these core reference documents still have a guiding significance on today's journalism and communication study and are the focus of the follow-up study. And there is also an academic inheritance relationship between these core reference documents which shows a clear knowledge accumulation effect.

INFLUENCE OF JOURNALISM AND COMMUNICATION PAPERS BY SUBJECT CATEGORY

The citation of a paper is often used to evaluate the academic influence of that paper. In this paper, to reveal the influence of journalism and communication research on other subjects, we carry out analysis of subject categories on the citation of the research papers included in SSCI. As mentioned above, the total number of journalism and communication research papers included in SSCI cited more than once is 14,389 during 2005-2014 and the total cited number is 122,672. Due to the limitation of the number of samples, we carried out analysis on the 5000 papers which were cited the most. These papers were incited 97,022 times and 50,499 references were cited, except for the 48,068 self-citation. The analysis results are shown in Table 7. Firstly, this shows that the degree of cross-level and mutual influence between journalism and communication studies and Psychology is quite high. Secondly, the research results of journalism and communication studies are also cited in business and economics, public environment occupational health, computer science, linguistics, sociology, library and information science, government law, education and teaching, Health Sciences, engineering, environmental ecology and other social sciences, which shows that the influence of journalism and communication studies is very ex-

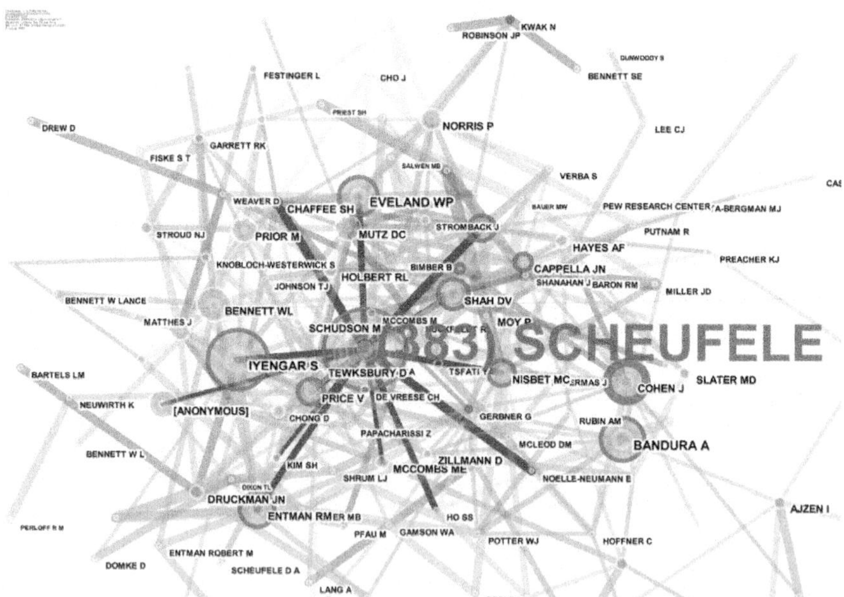

Figure 4: Relation map of high frequency authors of the journalism and communication papers.

Table 6: High frequency authors and their representative literatures of journalism and communication papers (Top 20)

Author	Total cited frequency	Representative literature	Representatives cited times
Scheufele, D.A.	383	Framing, agenda setting, and priming: The evolution of three media effects models (2007)	268
Ingra, S.	322	Television-news and citizens explanations of national affairs (1987)	95
Eveland, W.P.	253	Interactions and nonlinearity in mass communication: Connecting theory and methodology (1997)	44
Bandura, A.	245	A comparative test of status envy, social power, and secondary reinforcement theories of identificatory learning (1963)	109
Entman, R.M.	213	Blacks in the news - television, modern racism and cultural-change (1992)	158
Cohen, J.	204	Abuse and violence history of men and women in treatment for methamphetamine dependence (2003)	65
Price, V.	202	New values and public opinion: A theoretical account of media priming and framing (1997)	95
Shah, D.V.	177	Communication, context, and community - An exploration of print, broadcast, and Internet influences (2001)	177
Mcleod, J.M.	170	Understanding deliberation - The effects of discussion networks on participation in a public forum (1999)	81
Mutz, D.C.	165	The consequences of cross-cutting networks for political participation (2002)	165
Bennett, W.L.	162	Toward a theory of press-state relations in the united-states (1990)	102
Zaller, J.	160	Information, values, and opinion (1991)	87
Nisbet, M.C.	146	Pathways to political participation? Religion, communication contexts, and mass media (2003)	44
Norris, P.	139	"To entertain, inform, and educate": Still the role of public television (2001)	45
Prior, M.	138	Post-Broadcast Democracy: How Media Choice Increases Inequality in Political Involvement and Polarizes Elections (2007)	138
Chaffee, S.H.	122	Political knowledge and the campaign media of 1992 (1994)	96
Cappella, J.N.	113	Argument repertoire as a reliable and valid measure of opinion quality: Electronic dialogue during campaign 2000 (2002)	56
Ajzen, I.	109	Attitudes, personality and behavior (1988)	103
Petty, R.E.	108	Mass media attitude change: implications of the elaboration likelihood model of persuasion (2002)	41
Zillmann, D.	106	Female responses to provocation after exposure to aggressive and erotic films (1978)	20

Table 7: Distribution of journalism and communication citing articles (Top 20)

Subject category	Citation quantity	Proportion
Psychology	8999	21.036
Communication	8769	20.498
Business Economics	5166	12.076
Public Environmental Occupational Health	3024	7.069
Computer Science	2922	6.83
Social Sciences Other Topics	2913	6.809
Linguistics	2388	5.582
Sociology	2306	5.39
Information Science Library Science	2289	5.351
Government Law	2227	5.206
Education Educational Research	2102	4.914
Health Care Sciences Services	1648	3.852
Engineering	1282	2.997
Environmental Sciences Ecology	1202	2.81
Psychiatry	735	1.718
Biomedical Social Sciences	677	1.583
Family Studies	675	1.578
General Internal Medicine	651	1.522
Public Administration	579	1.353
Substance Abuse	552	1.29

tensive and the interdisciplinary study of the journalism and communication is becoming more and more powerful.

DISCUSSION

Through carrying out literature measurement analysis and descriptive statistical analysis on the journalism and communication research papers included in SSCI during 2005-2014 and combing related literatures, we revealed the basic situation of the research on the International journalism and communication in the last ten years: 1) The European and American countries represented by the United States, Britain and Holland occupy the dominant position leading the international journalism and communication study. While the study of journalism and communication in mainland China is lagging far behind the international level; 2) Business, Media, Internet and Information Science and so on are the most concerned areas of journalism and communication studies. Facebook and Twitter and so on are emerging research areas; 3) Internationally, the research on the journalism and communication shows the characteristic of problem-solving orientated and the micro application based, which pays great attention to the guiding role of the research on the educational practice, and has a relatively clear knowledge accumulation and academic inheritance path; 4) The influence of journalism and communication studies on other subjects is increasing, which shows the interdisciplinary characteristics of social science research from another side.

Through comparative analysis of domestic journalism and communication studies, we find the following phenomena and problems: 1) The international visibility and international level of the domestic journalism and communication studies are relatively low and the number of papers written by the authors from mainland China is only 183 among 14,389 samples. Although it may be related to the factors such as periodical source and language barrier, the key lies in the theory of the research itself is not strong and the depth of the research is not enough. 2) Domestic journalism and communication studies tend to take a more macro perspective and many research papers have been staying at the basic study on the theory of journalism and communication, business knowledge and development model, without reflecting the practical application of journalism and communication. Furthermore, the specific practice of journalism and communication in the business, economic and social livelihood and other areas needs to be strengthened. 3) The achievements of the domestic journalism and communication studies are more simple repetition and show obvious characteristics of knowledge fragmentation. Their theoretical foundation is weak and their effect on the knowledge accumulation and development of the journalism and communication is not obvious. 4) In the 20,647 journalism and communication research papers, only 234 papers were co-authored by Chinese authors and foreign authors, which showed deficiency in international cooperation and exchange. In order to change this situation, the researchers of journalism and communication need to establish the international awareness, to track and learn from the advanced research results and methods, to optimize the main content, structure and discipline distribution, to strengthen international cooperation and academic exchanges, and to strive to improve the international status of domestic journalism and communication studies and academic visibility on the basis of focusing on the specific situation in China.

REFERENCES

1. Chen, C. M. (2006). Citespace II: Detecting and Visualizing Emerging Trends and Transient Patterns in Scientific Literature. Journal of the American Society for Information Science & Technology, 57, 359-377. http://dx.doi.org/10.1002/asi.20317
2. Iyengar, S. (1987). Television News and Citizens' Explanations of National Affairs. American Political Science Review, 81, 815-831. http://dx.doi.org/10.2307/1962678
3. Li, W. (2013). The Publication Trends of the International Journal of Journalism and Communication: Measurement Analysis on the SSCI Articles. Publishing Research, 1, 85-89.
4. Li, W., Huang, P., & Li, X. J. (2013). International Research Advance of New Media Based on Mapping Knowledge Domain. Journal of Beijing University of Posts and Telecommunications (Social Sciences Edition), No. 2, 18-24.
5. Liao, S. Q., Shen, Q., Liu, C. Y. et al. (2014). Journalism and Communication Studies of China Mainland from 1998-2012. Journalism Bimonthly, 6, 70-82.
6. Liu, L., & Liu, N. C. (2009). Bibliometric Analysis of SSCI Publications of China from 1978-2007. Information Science, 10, 1590-1594.
7. Liu, Z. X., Liu, N. H., Ma, K. et al. (2013). Review of Journalism and Communication Research in China of the Year: Analysis Based on 9 Kinds of CSSCI Journals. Modern Communication (Journal of Communication University of China), 3, 41-48.
8. Persson, O. (1994). The Intellectual Base and Research Fronts of JASIS 1986-1990. Journal of the American Society for Information Science, 45, 31-38. http://dx.doi.org/10.1002/(SICI)1097-4571(199401)45:1<31::AID-ASI4>3.0

9. Scheufele, D. A., & Tewksbury, D. (2007). Framing, Agenda Setting, and Priming: The Evolution of Three Media Effects Models. Journal of Communication, 57, 9-20.

Chapter 10

SOCIAL MERCHANDISING: HUMAN TRAFFICKING IN BRAZILIAN SOAP OPERA

Denise Avancini Alves[1,2], Maria Helena Weber[2]

[1]Pontifical Catholic University of Rio Grande do Sul (PUCRS), Porto Alegre, Brazil

[2]Federal University of Rio Grande do Sul (UFRGS), Porto Alegre, Brazil

ABSTRACT

Human trafficking is one of today's largest shadow economies. This theme was included in plot of Salve Jorge, a soap opera in Brazil (broadcasted by Globo Network between October 2012 and May 2013). This article analyzes the social merchandising, an approach given to international human trafficking in entertainment venues of television, especially, from the telenovela Salve Jorge. The strategy of inclusion of social issues in the plots is recognized as social merchandising. So, it is in this privileged media space that the story of a social problem is also constituted. The study focuses on the discussion of the power of the telenovela to dramatize issues of public interest, having main broadcasting and audience of Salve Jorge. One seeks to question the maintenance and the impact of the subject of human trafficking as a dialogue between fiction and reality portrayed by Brazilian television. The show, Salve Jorge, is based on the real-life story of a Brazilian woman who was led to Israel and forced into prostitution. Therefore, human trafficking emerges as the central theme of this study over the main plot of Salve Jorge.

INTRODUCTION

Human trafficking should mean the "recruitment, transportation, transfer, harboring or receipt of persons, by means of the threat or use of force or other forms of coercion, of abduction, of fraud, of deception, of the abuse of power or of a position of vulnerability or of the giving or receiving of payments or benefits to achieve the consent of a person having control over another person, for the purpose of exploitation. Exploitation shall include, at a minimum, the exploitation of the prostitution of others or other forms of sexual exploitation, forced labor or services, slavery or practices similar to slavery, servitude or the removal of organs" (UN, 10 2004, p; 42). Generating, annually, more than 30 billion dollars, it is considered the third largest business in working capital in the world.

Human trafficking is a serious crime and one of today's largest shadow economies. It is one of the greatest violations of human rights today. Lured by the promise of a better life, people are recruited by criminal networks responsible for the third most lucrative illicit trade in the world, after the trafficking of drugs and weapons.

In terms of international classification, there are four traffic purposes recognized by the United Nations: sexual exploitation; removal of organs, tissues and body parts; slave labor; and servile marriage. For legal interpretation, trafficking can be configured as a kind of slavery, internationally coined under the term of "modern slavery". It is considered as a crime and is related to other criminal practices and human rights violations, serving not only the exploitation of slave labor, but also the international networks of commercial sexual exploitation, often linked to sexual tourism routes, with the involvement of specialized transnational gangs.

In Brazil, the issue was placed on the agenda by the federal government in 2004 with the publication of decrees to promulgate the UN convention against transnational organized crime and additional protocols. Since then, it has been discussed at the federal level with the launch of the National Policies to Counter Trafficking in Persons, as well as conducting symposiums to discuss the international problem. From 2005 to 2011, victims of trafficking in persons for sexual exploitation reached more than 450 cases mapped by the Ministry of Foreign Affairs, being considered as a business that presents variation accordingly to the world economy.

In media appropriation through entertainment, telenovelas take this issue as a central element. Human trafficking was addressed in Salve Jorge, written by Gloria Perez and broadcasted by Globo TV between October 22, 2012 and May 17, 2013. The inclusion of social issues in the plots of telenovelas is recognized as a social merchandising strategy. Therefore, it is in this privileged media space of fiction that the narrative of a social problem also constitutes itself.

In Brazil, the telenovela is part of one of the most popular narrative genres, settled in an effective way the routine of a large part of the Brazilian population, considering the high ratings and great penetration in the popular imagination.

Telenovela became the most popular product and one of the biggest sources of income in Brazilian television, especially at Globo Television. Moreover, the telenovela grew up addressing private life. Specifically Globo TV transformed the Brazilian telenovela into a consumer product for both national and international territories.

TELENOVELA IN BRAZIL

Telenovela is a cultural product; it influences people's habits and customs, positively or negatively, by communicating, informing and entertaining. According to La Pastina (1994) , telenovelas "have become very much a part of the fabric of the Brazilian society. It is hard to think of contemporary Brazil without thinking of telenovelas" because they are characterized as the main product of the culture industry, resulting from the television history and the culture of the country.

The consolidation of the telenovela as television's most popular and lucrative genre is closely related to a transformation in language by Brazilian authors, starting from the experience gained in radio and cinema. In Brazil, it is still possible to observe their great popular penetration, coupled with the fact that they have reached the foreign market, besides provoking controversy and mobilizing public opinion, being associated as the business card of the largest national television network.

"For nearly twenty years the telenovela has remained in that position, stating stylistic features and a way to make things which became known as 'Brazilian way', which mobilizes the national audience" (Hamburguer, 2011). The plot having its own time and being presented in chapter form causes the viewer to maintain a continuous interest. This seriality is one of the fundamental characteristics of the telenovela. The plot is presented to the viewer in daily episodes as "one story (or several interlaced and parallel narratives) which succeeds more or less linearly along all chapters" (Machado, 2001). Such characteristic is considered as a facilitator in that it establishes a routine that competes or occurs at the same time with and/or the other tasks of the home life and allows the viewer to track the sequence of the plot daily. Watching the telenovela becomes a ritual, a habit.

Brazilian telenovela, after achieving a considerable degree of credibility, has become a public space in which people debate representative issues of the country's own experience, thereby acting as a communication resource (Lopes, 2009). The telenovela, without abandoning the excitement and the characteristic pedagogical dimension of the melodramatic product, when approaching the limits of fiction with reality, has been being constituted with what Lopes (2009) designates as a communicative resource, bringing to the plot a repertoire of references recognized and shared by Brazilians. In this context, with the strategy of portraying contemporary social concerns in their plots, soap operas can promote or instigate discussions as to observe the Brazilian situation more accurately than in the newspapers.

Telenovela may act on the expansion of the audience capacities by using this narrative as a resource in everyday practices and interactions. Telenovela has become "a communication resource which, when activated, makes possible to share cultural rights, ethnic diversity and sociability, gaining greater awareness and motivation for practices against the conflicts and inequalities of Brazilian society" (Lopes, 2009).

In fiction, one cannot forget the true value, enhanced by Marques and Maia (2008) when they state, "even if we identify certain actions to exist only in the fiction realm, the feelings that move the characters, their gestures and intentions many times correspond to what we know about the world we inhabit".

This authenticity at narrating, interpreting or reproducing discussions of contemporary society is strengthened by what has been called the social merchandising that, in transposing the (re)reading of the real for the fiction, brings elements that support the maintenance of an aesthetic that is able to gather the aspects of a melodrama. Misery, violence, poverty, trafficking, prostitution, drugs, schizophrenia are hard issues that melodrama incorporates according to its aesthetic characteristic, being able to soften or enhance its appeal in accordance with the degree of reception acceptance.

The aesthetic dimension of the product is also underlined by Weber (2000) who states that "the fact that most of the population has been inoculated by the aesthetics of television, it becomes more vulnerable and receptive to the more easily assimilated speeches, with more known references: compact, passionate, standardized, advertising" (Weber, 2000). Along with this point of view, there is the seductive power of media, because "the media, with logic and power equivalent to the state and the capital, distinguishes itself from these by agility, insight, and naive and transparent seduction capacity. It can relativize the real—the story—showing it in a less bleak outlook, more comfortable, providing alibis to the citizens about the impossibility of change, because of the complexity of power and politics" (Weber, 2000).

In addition, it is worth reflecting on the power of frameworks, especially for a population portion. "Citizens with low levels of information can make consistent decisions, but only when the public debate is relatively open to a wide range of interpretations of the political reality" (Porto, 2007).

"Brazilian social merchandising employs three main strategies: the presentation of engrossing fictional stories that activate empathy for real-life people suffering some form of injustice; the use of key characters to model desired messages or behaviors; and the incorporation of realia—such as references to or images of actual events —to tie the imagined world of the televised drama to the spectator´s reality" (Atencio, 2014: p. 62).

This sui generis ability to synthesize the public and the private, the political and the domestic, news and fiction, male and female, is inscribed in the narrative of telenovelas, which combines formal conventions of documentary and television melodrama" (Lopes, 2009). The identification of real public figures with fictional characters are recurrent in telenovelas, there is a blurring of the boundaries between plots and real problems and the tendency towards a greater likelihood in storytelling. There is a continuous search for associating topics of public and private life referring to the merge of the public and private fields held by soap operas.

Telenovelas are studied further, especially Globo's, a Brazilian television channel that has a hegemonic position before other media.

GLOBO TV AND SOCIAL MERCHANDISING IN TELENOVELAS

Globo TV is the largest broadcaster in Brazil, balancing what is considered commercial success with artistic quality. According to OBITEL data (Ibero-American Observatory of Television Fiction), in Brazil, there are six national television broadcast networks, five being private—Globo, SBT, Record, Band and Rede TV!—and one public, TV Brasil. In 2012, except for two, all produced and exhibited television fiction.

Regarding the individual audience, Globo remains in the lead with 40.7% of broadcast television. The broadcaster is considered the largest producer of television fiction in the country. There are about 2500 annual hours of telenovelas and programs, and 1800 annual hours of television journalism.

In 2012, among televisions tuned exclusively on television channels, Globo obtained 44.7% share. The station also confirmed its hegemony on programs, and the 47 most seen programs in 2012 were from Globo. In addition, over 80% of the hours of fiction produced and displayed in 2013 were telenovela, increasing its weight in the making of the broadcast programming of Brazilian television.

The dominant themes in the main fictions in 2012 refer to the following contexts: "family relationships, revenge, ambition, adultery, identity revelations, disputes between social classes, racial, class and gender prejudice, child neglect, corruption" (Lopes, 2013: pp. 148-149). Globo TV has a consulting company responsible to the implementation of the social merchandising program in their soap operas. It is possible to see the evolution of the strategy of social merchandising by Globo during 1996 to 2005 (last ranking published), according Table 1.

In Salve Jorge, produced by Globo Network, the social merchandising was related to human trafficking.

SALVE JORGE AND HUMAN TRAFFICKING

Salve Jorge, written by Gloria Perez, debuted in prime time on Globo TV, on October 22, 2012, ending its display on May 17, 2013. With 179 chapters, the telenovela average audience was 33.6. Human trafficking is the social heart of the plot, opening the first chapter of the telenovela with scenes of an auction of the protagonist in Turkey (scenario-country where sexual exploitation is practiced with the tricked characters who lived in Rio de Janeiro). The victims of human trafficking for sexual exploitation are exploited by a gang with the 'justification' of debt acquired by the journey, family threat and restriction of access to documents, setting them up as illegal immigrants in that country.

The telenovela begins its first 30 seconds depicting images of Turkey. The scenes feature colorful plasticity, with pictures representing tourist areas of the country, especially the cities of Cappadocia and Istanbul. Right after, it presents the auction of a woman, who is recognized then as the protagonist of the plot, in a temporal projection of eight months of the narrative.

Table 1: Number of scenes using social themes in soap operas on Globo TV (1996-2005)

Period	*Health*	*Sexuality*	*Drugs*	*Gender Issues*	*Social Issues*	*Total*
1996	515	196	37	---	323	1071
1997	513	148	47	119	232	1059
1998	355	145	304	143	510	1457
1999	258	80	286	28	240	892
2000	47	96	51	42	344	580
2001	77	67	29	42	268	483
2002	238	139	273	153	607	1410
2003	208	159	129	257	601	1354
2004	73	91	28	199	617	1008
2005	277	544	63	135	532	1551
Total	**2561**	**1665**	**1247**	**1118**	**4274**	**10865**

Adapted from SCHIAVO, 2006 (p.4).

The scene is filmed inside a mansion, in a room, and, at the center, on a sort of platform, is the trafficked character—Morena, a single mother who lives with her mother and raises her child alone; this makes up the core of the plot (Figure 1). In the episode, she appears well made-up, dressed in elegant props and sensual clothing. Around, men of different nationalities (overlapping languages make the turn off the scene), wearing suits, smoking cigars, drinking and talking, admiring her beauty, but mostly the product she represents. Then, an interested man gets up and walks towards her in order to touch and smell the young woman. This same man makes the proposal and goes out with the trafficked woman who, in turn, shows revulsion and distress in the scene. The commodity is established. Soon after, another young woman enters the room, almost like a production line.

Adapted from SCHIAVO, 2006 (p.4).

Figure 1: Frames of the first chapter of Salve Jorge.

One can see that the first four minutes of Salve Jorge are intended to present the location where the plot will take place, with the climax being the auction of a trafficked woman. The auctioneer explains some features; among them, the age, they are over eighteen, and the fact that the trafficked woman is Brazilian. Such information reinforces or may be attached to the so-called guarantee of the legality of the activity (according to their age) and the nationality (Brazilian), considered an attribute because of the visibility of Latin women internationally.

International human trafficking has young Morena as its heroin, inhabitant of Complexo do Alemão (favela), in Rio de Janeiro, one of the main locations of the plot. She gets an offer to work in Turkey and, when she arrives in the country, she realizes that she had been trafficked, starting a struggle to get rid of the trafficking mafia and to see the head of the gang in Brazil, Livia Marine, arrested. Throughout the plot, Morena lives a complex love story with Theo, captain of the cavalry of the army, devoted to St. George, who wants to take on the relationship and raise as his the son of the young woman, Júnior.

The scenes displayed on December 4, 2012, show the moments experienced by Morena and the recruiter, then a friend, Wanda at the airport. Morena arrives in Turkey and comes across a group of foreign young women locked up. The girls, all deceived like her, are forced into prostitution in a nightclub. Angry, Morena attacks Wanda for having fooled her, becoming one of her main enemies (Figure 2).

The sequence of events demonstrates the crime of human trafficking for sexual exploitation: the profile of the victims (young women with financial difficulties), the emotional persuasion of the offenders to weave promises of a bright future and the incarceration in a closed nightclub or place without contact with the outside environment or the possibility to speak with relatives; who, at that time, can already be considered victims, because they are always coerced, besides all physical and psychological aggression.

The cast featured 91 characters plus extras to produce the most open scenes or those which reproduced the exploitation of the trafficked women. Regarding the locations, the main geographical areas of the plot were in Rio de Janeiro, especially in Complexo do Alemão, internationally, Turkey, mixing scenes of Cappadocia and Istanbul.

Concerning Complexo do Alemão's location, the view of the plot was marked by the favela pacification, with the presence of the cavalry of the Brazilian Army and its role in strengthening the process of UPPs (Pacifying Police Unit). Actors performed riding lessons, lived in the environmental army command to develop what is identified as laboratory preparation for telenovelas.

The geographical location of the narrative, then, is depicted in the first chapter, with shooting situations and the occupation of Complexo do Alemão (RJ). In comes also the cavalry of the army, which plays, as a result, the role of peacemaker in the favela. The scenes[1] blend fiction with pictures of the news coverage of Globo TV, with audios of journalists and media images that accompanied the performance of military forces in real-time, which took place on November 28, 2010. At that time, as well as media coverage, residents of the community told what was happening there through social networks (Figure 3).

The chapters, displayed from Monday through Saturday, were, in average, 75 minutes long. The telenovela has been exported to many countries, including Portugal and African countries, where Globo Network already has partnerships serving their entertainment products.

In the construction of the plot what one sees, in fact, are the contexts already established in the dramaturgical product composition: "beautiful, passionate, young, virtuous, protagonist heroes; failures of one and the other are superficial and always justified. Their virtues are enhanced by the exaggeration: they are workers, steadfast,

Figure 2: Frames of scenes showing trafficked people in Salve Jorge.

Figure 3: rames of complexo do alemão ando of the army training.

good parents, fighters, honest, loyal, courageous, and are always looking good" (Pallottini, 2000: p. 07). In Salve Jorge, the formula is not replaced. The subplots are presented, bringing love affairs, disaffections, sexuality envisaged in the action of trafficking and in seduction, the different dimensions of social class, discussions and family conflicts, kindness, public actions in the scope of the Army and the Federal Police, and the victory of good against evil or the sense of justice done as a supposed happy ending.

Besides the sexual exploitation of human trafficking, the telenovela deals with trafficking in babies, rescuing, in the plot, the story of a character who was illegally adopted and discovers her true path along the evolution of the chapters. The action of the Federal Police, added to the military interventions, is set into the plot, showing the theme from the point of view of the mapping process of gangs and involvement of the international agenda, given the magnitude of the crime.

In terms of scenery, the police station of the Federal Police is constantly triggered, with the presence of delegate Helô or her staff that maps the human trafficking scheme, both of sexual exploitation and of illegal adoption of babies. The links are established and the gang begins to be unraveled along the plot (Figure 4).

International spheres are also represented by the action of Interpol ? the International Criminal Police Organization—with the infiltration of an agent in the Turkish club, cooperating with the Federal Police in fighting the crime of trafficking. In the last chapter, the two teams come together and invade the establishment, arresting the gang and releasing the lured women.

In Salve Jorge, one can observe at least three dramatic arcs involving human trafficking: the victims of trafficking, the action of the gang and the actions of the Federal Police in tackling crime. These driven elements add in the configuration of Globo's social merchandising strategy. The dimension of reality in fiction, the correspondence with real situations, is evidenced by the telenovela by the display, at the end of some chapters, or even interacting with some characters throughout the plot (as in the case of the victims of trafficking in babies), of testimonials from relatives or victims of trafficking for sexual exploitation.

An example of this strategy is the testimony of the housekeeper Ana Lúcia Furtado, trafficked to Israel in 1998. She was a housekeeper and was the only breadwinner of her three children when, at the age of 24, she received a proposal of what she dreamed to be a better future: working as a waitress in Israel. However, she ended up as a prostitute in a nightclub and was the inspiration for the author Gloria Perez to shape the character of the protagonist, Morena.

In the story of Ana Lúcia, one can see the description of how the allurement took place: "I was in a party in Madureira, my friend Kelly and I, when we met Rosana... She approached us, bonded with us, when later, in the late evening, she made us a proposal to travel abroad, to work as waitresses at a diner in Israel. In the meantime, she had bonded with us, gone to our houses, met our families, become our friend" (Globo, 2013).

For the first time after her rescue, which took place in 1998, Ana Lúcia volunteered to tell all her drama to

Figure 4: Scenes from the federal police in action in Salve Jorge.

Globo, in a testimony after Chapter 85, aired on January 28, 2013. Ana Lúcia tells how the three months being held by the gang were and about the murder of her cousin, Kelly Martins, who went to Israel with her and inspired the character Jéssica.

The story of Ana Lúcia is often more dramatic than the fiction lived by Morena (Figure 5). She says that the contact with Gloria Perez is frequent and that she often recognizes, among the dialogues of the telenovela, sentences she told the writer. Ana Lúcia says, "I even joke that what the telenovela shows is a dream if compared to what we lived. In comparison to what we went through".

In November 2012, about a month after the debut of the telenovela, other real testimonials were inserted, testimonials from people who had experienced or closely followed the drama of who was trafficked. One can observe in Globo's website a video with the testimony of João Borges, father of trafficked Simone.

In one of the testimonials, the father João Borges tells the story of Simone Borges, who went to Spain hoping to make money. However, it was a farce and she was forced into prostitution. (...) As in fiction, the kidnappers took all Simone's money, her passport and kept her in captivity. With her, there were approximately 10 and 15 other Brazilian women living the same drama. Simone died in the same year she went to Spain, in 1996 (Globo, 2013).

Simone traveled to Spain on January 22, 1996, you know. And then she picked up. ... So, I've got an invitation to go to Spain to work and I wanted to go there because the salary there is $ 1200. When she arrived at the airport, they said: now the money you take from here (a thousand or so dollars), you give it to the pimp (...) to the woman who took you, and here you will work in a club (...) I did not know how many Brazilian women, 10 or 15 (...) all retained. They took the documents and forced them into prostitution (Globo, 2013).

The inclusion of testimonials on illegal adoption of babies is also observed. The disclosure of the NGO Missing in Brazil[2] is performed during the episode (Figure 6) displayed on November 8, 2012 and December 3, 2012, the testimony of Lior Wilk, a babies trafficking victim.

He is a young Israeli who wants to find out who his Brazilian biological parents are. In the scene, with the support of technology, Aisha, a young woman who was sold as a baby, talks to the boy who was trafficked in 1985. He says he loves his adoptive parents, but wonders how his life would be if he had continued in Brazil. Such doubts are played in the plot also by the character, giving voice to the international problem.

Beyond the intention to anchor reality in the television product itself, Globo Network expanded the possibilities of transmedia theme display, offering to the public the website ? on air during the airing of the novel ? coined as Disque Salve[3] (Dial Save) created in partnership with the NGO Viva Rio, to give information and help answer questions about trafficking and exploitation of people.

In this project, the NGO Viva Rio was responsible for operating the Dial Save, with the making of all the theoretical content on the subject (Figure 7), both for the web service and the call center (training teams, training on the subject, among others).

Figure 5: Trafficked women: in real life and in fiction.

According to Sandro Costa, coordinator of Save Dial at the NGO Viva Rio, the project recorded 456 cases in 22 weeks. In the 2013 work plan of the NGO, the project under the name Salve Jorge, had a budget estimated at R$ 650,000.00 by Globo Network. It is inferred that such an investment is set as a social support, thus, liable to

Figure 6: Scenes concerning illegal adoption.

Figure 7: Printscreen from dial save's website.

tax deduction. Therefore, it is clear that there is a transmedia ownership of the theme by the broadcaster, promoting its image as a company by linking social responsibility practices, besides increasing the visibility of their telenovela, guaranteeing an increase in audience.

In addition to the traditional serving of the telenovela on television, Globo Network has been investing in production of content for the web, seeking "the insertion and sustained growth of the Internet in Latin America and the accelerated use of virtual social networks[4] in the region, especially Facebook and Twitter" (OBITEL, 2014). Following this trend, the broadcaster, in addition to the chapters available for subscribers of G1, offered exclusive content viewing on its website, making supplementary materials to the plot available in digital environment, expanding the supply of the theme and extrapolating the television schedule.

Among the materials observed, there is the composition of a comic book telling the journey of a character that did not have a happy ending, expected in melodrama. This is the trafficked Jessica, who played an important role in the discussion on human trafficking; she did not make it until the end of the plot, though, being murdered throughout the display of Salve Jorge.

To keep the memory of the character alive and to extend the dynamic possibilities of interaction with fiction, Globo published on the telenovela website the stylized story in comics format (Figure 8), with the following title and helpline: "The Drama of Jessica: review the story of the trafficked girl in comics". "Blonde fought hard alongside Morena and ended up being murdered by Livia".

Figure 8: Image of the comic book: "The drama of Jessica".

The comic book summarizes the story of the character that, for having been inspired by a real case, takes on a new media space. In this case, Globo reproduced some scenes and developed an art of the frames, turning the serialization narrative into an edition specifically about a character. It shows a summary of Jessica's story and, by selecting her, it gives the character a parallel leading role, evidenced through a speech of contextual recovery through a narrator that translates the most emblematic scenes she lived in the plot.

In transposing the narrative text in a comic book of only character, the author offers her a degree of relevance, probably because she is an established actress, associated with the inspiration element of Kelly's life story, enticed and killed by a gang in Israel. Therefore, giving a new way of translating the narrative text into a comic book, it can transform the character Jessica into a superhero, commonly observed in this genre production. Moreover, in comic books with superheroes, there is the disguise feature to hide the identity of the protagonist. In this case, the cover is the very silence of the crime.

Another content offered in a transmedia way is in the Trafficking Dossier (Figure 9), which refers to a material available in the telenovela website that summarizes what the documentation of the characters involved in human trafficking in the plot would be.

According to the people responsible for production of content, there are three categories of bonding: trafficked, traffickers and victims. The website provides a brief overview of the profile of each character involved in the trafficking and complements the content with photos and videos.

The structure of the document refers to a visual aesthetic of police reports, with a technical data sheet of the characters, symbols and icons that refer to elements triggered by the legal sphere, as stamps and handcuffs.

Based on the drama of human trafficking observed in Salve Jorge, one can confirm that Globo Network, in its various derivations of melodrama, becomes an important element in building theme meanings in society, being responsible for giving light and voice to human trafficking issues, promoting its maintenance according to its marketing interest and rebuilding and reconfiguring social identities.

CONCLUSIONS

Television is an instrument to narrate history, society and to influence the ways of thinking of the public, mainly through the soap opera, which is considered as a cultural phenomenon in Latin America. The telenovela, as a popular genre, creates a public space to share experiences and national discussions (Lopes, 2012) and the representations in telenovelas tend to draw a parallel between the political and social realities. Salve Jorge is an example. Human trafficking has acquired importance, and, by giving voice and face to a story, and by inserting examples of lives stigmatized sexual identities or characters in violent situations, the soap opera reassures its role as a narrative capable of reflecting private dramas that, by gaining visibility into the public sphere, refer not to a single individual, but to a collective that is placed in relation to the mediated experience of the other, producing a perception of reality.

Figure 9: Trafficking dossier.

The ideological work of the telenovela is in the way to provide a representation of reality, triggering real elements out of the fictional ones. In Salve Jorge, besides the debate of the subject, the melodrama has brought to social merchandising this dimension with the inclusion of real testimonials.

The social merchandising in telenovelas is effective in the promotion and visibility of the theme that the very public debates because it affects the emotional, the playful. It comes effectively with the inclusion of facts and real elements in fiction, strengthening the role of rapprochement with the portrayed social truthfulness. In addition, the theme is turned into commodities in situations that go beyond serving, through the broadcaster products available on digital platforms such as the Comic of Jessica or the Trafficking Dossier. In this sense, the power of the soap opera is in the dramatization of issues of public interest, which, by being romanticized, gains permanence or longevity in the media agenda.

REFERENCES

1. Atencio, R. J. (2014). Memory's Turn: Reckoning with Dictatorship in Brazil. Wisconsin: The University of Wisconsin Press.

2. Globo (2005). Commercial Formats Guide (trad. Manual de formatos comerciais). Negócios Globo.

3. Globo (2013). Website G1. http://g1.globo.com/rio-de-janeiro/noticia/2013/02/mulher-que-inspirou-morena-de-salve-jorge-conta-o-drama-no-exterior.html

4. Hamburguer, E. (2011). Telenovelas and Interpretations of Brazil (trad. Telenovelas e Interpretações do Brasil). Lua Nova: Revista de Cultura e Política, São Paulo, N. 82, 61-86,.

5. La Pastina, A. (1994). Research on Soap Operas in Latin America. (trad. Pesquisa sobre audiência de telenovelas na América Latina). Revisão teórica e metodológica in Revista Brasileira de Comunicação/ INTERCOM, XVII, 17-37.

6. Lopes, M. I. V. (2009). The Soap Opera as a Communicative Resource (trad. A telenovela como recurso comunicativo). MATRIZes, 3, 21-47.

7. Lopes, M. I. V. (2012). Telenovela and Human Rights: Fiction Narrative as a Communicational Resource. In: A. V. Montie (Ed.), Comunicación y derechos humanos (pp. 175). International Association for Media and Communication Research (Alternatives Collection).

8. Lopes, M. I. V. (2013). Social Memory and Television Fiction in Ibero-Amercian Countries: Directory Obitel 2013 (trad. Memória social e ficção televisiva em países ibero-americanos: anuário Obitel 2013, Orozco Gomes, G. (Orgs.)). Porto Alegre: Sulina.

9. Machado, A. (2001) TV Taken Seriously (trad. Televisão levada a sério). São Paulo: Editora Senac.

10. Marques, A. C., & Maia, R. (2008). Emotional Appeal and Mobilization for Deliberation: The Homoerotic Link in Soap Operas (trad. Apelo emocional e mobilização para a deliberação: o vínculo homoerótico em telenovelas). In: Maia, R. (Org.). Media and Deliberation (trad. Mídia e Deliberação) (pp.380). Rio de Janeiro: Editora FGV.

11. Pallottini, R. (2000). Telenovelas: The Nices and the Bads (trad. Telenovela: os bons e os maus). In: Intercom-Congresso Brasileiro de Ciências da Comunicação. Manaus: Sociedade Brasileira de Estudos Interdisciplinares da Comunicação.

12. Porto, M. P. (2007). Television and Politics in Brazil: Globo and Interpretations of the Audience (trad. Televisão e Política no Brasil: a Rede Globo e as interpretações da audiência). Rio de janeiro: E-papers.

13. Weber, M. H. (2000) Communication and Political Spectacles (trad. Comunicação e espetáculos da política). Porto Alegre: Editora da Universidade, UFRGS.

Chapter 11

EXPLORING THE EFFECTIVENESS OF DISTRACTED DRIVING PSA (PUBLIC SERVICE ANNOUNCEMENT)

Valene Bummara[1], Jinbong Choi[2]

[1]School of Journalism & Mass Communication, Texas State University, San Marcos, TX, USA

[2]Department of Media & Communication, Sungkonghoe University, Seoul, South Korea

ABSTRACT

The issue of "distracted driving" has been a popular topic in research and the subject of numerous campaigns and laws. Fear appeals have commonly been utilized to prevent people, adolescents mainly, from engaging in such behavior. This paper examines the impact that a public service announcement featuring a fear appeal to discourage distracted driving has on the perceptions and intentions of a sample (N = 102) of Texas State University students. The students viewed a thirty- second PSA before completing a self-report questionnaire. Responses were analyzed to gauge the effectiveness of the PSA and look for the presence of gender differences and the third-person effect within the sample. This study focused specifically on the distracted behavior of text messaging while driving. Overall, students expressed the opinion that the PSA was believable and somewhat useful for preventing texting while driving. In line with past literature, males and females in this sample responded differently to the message, with females being more responsive. Contrary to past research, this study did not find support for the third-person effect.

INTRODUCTION

Given the pervasiveness of handheld technology in our society, there has been growing concern about the risks involved with using such devices, specifically cell phones, while operating a vehicle. This phenomenon, generally referred to as "distracted driving", is at the basis of numerous new traffic safety laws and campaigns aimed at preventing car accidents and loss of life on the road. In 2010, a national summit comprised of "safety experts, industry leaders and several U.S. senators" was held to examine what potential regulations could be enacted to solve this social danger (Wilson & Stimpson, 2010: p. 2213).

According to the National Highway Traffic Safety Administration (2011) , approximately 20% of the car crashes involving injuries in 2009 were reportedly due to distracted driving. Moreover, even though drivers of any age could suffer consequences of driving distracted, there seems to be a greater propensity for younger drivers to engage in this behavior. Recent statistics show that drivers under age 20 had the largest amount of fatal crashes as a result of distracted driving, followed by drivers age 20 to 29 (NHTSA, 2011).

In an attempt to combat this dangerous practice, various organizations concerned about public safety, such as municipal police departments, the Department of Transportation and even wireless telephone companies, have created advertisements and public service announcements. A public service announcement, or PSA, can be defined as, "a type of advertising, sponsored by either government agencies or other organizations, to promote causes and activities generally considered socially desirable" (Murry, Stam, & Lastovicka, 1996: p. 1). One tactic that is commonly found in these messages and studied in past research is the use of shocking content and/or appeals to fear (Brennan & Binney, 2010 ; Dahl, Frankenberger, & Manchanda, 2003 ; Hastings, Stead, & Webb, 2004 ; Lennon, Rentfro, & O'Leary, 2010). This tactic is relevant to the present study's topic because, according to Lewis, Watson, Tay and White (2007) , advertising on the issue of "road safety is particularly renowned for its use of physical threats in which drivers and passengers are often shown to be injured and killed as a result of unsafe and/or illegal behavior" (p. 203). However, debate over the effectiveness of these tactics as well as controversy about the extreme graphic content sometimes found in the ads still exists.

The present study aims to examine the effectiveness of a public service announcement against distracted driving on a convenience sample of college students attending Texas State University. This age group was selected for two reasons. First, most previous research in this area has utilized young adults in their samples (Dahl, Frankenberger, & Manchanda, 2003 ; Lennon, Rentfro, & O'Leary, 2010 ; Schoenbachler & Whittler, 1996). Second, this age group appears to be at the greatest risk, at least statistically, of being involved in a distracted- driving car crash (NHTSA, 2011). Cramer, Mayer and Ryan (2007) assert that "motor vehicle crashes are the leading cause of death and disability for young Americans" (p. 181). Thus, the present study will restrict participants to both males and females between the ages of 18 and 24. The subjects will be shown one time a thirty- second public service announcement from the National Highway Traffic Safety Administration's campaign against distracted driving. Afterwards, they will complete a self-report questionnaire regarding their perceptions of the ad and their intent to engage in cell-phone use while driving. The researcher will analyze the survey data quantitatively to answer three research questions as follows:

RQ 1: What is the impact of viewing an anti-distracted driving public service announcement on students' perceptions and intent?

RQ 2: Do responses to the PSA differ according to gender?

RQ 3: Is there evidence of the "third-person effect" within the data results?

LITERATURE REVIEW

What Is Distracted Driving?

Distracted driving is defined as, "any non-driving activity a person engages in that has the potential to distract him or her from the primary task of driving and increase the risk of crashing" (NHTSA, 2011). Distraction can be broken down into three overarching types. Visually distracted drivers avert their gaze from the road, manually distracted drivers remove their hands from the steering wheel, and cognitively distracted drivers lose focus while driving (NHTSA, 2011). This phenomenon is an important topic of study because it is prevalent in American society and can have grave consequences. The National Highway Traffic Safety Administration administered a survey in 2009 that reflected an increased frequency of electronic device use while people were driving (NHTSA, 2011). Moreover, recent research has shown that deaths resulting from distracted driving have risen more than 25% since 2005 (Wilson & Stimpson, 2010). And, as Gozzi (2011) points out, one can die by being a distracted driver themselves or as a victim of another individual driving in that manner. Therefore, organizations such as the National Highway Traffic Safety Administration have tried to create persuasive campaigns to reach drivers and tackle this hazardous activity. These campaigns generally fall under the umbrella term of social marketing.

1) Social marketing—its uses and appeals

The goal of social marketing is to "encourage changes in behavior that benefit the individual, community, and society at large" (Nicholson & Xiao, 2011: p. 2529). Advertisements in this category tend to promote real-life practices or ideas rather than products or services. Many government agencies and nonprofit organizations in the United States utilize social marketing; their prerogative is to induce those who view the advertisement (i.e. the American public) to behave in a way that is "socially desirable" (Lennon, Rentfro, &

O'Leary, 2010: p. 96). Brennan and Binney (2010) believe that these types of advertisements are useful to society because they promote individuals to consider others and act in their best interest. The present study focuses on a campaign encouraging safe driving, but advertisements exist on a number of other social issues such as environmental protection, drug abuse and safe sex practices.

2) Use of fear in advertising messages

A commonly used strategy in social cause advertising seems to be appealing to fear. Lennon, Rentfro and O'Leary (2010) define a fear appeal as "a persuasive communication attempting to arouse fear, promoting precautionary motivation and self-protective action" (p. 97). Advertisements that use these appeals influenceon "present viewers with the negative outcomes that they may experience as a result of engaging in the depicted unsafe and/or illegal behaviors" (Lewis, Watson, & Tay, 2007: p. 49). The goal behind this strategy is grounded in the notion that fear makes individuals feel tense and anxious, thus they will "seek ways to reduce these feelings" (LaTour & Zahra, 1989: p. 61). Previous research has looked at the ways in which fear is used and the effectiveness of doing so (Brennan & Binney, 2010 ; Hastings, Stead, & Webb, 2004 ; LaTour & Zahra, 1989 ; Lennon, Rentfro, & O'Leary, 2010 ; Lewis, Watson, Tay, & White, 2007).

For instance, Lewis, Watson and Tay (2007) claim that "threatening advertisements have been widely used in the social marketing of road safety" (p. 48). In their experimental study, Lennon, Rentfro and O'Leary (2010) had a very large sample of 840 adolescents view two separate fear-based advertisements discouraging distracted driving behaviors. The subjects in the study did find the illustrated behaviors to be "more distracting that they previously believed", a seemingly positive effect of the advertising appeal (Lennon, Rentfro, & O'Leary, 2010: p. 95). Yet, despite this response, the subjects also reported a higher level of intent to behave in the ways depicted in the ads; this reaction is known as the "boomerang effect" (Lennon, Rentfro, & O'Leary, 2010: p. 95). The boomerang effect can be seen as an adverse reaction to viewing a threatening advertisement. Still, some positive benefits have been found to exist from using fear-based or shocking content within advertisements. Dahl, Frankenberger and Manchanda (2003) analyzed college students' responses to controversial AIDS prevention advertisements. The results of their study showed that "shocking content in an advertisement significantly increases attention, benefits memory, and positively influences behavior" among the sample (Dahl, Frankenberger. & Manchanda, 2003: p. 268).

Relationship between Gender and Response to Fear Appeals

A focus of the previous literature on fear appeals in advertising is what, if any, differences exist with regard to gender as a variable. Seeing as both males and females have the capacity to engage in distracted driving and they are both included in the target audience of PSA's designed to discourage such behavior, it is reasonable to study how each gender responds to the social marketing messages they encounter.

Lennon, Rentfro and O'Leary (2010) found that the young men and women in their study's sample did not respond to the public service announcement they viewed in the same manner. The females reacted more favorably to the message and content in the announcement than did the males; furthermore, males believed that punitive measures by law enforcement, such as getting ticketed or arrested, were more useful means of preventing unsafe driving (Lennon, Rentfro, & O'Leary, 2010). In line with this research, Lewis, Watson and Tay (2007) used a questionnaire instrument to measure the behavioral intentions of a sample of 152 drivers in Australia both before and after they viewed two different, threatening advertisements promoting road safety. Again, the results of this study found the difference between genders to be significant. Males were significantly less likely to express intention to both decrease their driving speed and refrain from drinking under the influence of alcohol than were females (Lewis, Watson, & Tay, 2007: pp. 55-56). In their review of numerous studies that have utilized fear appeals, Lewis, Watson, Tay and White (2007) drew the conclusion that young males are considered a "high risk road user group" and threatening appeals aimed at them tend to emphasize physical danger (p. 213). However, males as a group "appear less influenced by physical appeals intending to target them" (Lewis, Watson, Tay, & White, 2007: p. 213). This issue presents a problem for social marketers because the advertisements they create are seemingly reached by primarily one gender instead of both. Related research on physical threat appeals has found that, when compared to other messages, adolescents react more positively to public service announcements "that depict negative social consequences" (Schoenbachler & Whittler, 1996: p. 52). Though Schoenbachler and Whittler (1996) looked specifically at PSA's designed to discourage the use of illegal drugs by adolescents, their findings could help in the creation of various other social marketing campaigns.

Concerns Regarding the Use of Fear Appeals

Despite the popular use of fear appeals in social marketing, and especially in road safety advertising, inconsistent opinions remain regarding the effectiveness of this strategy (LaTour & Zahra, 1989 ; Lewis, Watson, &

Tay, 2007 ; Lewis, Watson, Tay, & White, 2007). Lewis, Watson and Tay (2007) observe that "a substantial body of literature spanning over five decades attests to contradictory findings regarding the manner in which fear is related to persuasion" (p. 49). One possible reason for this inconsistency is described in LaTour and Zahra's (1989) review of fear-inducing advertisements. They note that not every individual responds to fearful messages in the same way; rather, "responses to fear appeals depend on the perceptions people develop concerning the enormity of the pending danger and on their evaluations of its effect" (LaTour & Zahra, 1989: p. 63). In other words, if an individual does not perceive the behavior depicted in a PSA to be dangerous or relevant to him/herself, the advertising message might be lost on that person. Another limitation described in prior research is that, although fear appeals seem to elicit viewers' attention, their capacity to induce real behavioral change in individuals is debatable (Lennon, Rentfro, & O'Leary, 2010 ; Lewis, Watson, Tay, & White, 2007). That is, advertising messages in this category may grasp audience awareness in the short-term, but may not necessarily accomplish the objective of enhancing driver safety in the long-term. In addition, some researchers believe that explicit, fear-arousing content in social marketing is not very effectual on their target audience because "today's youth have had much greater exposure than previous generations to graphic images and other fear messages" (Lennon, Rentfro & O'Leary, 2010: p. 96). In other words, one could argue that this cohort has been desensitized. With this in mind, it may be necessary for social marketing messages to either include more intense fear-arousing content or try an alternative approach altogether if they are to successfully impact young adults.

Beyond just debating its efficacy, past research has also considered what ethical issues can arise from the use of fear-based appeals in social marketing. Hastings, Stead and Webb (2004) chastise social marketers for their pervasive use of threatening messages and describe their concerns regarding the negative effects of these campaigns. Specifically they point out that "maladaptive responses", such as ignoring or suppressing the message within the advertisement, can occur in viewers and suggest that only those individuals who are psychologically healthy are actually persuaded by and benefit from such campaigns (Hastings, Stead, & Webb, 2004: pp. 974- 975). Moreover, they may have harmful effects for those members of society who are less psychologically stable or "vulnerable" (Hastings, Stead, & Webb, 2004: p. 975). Therefore, some scholars argue that, rather than using scare tactics to persuade people, "public health campaigns should focus more on instilling in audiences the belief that they are capable of exercising control over their health behavior and less on attempting to frighten them with fear appeals into ceasing, or not starting, deleterious health habits" (Anderson, 1995: pp.

205-206). In his study, Anderson (1995)exposed his subjects to PSA's that featured two different messages of self-efficacy as a means of preventing the act of driving drunk and one PSA that solely described the likelihood of being arrested for driving drunk. The results of this study demonstrated that participants who viewed the self-efficacy PSA's were better able to discourage others from driving under the influence of alcohol than were the participants who viewed the consequence-based control PSA (Anderson, 1995). These results, as well as the results of similar studies on this topic, seem to suggest that there is room for positive appeals in campaigns to prevent socially undesirable activities. However,Anderson's (1995) findings are limited in that his research was concerned with participants' ability to change the behavior of others, as opposed to modifying their own behavior.

THEORETICAL FRAMEWORK

Much of the prior research that studied the effectiveness of fear appeals to alter behavior has referenced two main theories as part of their conceptual frameworks. These two theories are the Protection Motivation Theory and the theory of the Third-Person Effect.

The Protection Motivation Theory, originally developed by Rogers (1983) , was described and then modified by Tanner, Hunt and Eppright (1991) . This theory attempts to explain and predict how individuals will respond to a communication message utilizing appeals to fear. Essentially, the theory posits that individuals will experience four processes when they are exposed to a threatening message: they evaluate how severe the threat is to them, the likelihood that the threat will affect them, how to eliminate or manage the threat, and whether they are able to perform the actions necessary to cope with the threat (Lewis, Watson, Tay, & White, 2007 ; Rogers, 1983 ; Tanner, Hunt, & Eppright, 1991). Believing Rogers' model to be limited in scope, Tanner, Hunt and Eppright (1991) altered the original Protection Motivation Model in their study of college students' responses to fear- provoking messages about sexually transmitted diseases. As cited by other researchers, their model considered "...the role of the social context of the coping response to a threat communication, introduced the notion that responses may be due to factors other than the communication itself, and emphasized, rather than minimized, the role of emotion" (Schoenbachler & Whittler, 1996: p. 38).

Another theory commonly referenced in the past literature is the Third-Person Effect. This theory, created by Davison (1983) , proposes that "people will tend to overestimate the influence that mass communications have on the attitudes and behavior of others" (p. 3). That is, people tend to "perceive that the media's greatest impact will not be on 'me' or 'you' but on 'them'—the third persons" (Davison, 1983: p. 3 ; Park & Salmon, 2005: p. 26). In their study of road safety advertisements, Lewis, Watson and Tay (2007) found the third-person effect to play out within their study participants. The male adolescents in their sample expressed the opinion that others would be more affected by the advertisements than they would be; females, on the other hand, expressed "reverse third-person effects" in that they believed the advertisements influenced themselves more than other people (p. 48). Park and Salmon (2005) measured the responses of a sample of 229 people to multiple news releases; these researchers also found support for the existence of the third-person effect in their experimental study.

METHOD

This study took a quantitative approach to examine the relationship between the independent and dependent variables, and answered the aforementioned research questions. A 30-second PSA against distracted driving from the National Highway Traffic Safety Administration served as the independent variable. The dependent variable was college students' reported intent to text while driving. A self-report questionnaire with 26 questions was developed to assess some demographic information about respondents, their perceptions of the PSA, and their intent to engage in a particular distracted driving behavior, text messaging while driving. The questionnaire focused mainly on the behavior of texting while driving because, according to the National Highway Traffic Safety Administration (2011) , it involves all three of the main distraction types mentioned previously. Qualifying questions were included to ensure that subjects fit into the sample criteria of students aged 18 - 24 attending Texas State University. The survey instrument also utilized items from a preexisting scale entitled the "Affective Response (General) Scale" (Bruner, 2009: p. 15). This semantic differential 5-point scale uses three items to measure a respondent's emotional reaction to a stimulus, in this case a PSA. A reliable construct, it has a reported Cronbach alpha of 0.95 (Bruner, 2009).

The researcher searched for and viewed several public service announcements online on the issue of distracted driving before selecting one to utilize in the present study. A thirty-second PSA from the National Highway Traffic Safety Administration's "Put it down" campaign entitled "BAM!" was chosen as the study's media clip because it was brief, current, and utilized a fear appeal. The ad discourages distracted driving by portraying three different drivers, each using a cellular telephone while driving, in what appears to be an everyday American setting. Suddenly, the ad shocks the audience by showing each driver crash their vehicle as a result of their distraction. The goal of the ad is to elicit fear and compliance into the audience by insinuating that they, too, could have a vehicle wreck on the road if they use their cell phones while driving. The PSA ends with the "Put it down" campaign logo and lists the NHTSA as the sponsor.

The PSA was shown one time to a convenience sample of 109 students in one large undergraduate level class and two small graduate level classes in the Mass Communication department at Texas State University in the fall of 2011. All students viewed the same PSA and were administered the same version of the questionnaire. The questionnaire was comprised of dichotomous (yes/no) questions to obtain background information, as well as Likert scale questions in which respondents indicated their level of agreement or disagreement regarding perceptions of the PSA, and demographic items. Intentions to engage in distracted driving were measured by asking students to rate their agreement or disagreement regarding the likelihood that they would text while driving and speak up when they were passengers with a driver who is texting. After all completed surveys were collected, it was determined that seven of the surveys either had incomplete responses or belonged to respondents out of the 18 - 24 age bracket. These questionnaires were removed from the sample. Thus, the final sample size in the study was 102 making the response rate for the surveys 93.5%. Data from the questionnaires was entered into and analyzed using the statistical software program, SPSS.

RESULTS & DISCUSSION

Characteristics of the Sample

Studying the dataset in SPSS led to some conclusions about the sample. First, with regard to descriptive characteristics, it was found that the sample was 42.2% male and 57.8% female. The modal classification within the dataset was "Junior", with 41.2% of respondents belonging to that category. In addition, freshman was 1%, sophomore was 22%, senior was 23%, and graduate student was 14%.

When asked the question, "How often do you write/read text messages while driving?" the majority of respondents (61.8%) answered that they did so "sometimes" and 10.8% answered "frequently". These statistics substantiate the claim that many young adults, by their own admission, are engaging in a very distracting behavior while driving. When asked to rate their agreement on the statement, "It is less dangerous to read text messages while driving than to write them", a slight majority (34.3%) reported that they "strongly disagree". However, the results for that question were mixed in that the proportion of respondents who answered either "somewhat disagree" or "somewhat agree" were roughly equivalent. When asked if they knew someone who had been involved in a car accident, injured or killed as a result of texting while driving, 75.5% of respondents answered "No" and 24.5% of them answered "Yes". Although it is a smaller proportion, the finding that approximately one-quarter of the sample personally knows someone who has been affected by distracted driving is notable.

Perceptions of the PSA

As part of RQ 1, some questions on the survey asked respondents to give their opinions regarding the PSA. The researcher first wanted to know how many individuals in the sample had previously seen the PSA used in the present study. The majority of respondents (76.5%) responded that they had never seen the PSA before, which supported the researcher's initial reasoning to select the particular PSA for the study. With regard to the content of the PSA, the following statistics were reported. 78.4% of respondents disagreed with the statement "The PSA is too graphic." This result could be explained by the fact that the particular PSA shown did not utilize extreme gore as some fear-arousing advertisements do; it could also reflect the notion mentioned in the previous literature that adolescents today are more accustomed to frightening appeals in the media. Approximately 60% of respondents reported they "strongly agreed" that "the PSA is believable" and that "the PSA should be played on television." When asked if they were able to discern which organization sponsored the PSA, just under one-quarter (24.5%) of the sample agreed that they could do so. This finding might be useful for social marketers to know if they aim to be transparent sponsors.

The "Affective Response (General) Scale" by Bruner (2009) included within the survey asked respondents to rate their emotional response to the PSA. Approximately 60% of the sample rated the PSA to be on the "Unpleasant" side. Roughly equivalent percentages of the sample expressed they "Liked" and "Disliked" the PSA with the modal response being "neutral". Almost 70% of the sample rated the PSA on the "Left me with a bad feeling" side of the scale. Table 1 shows the measures of central tendency for the three scale items.

Post-Viewing Intentions

The other part of RQ 1 concerned the impact of an anti-distracted driving PSA on student intentions. The data showed that 47.1% of students "somewhat agreed" and 16.7% "strongly agreed" that they were less likely to text while driving after viewing the PSA. Moreover, 42.2% of students "somewhat agreed" and 22.5% "strongly agreed" that they were more likely to speak up when they were passengers and a driver was texting. Based on

Table 1: Affective response (general) scale

	Unpleasant	Dislike	Left me with a bad feeling
Mean	2.29	3.01	2.12
Median	2.00	3.00	2.00

these results, it does seem as though the PSA evokes the sought after intentions in the sample.

Responses According to Gender

RQ 2 explored what, if any, differences exist between males and females with regard to their response after viewing the PSA. To do this, a chi-square test was run for gender and intention to text while driving. The results showed that a statistically significant relationship exists between these two variables (χ^2 = 23.867, p = 0.000). Another chi-square test was run for gender and intention to speak up when another driver is texting. Again, there was a statistically significant relationship found between these variables (χ^2 = 12.856, p = 0.012). Females agreed with the two intention measures more strongly than did males. These findings are in line with those of prior research, which have often found that males and females respond differently to PSA's using fear appeals, with females being more responsive.

Presence of the Third-Person Effect

The third research question sought to determine whether or not the third-person effect would occur within the sample of students. To explore this question, the data were analyzed for correlations between a question about a generalized audience (third-persons) and a question specific to the respondent (first-person). Results showed that a significant positive correlation existed between the variables measuring students' intention to text while driving after having seen the PSA and students' perception that viewing the PSA would help prevent the average 18 - 24 year old from texting while driving. A second significant positive correlation was found between the variables measuring students' perception that PSA's help to prevent texting while driving and their reported likelihood of thinking of the PSA they had viewed when they drove from now on. Both of these associations suggest that the third-person effect was not present in this sample because students' first-person opinions and their opinions concerning others moved in the same direction. These findings contradict those of previous research that have found strong evidence of students underestimating the effect PSA's have on themselves and overestimating the effects they have on generalized others.

CONCLUSIONS

In conclusion, the present study adds to previous research on this topic by exploring three research questions and contributing useful information pertaining to Texas State University students' perceptions and intentions after having viewed a fear-arousing PSA. Over half of the students perceived the PSA as "believable" and thought it would be beneficial to air on television. Most students in the sample "somewhat agreed" that, after watching the PSA, they were less likely to text while driving and more likely to speak up when they were passengers; this finding suggests a degree of effectiveness from the fear appeal. In line with past literature, a gender discrepancy did appear in responses to the PSA. Yet, the present study did not find support for the third-person effect.

This study has implications for social marketers and public safety organizations. The students in this sample reported that they did text while driving even though most students (44.1%) "strongly disagreed" that the PSA made texting while driving seemed more dangerous than it actually was. Therefore, creators of PSA's should investigate young adults' motivations behind engaging in distracted driving in order to better influence their behavior. Moreover, stronger emphasis should be placed on reaching males in the target audience, as they appear to respond less to public service announcement messages.

This study did have its limitations. First, it employed a nonrandom, convenience sample. The sample was comprised entirely of university students, who were critiqued as being "a relatively homogeneous group" (Lewis, Watson, & Tay, 2007: p. 58). Additionally, it would be better if sample were larger. By making these modifications, the study results could be generalized to the larger population. The present study lacked a pre-test to compare students' initial opinions to those after viewing the PSA. Finally, a main limitation was that reported intentions might not fully and accurately determine actual behavior in people. As quoted by Lewis, Watson, Tay amd White (2007), "while intentions are a good predictor of behavior, they are far from a perfect measure" (p. 212).

Future research could examine whether any differences in response to PSA's such as the one used here exist with regard to other demographic factors, such as whether one belongs to a majority or minority group. To learn if behavioral change actually occurs, study subjects could be involved in follow-up research with a qualitative research methodology. In this manner, students could describe their reactions to the PSA and their motivations to engage in distracted driving behaviors open-endedly. Moreover, since they tend to be the target audience, young adults could be helpful in designing the content and messages in distracted driving PSA's.

REFERENCES

1. Anderson, R. B. (1995). Cognitive Appraisal of Performance Capability in the Prevention of Drunken Driving: A Test of Self-Efficacy Theory. Journal of Public Relations Research, 7, 205-229. http://dx.doi.org/10.1207/s1532754xjprr0703_03
2. Brennan, L., & Binney, W. (2010). Fear, Guilt and Shame Appeals in Social Marketing. Journal of Business Research, 63, 140-146.http://dx.doi.org/10.1016/j.jbusres.2009.02.006
3. Bruner II., G. C. (2009). Marketing Scales Handbook: A Compilation of Multi-Item Measures for Consumer Behavior & Advertising Research, Volume 5. Fort Worth, TX: GCBII Productions. https://www.marketingscales.com/sites/default/files/v6sample.pdf
4. Cramer, S., Mayer, J., & Ryan, S. (2007). College Students Use Cell Phones While Driving More Frequently Than Found in Government Study. Journal of American College Health, 56, 181-184. http://dx.doi.org/10.3200/JACH.56.2.181-184
5. Dahl, D. W., Frankenberger, K. D., & Manchanda, R. V. (2003). Does It Pay to Shock? Reactions to Shocking and Nonshocking Advertising Content among University Students. Journal of Advertising Research, 43, 268-280.http://dx.doi.org/10.1017/S0021849903030332
6. Davison, W. (1983). The Third-Person Effect in Communication. Public Opinion Quarterly, 47, 1-15. http://dx.doi.org/10.1086/268763
7. Gozzi, J. (2011). Metaphors in Action: Distracted. ETC: A Review of General Semantics, 68, 110-111.
8. Hastings, G., Stead, M., & Webb, J. (2004). Fear Appeals in Social Marketing: Strategic and Ethical Reasons for Concern. Psychology & Marketing, 21, 961-986.http://dx.doi.org/10.1002/mar.20043
9. LaTour, M., & Zahra, S. (1989). Fear Appeals as Advertising Strategy: Should They Be Used? The Journal of Consumer Marketing, 6, 61-70. http://search.proquest.com/docview/220130827?accountid=5683http://dx.doi.org/10.1108/EUM0000000002548
10. Lennon, R., Rentfro, R., & O'Leary, B. (2010). Social Marketing and Distracted Driving Behaviors among Young Adults: The Effectiveness of Fear Appeals. Academy of Marketing Studies Journal, 14, 95-113.
11. Lewis, I., Watson, B., & Tay, R. (2007). Examining the Effectiveness of Physical Threats in Road Safety Advertising: The Roles of the Third Person Effect, Gender, and Age. Transportation Research Part F: Traffic

Psychology and Behaviour, 10, 48-60.http://dx.doi.org/10.1016/j.trf.2006.05.001

12. Lewis, I., Watson, B., Tay, R., & White, K. M. (2007). The Role of Fear Appeals in Improving Driver Safety: A Review of the Effectiveness of Fear-Arousing (Threat) Appeals in Road Safety Advertising. International Journal of Behavioral Consultation and Therapy, 3, 203-222. http://dx.doi.org/10.1037/h0100799
13. Murry, J., Stam, A., & Lastovicka, J. (1996). Paid-versus Donated-Media Strategies for Public Service Announcement Campaigns. Public Opinion Quarterly, 60, 1-29.http://dx.doi.org/10.1086/297737
14. National Highway Traffic Safety Administration (2011). Distracted Driving.http://distraction.gov/
15. Nicholson, M., & Xiao, S. H. (2011). Consumer Behavior Analysis and Social Marketing Practice. The Service Industries Journal, 31, 2529-2542.http://dx.doi.org/10.1080/02642069.2011.531124
16. Park, H. S., & Salmon, C. T. (2005). A Test of the Third-Person Effect in Public Relations: Application of Social Comparison Theory. Journalism and Mass Communication Quarterly, 82, 25-43. http://dx.doi.org/10.1177/107769900508200103
17. Rogers, R. W. (1983). Cognitive and Physiological Processes in Fear Appeals and Attitude Change: A Revised Theory of Protection Motivation. In J. T. Cacioppo, & R. E. Petty (Eds.), Social Psychophysiology: A Sourcebook (pp. 153-176). New York: Guilford Press.
18. Schoenbachler, D., & Whittler, T. (1996). Adolescent Processing of Social and Physical Threat Communications. Journal of Advertising, 25, 37-54.http://dx.doi.org/10.1080/00913367.1996.10673511
19. Tanner, J. F., Hunt, J. B., & Eppright, D. R. (1991). The Protection Motivation Model: A Normative Model of Fear Appeals. The Journal of Marketing, 55, 36-45.http://dx.doi.org/10.2307/1252146
20. Wilson, F. A., & Stimpson, J. P. (2010). Trends in Fatalities from Distracted Driving in the United States, 1999 to 2008. American Journal of Public Health, 100, 213-219.http://dx.doi.org/10.2105/AJPH.2009.187179

Chapter 12

HIERARCHICAL VALUE MAPS OF SMART PHONES, PORTAL SITES, AND SOCIAL NETWORK SERVICES BASED ON USER INVOLVEMENT

Sang Hee Kwon[1], Min Kyung Cha[1], Seo Young Lee[2*]

[1]Sungkyunkwan University, Seoul, Korea

[2]Yonsei University, Seoul, Korea

ABSTRACT

This study compares the hierarchical value maps (HVMs) for portal sites, smart phones, and social network services (SNSs) according to means-end chain theory. Means-end chain theory offers insights into how a media product satisfies the personal values of consumers. We derive the HVM for each media and investigate the effect of involvement on the HVM structure. A total of 424 individuals were queried for their opinions on the attributes, functional consequences, psychological consequences, and value of each media product through association pattern technique laddering. These elements constitute the value chain structure. Our findings show that the value of each media is determined by involvement levels. For each media, high-involvement user groups regard self-satisfaction as the most important value they aspire for. This study determines that different levels of involvement do not affect the relationships among the elements of the value chain. HVMs for smart phones, portal sites, and SNSs are focused on a special value. However, the level of involvement generally does not seem to alter the structures of HVMs.

INTRODUCTION

In today's media-diverse world, technology has spawned a plethora of products and services, each with their own values and usage. Usage value has a large bearing over many aspects of a product or service. Moreover, user needs evolve as the media environment evolves. Users tend to be financially self-sufficient and intellectually sophisticated; thus, their aspirations resonate with the high levels of Maslow's hierarchy of needs (Maslow, 1943; Baudrillard, 1970) , such as desire to belong, respect, and self-actualization. New media creates shifts in the psychological needs of users along with their intentions for media use. Media usage will continue to evolve because technological advances enable easy access to content through different types of media at a low price.

We are interested in the selection of communication medium of users, who are influenced not only by the attributes of the medium but also by their psychological needs and values.

Given that user intention is the dominant motivation that drives media consumption, we must understand the motives, needs, and values of consumers. In particular, we should consider the services that media should provide as time passes and values change.

Consumer motives, needs, and values are particularly pertinent in the current media environment, where we see the proliferation of new media products, services, and functionality. Understanding consumer values provides media companies an advantage in the fiercely competitive consumer IT industry.

Christensen and Olson (2001) say that consumers prefer media services or functions involving consequences that are congruent with their personal values; in other words, the cognitive structures behind a consumers' personal values, and goals. This concept is the basis behind means-end chain theory, whereby the motivation of consumers in choosing a product is determined by the attributes and consequences that are in line with their personal values (Gutman, 1982; Peter & Olson, 2005) .

This study aims to understand the consumer decision-making process that underlies the value structure in the choice of using smart phones, portal sites, and social network services (SNSs). In addition, this study examines the effect of involvement on value structure.

We can observe rapid developments in media products and services and the tremendous enrichment of functionality. Understanding consumer values provides an advantage to media companies racing to stay ahead in the fiercely competitive consumer IT industry.

THEORETICAL BACKGROUND

Means and Chain Approach on Adoption of Smart Media

Means-ends chain theory links a chain of attributes, consequences, and values to define the relationship between motives and goal states of consumers (Gutman, 1981) . Attributes are the specific, concrete, and physical traits of a product.

Consequences are the attributes of a product with perceived benefits. Value is linked to the abstract goals of an individual (ter Hofstede, Audenaert, Steenkamp, & Wedel, 1998) . Through the aforementioned relationship, we can construct a hierarchical value map (HVM) of the consumer decision-making process by considering not only the visual aspects of attributes but also the psychological, abstract, and symbolic steps to delve deep into the inner motives behind consumer behavior (see Table 1).

HVM provides a holistic framework to understand the choices made by media consumers. An HVM begins with product attributes and ends in personal values (Woodruff & Gardial, 1996) .

Involvement is defined as an individual's internal desire and interest for a product. It determines motivation, which may influence the goals that individuals strive for (Celsi & Olson, 1988) . Involvement causes a differing perception of products and individual values (Petty & Cacioppo, 1986) because the matters that users consider important affect their motivations for information processing, attributes, and consequences. Differences in motivation affect the desires and satisfaction of individuals (Petty & Cacioppo, 1986) . Through this process, involvement affects attributes, consequences, and values, namely, the overall means-end chain structure.

Table 1: Levels of abstraction

Level of Abstraction	3 Steps	6 Steps	4 Steps
Abstract	Value	Terminal values Instrumental values	Values
↕	Consequences	Psychological consequences Functional consequences	Psychological consequences Functional consequences
Concrete	Attributes	Abstract attributes Physical attributes	Attributes

In the present study, we investigate the supposition that involvement has an effect on any segment of HVM for media products. Accordingly, we propose the following research questions:

1) How does involvement affect media (smart phone, portal sites, and SNSs) users' perception of items in the four categories, namely, attributes, functional consequences, psychological consequences, and values?
2) Does involvement affect media (smart phones, portal sites, and SNSs) users' perception of the relationships among the categories, namely, attributes, functional consequences, psychological consequences, and values?
3) Does involvement change the HVM for users of smart phones, portal sites, and SNSs?

METHODOLOGY

Laddering Interview Method

Means-end chain theory was used to analyze the perception of users on smart phones, portal sites, and SNSs. User groups were queried on a list of items in each of the three categories (attributes, benefits, and values), relationships, and associations among the categories. The key variable involvement was used to assess if an influence exists on the value structure for media usage.

Consumers must understand how the attributes and benefits (consequences) of media relate to their inner values. To this end, researchers developed laddering as a method to investigate the minds of consumers. Laddering questionnaires can be either soft laddering or hard laddering(Grunert & Grunert, 1995) . Soft laddering involves one-on-one in-depth interview to assess the psychological disposition of respondents (Grunert & Grunert, 1995) . Hard laddering is a quantitative research method capable of overcoming the limitations of soft laddering. Numerous hard laddering techniques exist, but association pattern technique (APT) is the most sophisticated research method. In this study, we used APT laddering method to collect data for our means-end chain analysis.

First, we developed a list of attributes, functional consequences, psychological consequences, and values for measurements that are relevant for users of smart phones, portal sites, and SNSs. The items for these categories were extracted from a review of current literature. APT laddering was used to determine the relationships of items among categories (i.e., attributes-functional consequences, functional consequences-psychological consequences, and psychological consequences-value) for each media and establish a complete picture of the value structure. We also investigated the involvement factor for each media through a modified version of the Zaichkowsky personal involvement index (Zaichkowsky, 1985; Celsi & Olsen, 1988; Petty & Cacioppo, 1986; Huber, Beckmann, & Hermann, 2004) . We used SPSS 18.0 software and derived an average involvement score of 5.1773 for smart phones, 4.9008 for portal sites, and 4.3358 for SNSs. Media involvement scoring below the average score was categorized as low involvement. Conversely, media involvement scoring higher than the average was considered high involvement.

Frequency scoring is commonly used in APT laddering to extract the value structure from survey participants. Survey respondents marked in the implication matrix all the relationship pairs (e.g., attributes-functional consequences, psychological consequences-value) that are relevant to a consumer. The frequency score summarized the total number of times a relationship pair was marked by all survey respondents. However, the implication matrix can be quite complex and can be filled with unimportant relationships. To lessen the number of frequency scores, means-end chain theory only extracted the relevant relationships for the construction of the HVM diagram. Unimportant relationships were ignored.

Given that all important relationships (i.e., attributes, consequences, and values) for each item were extracted, we developed a comprehensive HVM summarizing the relationship between motivation and behavior (ladder).

RESEARCH RESULTS

In this study, 424 individuals were surveyed about their use of smart phones, portal sites, and SNSs. The survey was conducted from April 2, 2014 to May 5, 2014. Most respondents were in their 20s (70.5%). In total, 55.7% were female and 44.3% were male. The most commonly used smart phone was Galaxy (49.1% of respondents). In total, 54.7% of portal sites used Daum, and 93.9% of users used Kakao Talk.

Results for Research Question 1

Table 2 shows the frequencies of smart phone functional consequences. We could not determine any significant difference ($\chi^2 = 9.066$, $p = 0.526$) between high and low involvements through the chi-square test. This finding indicates that user perception of smart phone functional consequence is not dependent on the involvement factor.

Table 2: Cross tabulation of functional consequence involvement for smart phones

Items	Involvement				Total	
	High Involvement		Low Involvement			
Daily life support	194	(11.8%)	223	(12.2%)	417	(12.0%)
Self-expression	136	(8.3%)	139	(7.6%)	275	(7.9%)
Social relationship	179	(10.9%)	205	(11.2%)	384	(11.1%)
Mutual communication	179	(10.9%)	197	(10.8%)	376	(10.8%)
Speedy information retrieval/content acquisition	174	(10.6%)	194	(10.6%)	368	(10.6%)
Variety of information and content/acquisition	175	(10.6%)	198	(10.8%)	373	(10.7%)
Personal information and content storage	162	(9.8%)	179	(9.8%)	341	(9.8%)
Sharing information/content	112	(6.8%)	128	(7.0%)	240	(6.9%)
Work (mobile office)	148	(9.0%)	165	(9.0%)	313	(9.0%)
Entertainment	186	(11.3%)	199	(10.9%)	385	(11.1%)
Total	1645	(100.0%)	1827	(100.0%)	3472	(100.0%)

$\chi^2 = 9.066$, $p = 0.526$.

Involvement affects user perception of psychological consequence for smart phone users (see Table 3). The results of the chi-square test showed no significant difference ($\chi^2 = 14.112$, $p = 0.294$) in the frequency of high- and low-involvement user groups.

The most important smart phone values are shown in Table 4. Involvement has an influence on people's perception of value ($\chi^2 = 26.302$, $p < 0.01$).

The functional consequence involvement for portal sites (Table 5) indicates that the high-involvement group has a statistically significant difference with the low-involvement group ($\chi^2 = 26.656$, $p = 0.003$).

For portal site users, involvement does not affect psychological consequence items ($\chi^2 = 15.810$, $p = 0.200$; see Table 6).

Involvement levels have an effect on value items for portal site users (see Table 7; $\chi^2 = 26.123$, $p = 0.01$).

No statistical significance exists between high- and low-involvement SNS user groups for functional items ($\chi^2 = 12.451$, $p = 0.256$; see Table 8).

The high-involvement user group has no statistically significant difference with the low-involvement user group for psychological consequence items of SNS users ($\chi^2 = 17.353$, $p = 0.136$; see Table 9).

Finally, the important values pursued by SNS users are shown in Table 10. The high-involvement user group has a high statistically significant difference with the low-involvement user group ($\chi^2 = 35.834$, $p = 0.000$).

Results for Question 2

After the text edit has been completed, the paper is ready for the template. Duplicate the template file by using the Save As command, and use the naming convention prescribed by your journal for the name of your paper. In this newly created file, highlight all of the contents and import your prepared text file. You are now ready to style your paper.

Impact of Involvement on the Means and Chains Relationships for Smart Phone User

As shown in Table 11, the ranking of the most important relationships between attributes and functional consequences for smart phone users were very similar for both the high and low involvement groups; with the top three relationship for both groups being time/alarm-daily life support, calendar/diary/memo-daily life support and game-entertainment.

Table 3: Cross tabulation of psychological consequence involvement for smart phones

Item	Involvement				Total	
	High		Low			
Self satisfaction	152	(10.8%)	185	(12.3%)	337	(11.6%)
Self pride	64	(4.5%)	60	(4.0%)	124	(4.3%)
Self cultivation	124	(8.8%)	126	(8.4%)	250	(8.6%)
Sincerity	80	(5.7%)	80	(5.3%)	160	(5.5%)
Individual personality	117	(8.3%)	114	(7.6%)	231	(7.9%)
Desire to possess	82	(5.8%)	72	(4.8%)	154	(5.3%)
Well-rounded social life	174	(12.4%)	195	(13.0%)	369	(12.7%)
Convenience	188	(13.4%)	206	(13.7%)	394	(13.6%)
Trust	77	(5.5%)	86	(5.7%)	163	(5.6%)
Preference	95	(6.8%)	97	(6.5%)	192	(6.6%)
Interest	160	(11.4%)	178	(11.9%)	338	(11.6%)
Trendy/sophisticated	94	(6.7%)	101	(6.7%)	195	(6.7%)

$\chi^2 = 14.112, p = 0.294.$

Table 4: Cross tabulation of value and involvement for smart phones

Item	Involvement				Total	
	High		Low			
Self-realization	162	(9.6%)	174	(9.5%)	336	(9.6%)
Vibrant life	157	(9.3%)	188	(10.3%)	345	(9.8%)
Self-satisfaction	180	(10.7%)	190	(10.4%)	370	(10.5%)
Self-respect	133	(7.9%)	157	(8.6%)	290	(8.3%)
Sense of belonging	116	(6.9%)	140	(7.6%)	256	(7.3%)
Being well-respected	134	(8.0%)	118	(6.4%)	252	(7.2%)
Fun and enjoyment	164	(9.8%)	189	(10.3%)	353	(10.0%)
Warm relationship with others	167	(9.9%)	184	(10.0%)	351	(10.0%)
Empowerment	125	(7.4%)	134	(7.3%)	259	(7.4%)
Happiness	162	(9.6%)	163	(8.9%)	325	(9.3%)
Inner Balance	111	(6.6%)	101	(5.5%)	212	(6.0%)
Aesthetic aspect	71	(4.2%)	93	(5.1%)	164	(4.7%)
Total	1682	(100.0%)	1831	(100.0%)	3513	(100.0%)

$\chi^2 = 26{,}302, p < 0.01.$

Table 5: Cross tabulation of functional consequence and involvement for portal sites

Item	Involvement				Total
	High		Low		
Daily life support	188	(11.6%)	205	(12.6%)	393 (12.1%)
Self-expression	104	(6.4%)	109	(6.7%)	213 (6.5%)
Social relationship	131	(8.1%)	130	(8.0%)	261 (8.0%)
Mutual communication	136	(8.4%)	132	(8.1%)	268 (8.2%)
Speedy information retrieval/content acquisition	191	(11.8%)	194	(11.9%)	385 (11.8%)
Variety of information and content/acquisition	187	(11.5%)	194	(11.9%)	381 (11.7%)
Personal information and content storage	170	(10.5%)	172	(10.6%)	342 (10.5%)
Sharing information/content	163	(10.0%)	147	(9.0%)	310 (9.5%)
Work (mobile office)	168	(10.3%)	152	(9.3%)	320 (9.8%)
Entertainment	187	(11.5%)	192	(11.8%)	379 (11.7%)
Total	1625	(100.0%)	1627	(100.0%)	3252 (100.0%)

$\chi^2 = 26.656, p = 0.003.$

Table 6: Cross tabulation of psychological consequence and involvement for portal site users

Items	Involvement				Total	
	High		Low			
Self-satisfaction	152	(14.5%)	158	(15.0%)	307	(14.8%)
Self-pride	64	(6.8%)	56	(5.3%)	126	(6.1%)
Self-cultivation	124	(11.3%)	105	(10.0%)	221	(10.6%)
Sincerity	80	(7.0%)	74	(7.0%)	146	(7.0%)
Individual personality	117	(10.2%)	93	(8.9%)	198	(9.5%)
Desire to possess	82	(7.6%)	72	(6.9%)	150	(7.2%)
Well-rounded social life	174	(17.3%)	191	(18.2%)	368	(17.7%)
Convenience	188	(18.4%)	204	(19.4%)	393	(18.9%)
Trust	77	(8.5%)	88	(8.4%)	175	(8.4%)
Preference	95	(8.6%)	102	(9.7%)	190	(9.2%)
Interest	160	(16.3%)	166	(15.8%)	333	(16.0%)
Trendy/sophisticated	94	(8.3%)	79	(7.5%)	164	(7.9%)
Total	1026	(100.0%)	1050	(100.0%)	2076	(100.0%)

$\chi^2 = 15.810, p = 0.200.$

Table 7: Cross tabulation of value and involvement for portal sites users

Items	Involvement				Total	
	High		Low			
Self-realisation	162	(9.8%)	172	(10.4%)	334	(10.1%)
Vibrant life	166	(10.0%)	171	(10.3%)	337	(10.2%)
Sense of accomplishment	177	(10.7%)	168	(10.1%)	345	(10.4%)
Self-respect	138	(8.3%)	144	(8.7%)	282	(8.5%)
Sense of belonging	122	(7.3%)	116	(7.0%)	238	(7.2%)
Being well-respected	120	(7.2%)	116	(7.0%)	236	(7.1%)
Fun and enjoyment	176	(10.6%)	163	(9.8%)	339	(10.2%)
Warm relationship with others	162	(9.8%)	166	(10.0%)	328	(9.9%)
Empowerment	123	(7.4%)	113	(6.8%)	236	(7.1%)
Happiness	158	(9.5%)	156	(9.4%)	314	(9.5%)
Inner balance	93	(5.6%)	95	(5.7%)	188	(5.7%)
Aesthetic aspect	63	(3.8%)	77	(4.6%)	140	(4.2%)
Total	1660	(100.0%)	1657	(100.0%)	3317	(100.0%)

$\chi^2 = 26.123, p = 0.01.$

Table 8: Cross tabulation of functional consequence and involvement for SNS users

Items	Involvement				Total	
	High		Low			
Daily life support	199	(13.0%)	198	(13.3%)	397	(13.2%)
Self-expression	154	(10.0%)	146	(9.8%)	300	(9.9%)
Social relationship	106	(6.9%)	112	(7.5%)	218	(7.2%)
Mutual communication	207	(13.5%)	203	(13.7%)	410	(13.6%)
Speedy information retrieval/content acquisition	183	(11.9%)	173	(11.7%)	356	(11.8%)
Variety of information and content/acquisition	147	(9.6%)	151	(10.2%)	298	(9.9%)
Personal information and content storage	149	(9.7%)	124	(8.4%)	273	(9.0%)
Sharing information/content	73	(4.8%)	77	(5.2%)	150	(5.0%)
Work (mobile office)	137	(8.9%)	126	(8.5%)	263	(8.7%)
Entertainment	179	(11.7%)	174	(11.7%)	353	(11.7%)
Total	1534	(100.0%)	1484	(100.0%)	3018	(100.0%)

$\chi^2 = 12.451, p = 0.256.$

Table 9: Cross tabulation of psychological consequence and involvement for SNS users

Items	Involvement				Total	
	High		Low			
Self-satisfaction	162	(11.0%)	163	(11.9%)	325	(11.4%)
Self-pride	64	(4.3%)	59	(4.3%)	123	(4.3%)
Self-cultivation	104	(7.1%)	99	(7.2%)	203	(7.1%)
Sincerity	128	(8.7%)	122	(8.9%)	250	(8.8%)
Individual personality	80	(5.4%)	64	(4.7%)	144	(5.1%)
Desire to possess	183	(12.4%)	171	(12.5%)	354	(12.4%)
Well-rounded social life	164	(11.1%)	147	(10.7%)	311	(10.9%)
Convenience	182	(12.3%)	181	(13.2%)	363	(12.8%)
Trust	69	(4.7%)	54	(3.9%)	123	(4.3%)
Preference	85	(5.8%)	81	(5.9%)	166	(5.8%)
Interest	174	(11.8%)	163	(11.9%)	337	(11.8%)
Trendy/sophisticated	79	(5.4%)	66	(4.8%)	145	(5.1%)
Total	1474	(100.0%)	1370	(100.0%)	2844	(100.0%)

$\chi^2 = 17.353, p = 0.136.$

Table 10: Cross tabulation of value and involvement for SNS users

Items	Involvement				Total	
	High		Low			
Self-realisation	149	(8.9%)	158	(9.8%)	307	(9.3%)
Vibrant life	174	(10.4%)	157	(9.8%)	331	(10.1%)
Sense of accomplishment	182	(10.9%)	163	(10.1%)	345	(10.5%)
Self-respect	138	(8.2%)	135	(8.4%)	273	(8.3%)
Sense of belonging	141	(8.4%)	125	(7.8%)	266	(8.1%)
Being well-respected	135	(8.1%)	120	(7.5%)	255	(7.8%)
Fun and enjoyment	173	(10.3%)	170	(10.6%)	343	(10.4%)
Warm relationship with others	180	(10.7%)	177	(11.0%)	357	(10.9%)
Empowerment	106	(6.3%)	101	(6.3%)	207	(6.3%)
Happiness	167	(10.0%)	139	(8.6%)	306	(9.3%)
Inner balance	80	(4.8%)	88	(5.5%)	168	(5.1%)
Aesthetic aspect	50	(3.0%)	77	(4.8%)	127	(3.9%)
Total	1675	(100.0%)	1610	(100.0%)	3285	(100.0%)

$\chi^2 = 35.834, p = 0.000.$

Table 11: Implication matrix of relationships between attributes and functional consequences for smart phone users by invol- vement

Items	Involvement				Total	
	High		Low			
Time/alarm-daily life support	183	(12.2%)	222	(13.1%)	405	(12.7%)
Calendar/diary/memo-daily supp life support	172	(11.5%)	200	(11.8%)	372	(11.7%)
Game-entertainment	168	(11.2%)	188	(11.1%)	356	(11.2%)
Maps/navigation-daily life support	151	(10.1%)	177	(10.5%)	328	(10.3%)
Electronic commerce-daily life support	147	(9.8%)	154	(9.1%)	301	(9.5%)
Internet surfing-speedy information retrieval/contents acquisition	137	(9.2%)	150	(8.9%)	287	(9.0%)
Internet surfing-variety of information/content acquisition	137	(9.2%)	137	(8.1%)	274	(8.6%)
Voice call/video call-social relationship	135	(9.0%)	141	(8.3%)	276	(8.7%)
SNS use-social relationship	134	(9.0%)	172	(10.2%)	306	(9.6%)
Voice call-telephone call/mutual communication	132	(8.8%)	148	(8.8%)	280	(8.8%)
Total	1496	(100.0%)	1689	(100.0%)	3185	(100.0%)

$\chi^2 = 35.834, p = 0.000.$

As shown in Table 12, the top three functional consequence-psychological consequence relationships for high and low involvement groups are entertainment-fun, followed by mutual communication-Well-rounded social life and social Relationship-Well-rounded social life. There was very little difference in how the high and low involvement groups rated importance of the lesser ranked relationships.

As shown in Table 13, the top three psychological consequences relationships for both high and low users are well-rounded social life-warm relationship with others, interest-Fun and enjoyment and Preference (taste)-hap- piness. There was very little difference between how the high and low involvement groups ranked the other 7 relationships.

Table 12: Implication matrix of relationships between function consequences and psychological consequences for smart phone users by involvement

Items	Involvement				Total	
	High		Low			
Entertainment-fun	134	(12.0%)	151	(11.4%)	285	(11.7%)
Mutual communication-well-rounded social life	129	(11.5%)	149	(11.2%)	278	(11.4%)
Social Relationship-well-rounded social life	127	(11.4%)	149	(11.2%)	276	(11.3%)
Work (mobile office)-convenience	123	(11.0%)	123	(9.3%)	246	(10.1%)
Daily life support-convenience	115	(10.3%)	139	(10.5%)	254	(10.4%)
Speed information retrieval/content acquisition-convenience	109	(9.7%)	131	(9.9%)	240	(9.8%)
Personal information content storage-convenience	99	(8.9%)	117	(8.8%)	216	(8.8%)
Variety of information/content acquisition-convenience	98	(8.8%)	133	(10.0%)	231	(9.5%)
Self-expression-self satisfaction	95	(8.5%)	127	(9.6%)	222	(9.1%)
Sharing info/contents-convenience	89	(8.0%)	107	(8.1%)	196	(8.0%)
Total	1118	(100.0%)	1326	(100.0%)	2444	(100.0%)

Table 13: Implication matrix of relationships between psychological consequences and value for smart phone users by invol- vement

Items	Involvement				Total	
	High		Low			
Well-rounded social life-warm relationship with others	111	(14.2%)	132	(15.5%)	243	(14.9%)
interest-fun and enjoyment	95	(12.2%)	110	(12.9%)	205	(12.6%)
Preference (taste)-happiness	81	(10.4%)	83	(9.8%)	164	(10.1%)
interest-happiness	85	(10.9%)	73	(8.6%)	158	(9.7%)
Self-cultivation-self accomplishment	87	(11.2%)	70	(8.2%)	157	(9.6%)
Trust-warm relationship with others	65	(8.3%)	81	(9.5%)	146	(9.0%)
Preference/taste-fun and enjoyment	72	(9.2%)	73	(8.6%)	145	(8.9%)
Self-cultivation-self-realisation	62	(7.9%)	83	(9.8%)	145	(8.9%)
Self-pride-self accomplishment	62	(7.9%)	76	(8.9%)	138	(8.5%)
Convenience-vibrant life	60	(7.7%)	69	(8.1%)	129	(7.9%)
Total	780	(100.0%)	850	(100.0%)	1630	(100.0%)

Impact of Involvement on the Means and Chains Relationships for Portal Site Users

As shown in Table 14, the three most important attributes to functional consequences relationships for portal sites for both high and low involvement groups are game-daily life support, maps-daily life support followed by multimedia content-entertainment. There were differences in how the low and high involvement groups rated the lower rank items.

As shown in Table 15, the three most important relationships between psychological consequences and functional consequences for the high involvement group are work (mobile office)-Convenience, social relationship-vibrant life followed by mutual communication-vibrant life. For the low involvement group, the most important relationships are social relationship-vibrant life, mutual communication-vibrant life followed by daily life support-convenience.

As shown in Table 16, the three most important relationships between psychological consequences and values were the same for both the high and low involvement groups; which were pursuing personal character-warm relationship with others, interest-fun and enjoyment followed by self-satisfaction-self realization.

Table 14: Implication matrix of relationships of attributes and functional consequences for portal site users by involvement

Items	Involvement				Total	
	High		Low			
Internet surfing-daily life support	96	(5.9%)	117	(7.1%)	213	(6.5%)
Internet surfing-seedy information retrieval/content acquisition	124	(7.7%)	125	(7.6%)	249	(7.6%)
Cloud-Information/content-personal storage	125	(7.7%)	114	(7.0%)	239	(7.3%)
News/life information-speedy information retrieval/content acquisition.	127	(7.9%)	128	(7.8%)	255	(7.8%)
News/life information—a variety of information/content acquisition	118	(7.3%)	108	(6.6%)	226	(6.9%)
Knowledge dictionary/variety of information/content acquisition	109	(6.7%)	110	(6.7%)	219	(6.7%)
Multimedia content-entertainment	130	(8.1%)	132	(8.1%)	262	(8.1%)
Game-daily life support	145	(9.0%)	148	(9.1%)	293	(9.1%)
Maps-daily life support	145	(9.0%)	148	(9.1%)	293	(9.1%)
e-commerce/daily life support	127	(7.9%)	143	(8.8%)	270	(8.3%)
Total	1608	(100.0%)	1629	(100.0%)	3237	(100.0%)

Table 15: Implication matrix of relationships of psychological consequences and functional consequences for portal site users by involvement

Items	Involvement				Total	
	High		Low			
Daily life support-convenience	106	(10.3%)	139	(12.3%)	245	(11.3%)
Self-expression-self satisfaction	95	(9.2%)	103	(9.1%)	198	(9.2%)
Social relationship-vibrant life	125	(12.2%)	145	(12.8%)	270	(12.5%)
Mutual communication-vibrant life	125	(12.2%)	141	(12.5%)	266	(12.3%)
Speedy information retrieval/content acquisition-convenience	120	(11.7%)	134	(11.8%)	254	(11.8%)
Variety of information/content acquisition-convenience	115	(11.2%)	119	(10.5%)	234	(10.8%)
Information content storage-convenience	110	(10.7%)	119	(10.5%)	229	(10.6%)
Sharing info/contents-convenience	101	(9.8%)	108	(9.5%)	209	(9.7%)
Work (mobile office)-convenience	131	(12.7%)	124	(11.0%)	255	(11.8%)
Total	1028	(100.0%)	1132	(100.0%)	2160	(100.0%)

Table 16: Implication matrix of relationships of psychological consequences and values for portal site users by involve- men

Items	Involvement				Total	
	High		Low			
Self-satisfaction-self-realisation	91	(10.8%)	93	(11.7%)	184	(11.3%)
Self-pride-self accomplishment	78	(9.3%)	65	(8.2%)	143	(8.8%)
Self-cultivation-self accomplishment	82	(9.8%)	65	(8.2%)	147	(9.0%)
Integrity-self accomplishment	59	(7.0%)	69	(8.7%)	128	(7.8%)
Pursuing personal character-warm relationship with others	112	(13.3%)	127	(16.0%)	239	(14.6%)
Desire to possess-vibrant life	66	(7.9%)	75	(9.5%)	141	(8.6%)
Well-rounded social life-warm relationship with others	65	(7.7%)	74	(9.3%)	139	(8.5%)
Preference taste-fun and enjoyment	80	(9.5%)	69	(8.7%)	149	(9.1%)
Interest-fun and enjoyment	116	(13.8%)	97	(12.2%)	213	(13.1%)
Interest-happiness	90	(10.7%)	59	(7.4%)	149	(9.1%)
Total	839	(100.0%)	793	(100.0%)	1632	(100.0%)

Impact of Involvement on the Means and Chains Relationships for SNS Users

For SNS users, Table 17 shows the importance rankings of the relationships between the attributes and functional consequences were the exactly the same for both the high and low involvement groups. The three most important relationships were my account/scheduling-daily life support, online social networking-social relationships and friends/institution introduction-social relationships.

Table 18 shows the two most important relationships between psychological consequences and functional consequences for bothe the high and low involvement groups were mutual communication-well-round social life followed by a variety of information/content acquisition-convenience. Minor differences appeared in the ranking of lesser important items.

Table 19 shows the three most important relationships between psychological consequences and value for both the low and high involvement groups are Well-rounded social life-Friendly relationship with others, desire to possess-warm relationship with others followed by interest-fun and enjoyment. Minor differences appeared in the ranking of lesser important items.

Results for Research Question 3

Question 3 aims to construct HVMs through means-end chain theory and to connect the relationships among the categories (attributes, functional consequences, psychological consequences, and value) of smart phones, portal sites, and SNSs. The results for Question 3 is used to generate goal hierarchy for using smart media and incorporates the results obtained in Questions 1 and 2.

The HVM for high-involvement smart phones users is shown in Figure 1. The most important ladders are game-entertainment-interest-fun and enjoyment, games-entertainment-interest-happiness, time/alarm-daily life support-convenience-vibrant life, calendar/memo/diary-daily life support-convenience-vibrant life, and map navigation-daily life support-convenience-vibrant life.

Figure 2 shows that the HVM for low-involvement users is similar to that for high-involvement users. This finding indicates that involvement is not a key factor for smart phone users. Smart phone users derive convenience value from the attributes on offer, such as voice call/video call. For smart phone game players, the values derived by these users are fun, enjoyment, and happiness.

Figure 3 and Figure 4 show that the HVM of portal site users is simpler than that of smart phone users. However, a focus on convenience exists at the psychological consequences stage.

Figure 5 and Figure 6 show that the HVM of SNS users is different from that of portal sites or smart phone users. The connections between each step are spread diversely. Many ladders are linked to the "warm relationship with others" value.

Table 17: Implication matrix of relationships of attributes and functional consequences for SNS users by involvement

Item	Involvement				Total	
	Low		High			
My account/scheduling-daily life support	168	(9.4%)	170	(10.0%)	338	(9.7%)
Online social networking-social relationships	178	(9.9%)	165	(9.7%)	343	(9.8%)
Friends/institution introduction-social relationships	132	(7.4%)	146	(8.6%)	278	(8.0%)
Friends/institution searching-social relationships	133	(7.4%)	123	(7.2%)	256	(7.3%)
Aggregation of news-speedy information retrieval/content acquisition	97	(5.4%)	95	(5.6%)	192	(5.5%)
Mentionor comments-social relationships	115	(6.4%)	120	(7.0%)	235	(6.7%)
Mention or comments-mutual communication	106	(5.9%)	90	(5.3%)	196	(5.6%)
Sns game-entertainment	168	(9.4%)	156	(9.2%)	324	(9.3%)
E-commerce-daily life support	142	(7.9%)	136	(8.0%)	278	(8.0%)
Send gifts and items-social relationship	149	(8.3%)	133	(7.8%)	282	(8.1%)
Total	1790	(100.0%)	1703	(100.0%)	3493	(100.0%)

Table 18: Implication matrix of relationships between psychological consequences and functional consequences for SNS Users by Involvement

Items	Involvement				Total	
	Low		High			
Daily life support-convenience	88	(7.7%)	93	(7.9%)	181	(7.8%)
Self-expression-self satisfaction	103	(9.0%)	111	(9.4%)	214	(9.2%)
Social relationships-well-rounded social life	83	(7.2%)	72	(6.1%)	155	(6.7%)
Mutual communication-well-rounded social life	129	(11.3%)	136	(11.5%)	265	(11.4%)
Speedy information retrieval/contents acquisition-well-rounded social life.	104	(9.1%)	117	(9.9%)	221	(9.5%)
Speedy information retrieval/contents acquisition-empathy	101	(8.8%)	83	(7.0%)	184	(7.9%)
A variety of information/contents acquisition-convenience	109	(9.5%)	116	(9.8%)	225	(9.7%)
Information/contents individual storage-convenience	108	(9.4%)	107	(9.1%)	215	(9.3%)
Sharing info/contents-convenience	94	(8.2%)	107	(9.1%)	201	(8.6%)
Work (mobile office)-convenience	74	(6.5%)	83	(7.0%)	157	(6.8%)
Total	1146	(100.0%)	1178	(100.0%)	2324	(100.0%)

Table 19: Implication matrix of relationships between psychological consequences and value for SNS users by involvement

Items	Involvement				Total	
	Low		High			
Self-satisfaction-self realisation	88	(9.7%)	90	(10.4%)	178	(10.0%)
Self-pride-self accomplishment	88	(9.7%)	75	(8.6%)	163	(9.2%)
Self-cultivation-self realisation	65	(7.1%)	78	(9.0%)	143	(8.0%)
Self-cultivation-self accomplishment	82	(9.0%)	60	(6.9%)	142	(8.0%)
Desire to possess-warm relationship with others	116	(12.7%)	118	(13.6%)	234	(13.2%)
Well-rounded social life-friendly relationship with others	121	(13.3%)	121	(13.9%)	242	(13.6%)
Trust-warm relationship with others	81	(8.9%)	79	(9.1%)	160	(9.0%)
Preference taste-happiness	89	(9.8%)	67	(7.7%)	156	(8.8%)
Interest-fun and enjoyment	107	(11.8%)	115	(13.2%)	222	(12.5%)
Interest-happiness	73	(8.0%)	66	(7.6%)	139	(7.8%)
Total	910	(100%)	869	(100%)	1779	(100%)

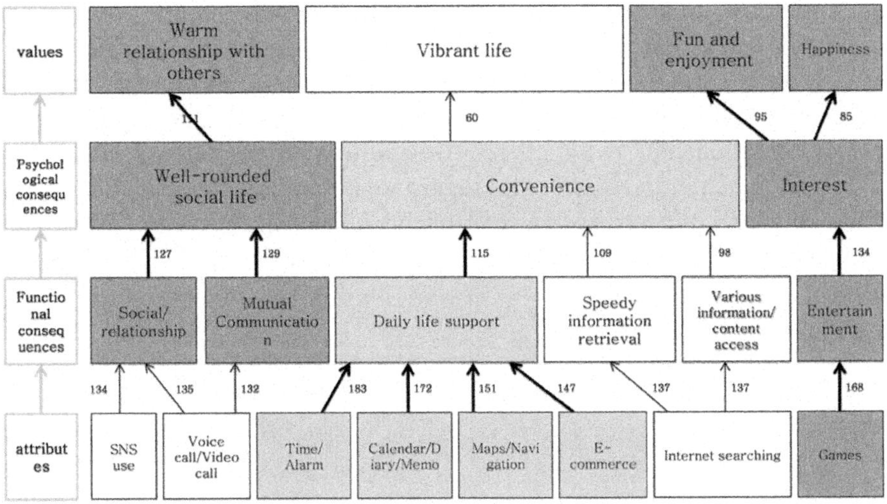

Figure 1: HVM for high-involvement smart phone users.

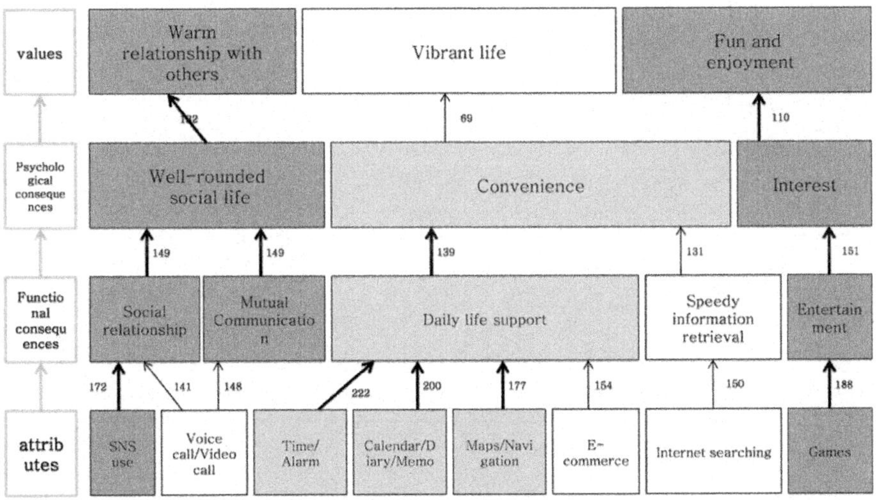

Figure 2: HVM for low-involvement smart phone users.

DISCUSSIONS

In this study, we derived the HVMs of smart phones, portal sites, and SNSs depending on user involvement based on the concept of involvement and means-chain theory. We identified differences in values among users in the high-involvement group and users in the low-involvement group for all media types.

The most important value for the high-involvement group is self-accomplishment. The members of the high- involvement group tend to be very active users who use media as a means to achieve their goals. The most important values for the low-involvement group are self-realization and friendly relationships with others. In addition, high-and low-involvement HVMs are apparently similar with regard to motivation and behavior of media users. However, the perceptions of attributes, consequences, and utilization of media show differences depending on involvement.

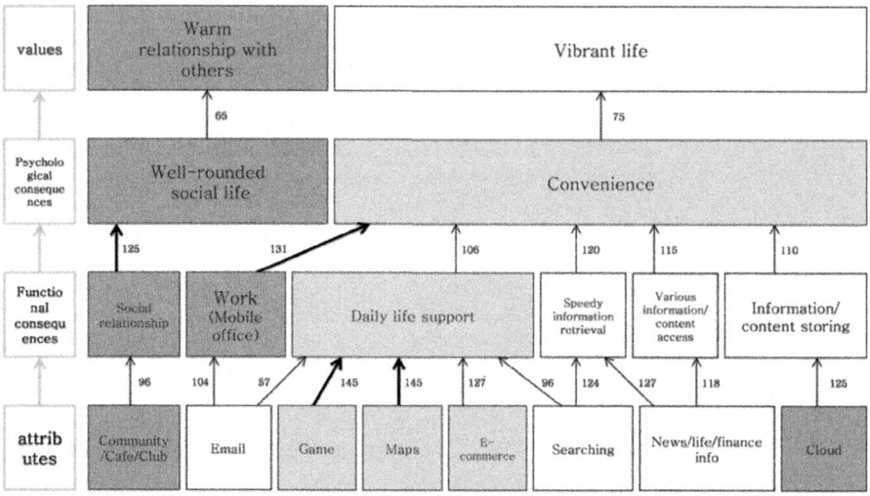

Figure 3: HVM for high-involvement portal site users.

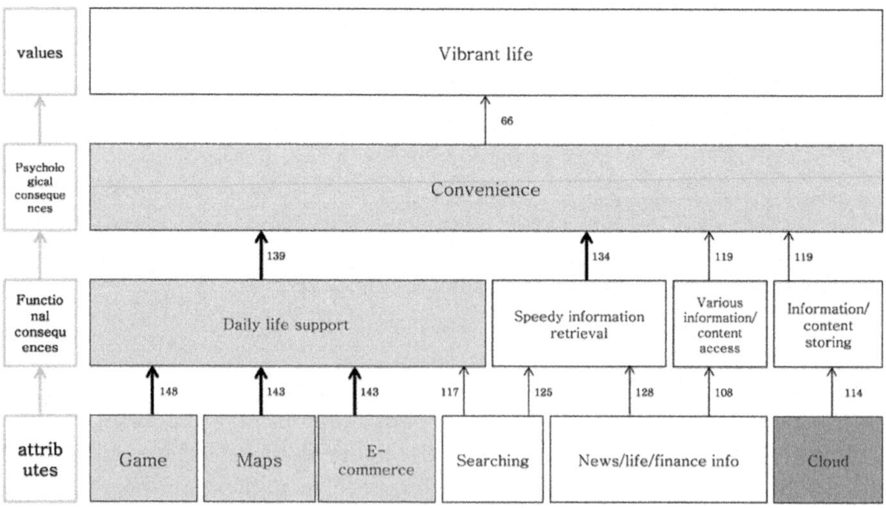

Figure 4: HVM for low-involvement portal site users.

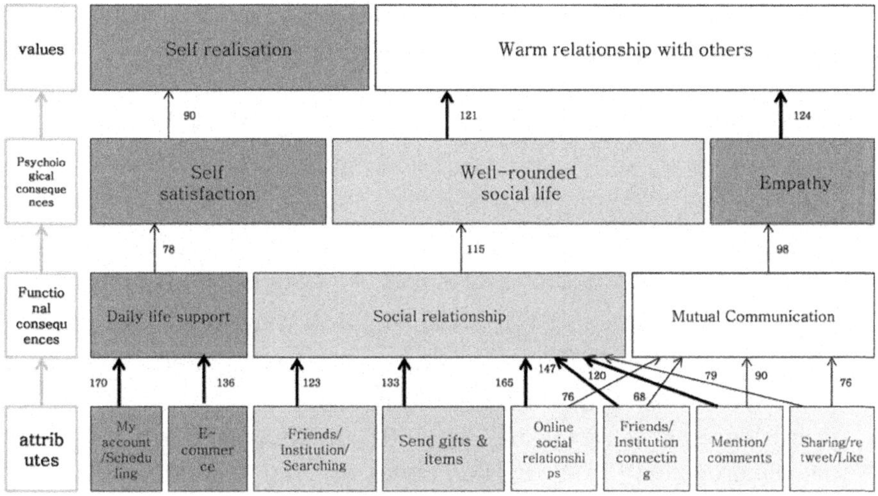

Figure 5: HVM for high-involvement SNS users.

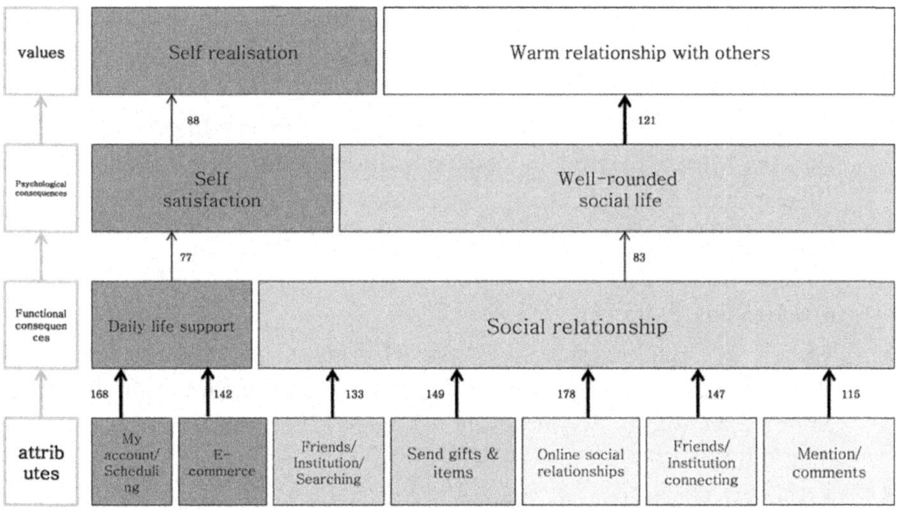

Figure 6: HVM for low-involvement SNS users.

The implication of the research findings is that different usage values exist in cyber media. The result shows that the basic values for smart phone users are social life support, entertainment, social relationship, and interaction communication. In comparison, the important values for portal site users are quick information acquisition, supporting daily life, and a variety of information/content acquisition and entertainment. The HVMs of smart phones, portal sites, and SNSs were compared with one another, and the result shows that they have different value chains.

The final values of users are also influenced by the characteristics and functional strength of media. New communication devices constantly attempt to meet the basic human desire for communication because desire drives the demand for new social smart devices.

REFERENCES

1. Baudrillard, J. (1970). The Consumer Society: Myths and Structures. Theory, Culture & Society. New York: Nottingham University.
2. Celsi, R. L., & Olson, J. C. (1988). The Role of Involvement in Attention and Comprehension Processes. Journal of Consumer Research, 15, 210-224.http://dx.doi.org/10.1086/209158
3. Christensen, G. L., & Olson, J. C. (2001). Involved with What? The Impact of Heterogeneity in Goal Hierarchies on High Enduring Involvement. Advances in Consumer Research, 28, 392.
4. Grunert, K., & Grunert, S. (1995). Measuring Subjective Meaning Structures by the Laddering Method: Theoretical Considerations and Methodological Problems. International Journal of Research in Marketing, 12, 209-225. http://dx.doi.org/10.1016/0167-8116(95)00022-T
5. Gutman, J. (1981). A Means-End Model for Facilitating Analysis of Product Markets Based on Consumer Judgement. Advances in Consumer Research, 8, 116-121.
6. Gutman, J. (1982). A means-End Chain Model based On Consumer Categorisation Processes. Journal of Marketing, 46, 60-72. http://dx.doi.org/10.2307/3203341
7. Huber, F., Beckmann, S. C., & Herrmann, A. (2004). Means-End Analysis: Does the Affective State Influence Information Processing Style? Psychology & Marketing, 21, 715-737. http://dx.doi.org/10.1002/mar.20026
8. Maslow, A. (1943). A Theory of Human Motivation. Psychological Review, 50, 370-396.http://dx.doi.org/10.1037/h0054346
9. Peter, J. P., & Olson, J. C. (2005). Consumer Behaviour and Marketing Strategy (7th ed). New York: McGraw-Hill/Irwin.
10. Petty, R. E., & Cacioppo, J. T. (1986). Communication and Persuasion: Central and Peripheral Routes to Attitude Change. New York: Springer-Verlag.http://dx.doi.org/10.1007/978-1-4612-4964-1
11. ter Hofstede, F., Audenaert, A., Steenkamp, J. E. M., & Wedel, M. (1998). An Investigation into the Association Pattern Technique as a Quantitative Approach to Measuring Means-End Chain. International

Journal of Research in Marketing, 15, 37-50.http://dx.doi.org/10.1016/S0167-8116(97)00029-3

12. Woodruff, R. B., & Gardial, S. F. (1996). Know Your Customer: New Approaches to Understanding Customer Value and Satisfaction. Cambridge, MA: Blackwell Publishers, Inc.
13. Zaichkowsky, J. L. (1985). Measuring the Involvement Construct. Journal of Consumer Research, 12, 341-352. http://dx.doi.org/10.1300/J047v06n04_05

Chapter 13

MAPPING TRAJECTORIES OF ATTENTION TO DRUG RELATED ISSUES IN ESTONIAN MAIN DAILIES

Marianne Paimre

Department of Law, University of Tartu, Tartu, Estonia

ABSTRACT

Illicit drugs have been a burning social issue in Estonia over the last fifteen years. Estonia has taken the lead in Europe with regard to drug-related deaths and prevalence of HIV among injecting drug users. Experimental drug use among Estonian students is more widespread than the European average. It is important to study press coverage, because according to agenda setting theory, the media plays an important role in influencing the salience of social issues on the public agenda. The aim of this article is to map fluctuations in attention received from Estonian two major dailies to different drug related issues during the last 25 years. The author focuses on issues highlighted in national and international drug reports such as drug addiction, drug related crime, spread of HIV among addicts, drug-induced deaths, drug problem in schools etc. Content analysis of almost 1000 press articles reflecting drug problems in Estonia was carried out from 1990 to 2014. The study revealed that since 1995, attention received from the major newspapers to drug related crime has been high and quite stable compared to other drug issues. Press interest with regard to problem drug use and HIV was notice a bleat the turn of the millennium and in the beginning of the new century, but almost lost by 2014. More intense periods of coverage were triggered by specific events. Only a few articles have reflected drug induced death despite the fact that Estonia is the undisputed leader in the EU regarding this indicator. This reflects that the coverage was not been in line with the drug situation in Estonia. It seems that the attention of the press depends rather on newsworthiness of the issue and the agenda setting processes.

INTRODUCTION

Drug addiction has been one of the burning social issues in Estonia over the past decades. By today, Estonia has taken the lead in Europe with regard to drug-related deaths and prevalence of HIV among injecting drug users. Experimental drug use among Estonian students is more widespread than the European average. Despite efforts at the national level, use of illicit drugs among the population has grown in the new millennium (NIHD, 2014) . It has been suggested that drug problems will not diminish as long as the general public fails to recognize their importance (NIHD, 2005; Ministry of the Interior, 2014) . Some blame could be placed on the media for downplaying the problem (Ibid).

According to the agenda setting theory, the urgency the public attributes to a problem is very much conditioned by the prominence the media accords to it (McCombs & Shaw, 1972; McCombs & Reynolds, 2002; Schäfer et al., 2014: p. 153). The print media is an important factor in raising awareness about social issues including drugs (Bell, 1985; Coleman, 1993; Edwards, 1995; Crano & Burgoon, 2002; McQuail, 2010) . Major newspapers could play a prominent role in determining public opinion about illicit drugs and shaping relevant public policies (Fan, 1996; Lawrence et al., 1999; Blood et al., 2003; Watts, 2003; Hoffman & Slater, 2007). Thus, it is necessary to explore how drug issues are reported in national dailies.

Several scholars have studied press coverage on illicit drugs across the world. The multidimensional and complex nature of the research question has given rise to a variety of methodologies and approaches. Many scientists have analyzed the context, in which illegal drugs have been represented in the media as well as the prevalent attitudes regarding drug use (e.g. Törrönen, 2004; Manning, 2006; Bright et al, 2008; Hellman, 2010; Hughes et al., 2010). Other researchers have focused on the interconnections between media coverage, public opinion and public policies(Shoemaker et al., 1989; Deseran & Orcutt, 2009) . Qualitative studies concentrating on some significant case have been rather commonplace (McArthur, 1999; Lawrence et al., 1999; Elliott & Chapman, 2000) . Scientists have often blamed the media for the sensational, biased and one-sided angle characteristic of their drug accounts which could exert a disorienting effect on the public perception of the issue (Craig, 1981; Murji, 1998; Chermak, 1997; Manning, 2006; Noto et al., 2006; Bright et al., 2008; Taylor, 2008) . Only some scholars have concentrated on changes in media coverage of drug issues (e.g. Fan, 1996; Hellman, 2010; Hughes et al., 2010). There is lack of longitudinal studies in this field. This article hopes to fill the gap in this respect.

In the US, Gonzenbach (1996) tracked trajectories of attention to the whole drug issue provided by the public, government, the president and the media in the 1980s using a five-stage model of issue attention cycle introduced by A. Downs. However, the US has faced the drug problem already many decades by then. Thus he does not focus on formation of the drug issue, but instead takes a period when the cycle emerged clearly. In Estonia, it is possible to study the development of the mediated drug discourse from the very beginning, because drugs entered the public agenda relatively late compared to the Western societies, only in the 1990s (Paimre, 2013) . In this study, simplified version of attention cycle (McComas & Shanahan, 1999) with three phases of media interest (waxing attention, maintenance, and waning attention) is used in order to explore changes in press attention to drug problems in Estonia. It could be argued that issue cycles (see e.g. Djerf-Pierre, 2011) are under scrutiny in this article.

The aim of this study is to map fluctuations in newspaper coverage of different issues related to illicit drugs (addiction, drug crime, spread of HIV among addicts, drug-induced deaths, drug problem in schools etc.) in post-Soviet Estonia (1990-2014). Thus the article focuses on the press coverage of drug problems, but not on the attention received by the political institutions or public. The author poses the following question: How has press concern to various issues related to drugs changed during the past quarter century? Has press attention generally been in line with real-world indicators? What kind of events has triggered “spikes”?

Some scholars have indicated to “issues” broadly defined in their analysis to the whole ecological domain (e.g. Downs as cited in Djerf-Pierre, 2011), the others have been concentrated on some single issue (e.g. Shanahan & McComas, 1997). In this article, coverage of several sub-issues of the whole illicit drug domain is under scrutiny. When studying media coverage on drugs scholars have often focused on representations of different substances (e.g. Sznitman & Lewis, 2015;EMCDDA, 2005; Manning, 2006). The author of this article does not concentrate on different substances, but instead focuses on the coverage of different social problems induced by (or attendant to) illicit substances and their use (e.g. drug addiction, drug related crime etc.).

SAMPLE AND METHOD

Sample

Two national dailies with the largest circulations, Postimees (PM) and Eesti Päevaleht (EPL) were selected for the research. Their predecessors Edasi and Noorte Hääl were under scrutiny in 1990. Articles from 1990-2000 were retrieved by reviewing publications stored in the library with the aim of identifying all the stories reporting on drugs in Estonia. By 2000 most of the print newspapers had also developed their online editions and as of 2005 it became possible to use online keywords search.

The search results were extracted for the sample to include only stories with substantive content on illicit drugs focusing on the relevant situation in Estonia. If the article featured both in the print and online paper, it counted as one. All the types of articles (editorials, news, opinion articles, features etc. are involved) reporting illicit drug problem in Estonia were included. All together 962 articles were analyzed from the period 1990-2014.

Method

A formalized content analysis was used as the method in this study (Riffe et al., 2005) . Quantitative analysis of media texts can enable large samples to be analyzed and thereby reducing the potential for sampling bias (Hansen, 1998; Hughes et al., 2011: p. 286). All the 962 articles were analyzed according to coding rules developed by the author. The main categories were the themes of articles (e.g. addiction; spread of infectious diseases; drug problem in schools; cannabis regulation; drug related crime; prevention; some other topic) and sub-topics. The author's main interest was to find out how many articles on various subjects were published in various years. Additionally, categories such as sources of information (e.g. government, parliament, police, court, treatment centres, NGO-s, media, citizens etc.), types of the article and level of the problem were used. 10% of articles (n = 96) were tested for reliability by the other coder. Value of Scott's π was 0.88.

OVERVIEW OF THE DEVELOPMENT OF DRUG RELATED ISSUES IN ESTONIA

With a view to comparing and contrasting the changes in the media coverage of the Estonian drug situation, the author firstly offers a short overview of the development of the drug related problems in Estonia. Illegal drugs became more widespread in Estonia only as late as a couple of decades ago. The number of problem drug users went up, drug-related crime took off, students started to express a closer interest in experimenting with illegal drugs in the 1990s (PHARE, 1998) . There were many reasons contributing to the spreading of illicit drugs in Eastern-Europe e.g. more travel opportunities opened up, illegal substances became more accessible etc. (Ibid).By the turn of millennium, all the indicators reflecting drug problems have increased considerably. Drug problems in Estonia that have been mentioned repeatedly in the international and national reports have been discussed in more detail below.

Problem drug use. By mid-1990s data collected from medical institutions revealed a significant rise in problem drug use. 24.5 drug users to a hundred thousand inhabitants were registered in 1995 by hospitals. By comparison the corresponding average figure for 1960s was only 3.5 and for 1970s 6.2 (PHARE, 1998: p. 31) . By 1996 the number had risen to 51.6 and by 1997 72.8 already (Ibid). The baseline in drug statistics has shifted considerably over time making it difficult to compare the earlier indicators with the more recent ones. In the 21th century, the use of opiates and amphetamine in Estonia has been significant (UNODC, 2011: p. 52; UNODC, 2013; OECD, 2014: p. 53) . Estonia has been among the EU countries with the highest rates of injecting drug use(EMCDDA, 2014: p. 47) .

Spread of HIV and other diseases. The above issue is closely linked to the transmission of infectious diseases among addicts. Isolated instances of HIV carriers among IDUs were recorded already as early as in 1997 and 1998 (NIHD, 2009) . At the turn of the millennium there was an upsurge in recorded numbers of IDUs with HIV. The incidence figure for 2000 was 354 compared to 1340 in 2001 (NIHD, 2011) , which is frightfully many for a country with a population of 1.3 million. By 2010 the figure has dropped to 62. Despite the government's efforts to tackle the acute problem and the recession in statistics, Estonia still tops the EU for this particular indicator (EMCDDA, 2014: p. 47; UNODC, 2014: p. 8) .

Drug induced death. In the 2000s, Estonia has become Europe's run-away leader in drug deaths(EMCDDA, 2014; NIHD, 2014) . The mortality rate is twice that of second placed Norway. In 2000, 31 drug induced deaths were recorded, 57 respectively in 2005. A total of 101 people died due to using drugs in Estonia in 2010 (this was 133 people in 2009). The number of drug-induced deaths in Estonia soared in 2012 (123 cases). The National Institute of Health has reported that overdoses are the predominant cause of death. Fentanyl, which is produced mainly in neighboring Russia, has been the underlying cause of death in most cases (NIHD, 2014) . At the moment Estonia ranks 4th in the world with respect to this particular indicator (data from NIHD).

Drug use by adolescents. Experimenting with softer drugs (e.g. cannabis, ecstasy etc.) by youth has spread significantly during last decades. Only 7% of the 15 - 16 year-old adolescents has experimented with drugs according to the 1995 ESDPAD survey (NIHD, 2002: p. 18) . In 1999 the indicator was 15% already and in 2003 24% respectively. By 2011 third (32%) of the 15 - 16 year-old schoolchildren reported having tried some illicit drug in their lifetime which exceeds the European average (ESPAD, 2012) . The spike in drug use came to a halt in 2011. Thus the problem has rapidly grown during the 1990s and 2000s, but now is finally slowing. However a new problem has emerged lately—handling of illicit drugs by minors has exhibited an upward trend in recent years (Ministry of Justice, 2015) .

Drug related crime. The number of drug-related offences started to increase considerably since the second half of the 1990s. A dramatic growth in recorded drug offences occurred at the beginning of 2000s. When in 1997 only 114 offences were officially recorded (twice more than in 1995), then the corresponding figure for 2001 amounted to 2301 (data from the Ministry of Justice). After the peak year this number has not exceeded 1600 per annum. The downward trend is most likely attributable to the fact that drug abuse was no longer deemed an offence subject to criminal punishment. In 2010, 957 drug offences were registered, in 2014 was the indicator 1218 (Ministry of Justice, 2015) . However, compared with the other European countries, drug seizures do not seem to be a major problem in Estonia (EMCDDA, 2014: p. 79) .

Thus, almost from the nonexistence, drug problems have increased rapidly in Estonia during recent decades. The state has reacted to the drug problems since the second half of the 1990s (Paimre, 2013) . The first drug prevention program was launched in 1997. In 2014, the latest drug strategy document was introduced by the Ministry of Interior (2014) which compared to previous versions of Estonian drug strategies, introduces softer measures in combating drugs.

Despite efforts at the national level, drug problems have not reduced noticeably in Estonia. Sociologists have proposed that the relatively modest success in the prevention arena can be attributed to the fact that the general public fails to recognize drug-addiction as a serious evil(Saar, 2012) . The media reporting on drug issues could have some impact on this (Ibid). It is known that media content is important source of information for most people in several social issues(Sato & Campbell, 2014: p. 20) .

RESULTS OF THE ANALYSIS OF THE PRESS ARTICLES

As indicated in the previous chapter, problems related to illicit drugs started to surface more in the newly independent Estonia at the beginning of 1990s. Yet by the summer of 1995 they had hardly ever garnered any attention in the two major national dailies, which did not correspond to the real world indicators. The press "discovered" illicit drugs in 1995 (see Figure 1). Since that time, issues related to illicit substances have been quite newsworthy for the Estonian main dailies. E.g. during the 2000s, every other day an article has appeared on drug problems in the major dailies. The coverage of various sub-issues is examined in more detail below.

Drug related crime. The bulk of analyzed articles (52%) during 1990-2014 focused on the association between drugs and criminality. By comparison, articles on drug problem in schools comprised only 11%. Drug related crime has attracted the attention of the dailies since 1995. Illicit drugs were represented only once in analyzed papers (PM 19. June 1995) in thefirsthalf of 1995, but in the second half of the year, already 64 articles appeared. Most of them (81%) reflected drug related crimes. The surge of interest was not attributable to the growing number of registered drug related offences, but resulted from two dramatic drug-related events directly affecting Estonia. The first case was about the arrest of Estonian drug smugglers in Bangkok which generated 49 articles in PM and EPL in the second half of the year. In august 1995, criminal investigation department executives cut down the poppy crop in the field of a South-Estonian farmer which was the second most intensively covered case (with 41 articles). Selection of voices reflected the importance of the issue for Estonian journalists, e.g. the police accounted for 85% of the sources mentioned in articles in 1995, various ministries 19% and the government 8% respectively. The articles consisted mainly of news (72%) next to occasional opinion pieces (5%) and interviews (7%). This was the beginning of the period of waxing press interest in respect to the subject.

By 2000 and 2005 the amount of articles on drug crime has substantially increased (139 and 125 articles respectively), thus the press concern for drug crime has reached to the maintenance phase. Routine news accounted for the majority of articles on drug crime theme (80%). By 2010 attention by press has decreased (99 articles), but rose again by 2014 (109). Typical headlines of the new millennium regarding drug offences included e.g. "Smugglers of large quantities of amphetamine face punishment" (PM, 10. Sept. 2010); "Court sentenced cannabis cultivators to imprisonment" (PM, 7. Dec. 2014); "A young man high on drugs and without a driving license caused a serious accident in the calm traffic area" (PM., 30. Oct. 2014). Drug offences committed by Estonians in neighboring Finland have been especially newsworthy (e.g. PM, 8. March 2010; 8. Oct. 2010; 23. Nov. 2010, etc.). EPL, reportedly more focused on social issues, did not cover drug-related crime incidents as avidly as PM did.

In recent years, two young Estonian girls caught with nearly six kilos of cocaine in Peru in October of 2013 made the news on several occasions. Although after 1995 many Estonians have been arrested for drug smuggling all around the globe, the media coverage of this case did not fall far behind the 1995 incident in its intensity. A severe punishment (almost nine years in a Peruvian prison) awaiting for the girls in South-America seemed for the journalists to be in stark contrast with their youth and naivety (e.g. EPL, 13. Feb. 2014). In 2014, the fact that the Nigerian citizen responsible for recruiting the two Estonians as drug mules went on trial triggered the media interest for a while (EPL, 25. Nov 2014; 5. Dec. 2014 etc.).

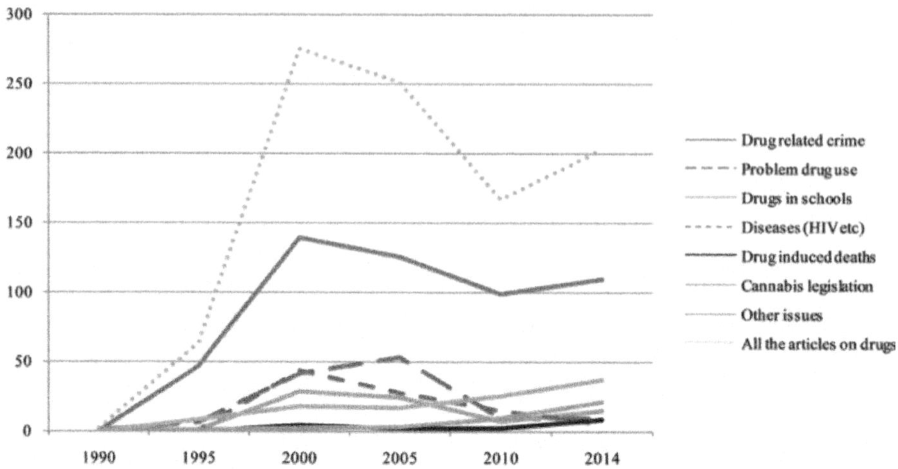

Figure 1: Trajectories of attention to drug related issues by Estonian dailies 1990-2014 (N = 962).

In 91% drug related crime was discussed on state level (the state should to smth. to solve the problem). The public has supposedly inferred from the coverage brought to them over the last decades that drugs and criminal conduct are inextricably linked and that drug related crime is the most burning issue in respect to drugs in Estonia.

Addiction/problem drug use. A new and fascinating subject that captured the media's attention in 2000 was problem drug use. 41 articles focused on this aspect in 2000. All together 120 articles (13%) covered this topic in 1990-2014. Press interest was even highest in 2005 (53 articles). 25 stories appeared on the local municipality's failed attempt to establish a day center for drug addicts in 2005. Indeed, the city of Tallinn had unveiled a plan to open a European style low threshold center, but it was derailed by the fierce opposition from local residents. The papers weighed both sides of the argument at the time. A marked change towards a more tolerant attitude of journalists to addicts originates from that period (see e.g. PM 11. May 2005 and 7. July 2005). However, by 2010 the "assistance and support" angle had lost its journalistic appeal. By 2014 the media interest has disappeared, only 10 articles appeared.

In many articles (35), addicts were portrayed as posing a serious threat to the welfare of the general public (e.g. PM, 11. Oct. 2000 and 18. Dec. 2000; EPL, 23. March 2010; PM, 14. June 2010 etc.). For instance, there were rumours going around that in order to clean their needles, addicts frequented supermarkets and used vegetables for disinfection purposes, consequently exposing all of us to AIDS and hepatitis or that they got a kick out of attacking innocent citizens in the streets with their used syringes (PM, 3. Nov. 2000 and EPL, 11. Oct. 2000). In 2014 there were media reports on how residents of an apartment building objected to the setting up of an automatic needle dispensing machine in their stairwell (EPL, 26. June 2014). Revealing police stats regarding the majority of thieves in Tallinn having a drug problem does very little to help local residents become more tolerant towards addicts (EPL, 29. July 2014).Such an approach was evident throughout 2010 and 2014 (e.g. EPL, 29. July 2014; PM, 14.06. 2010 etc.). In 2014 female addicts received more media attention than ever before e.g. how doctors and midwives are struggling with mothers-to-be arriving in maternity hospitals while high on drugs (e.g. EPL, 15. Dec. 2014). The proposal to replace imprisonment with addiction treatment for drug offences has been on the table since 2010 (PM, 17. March, 2010).

21% of articles on this theme depicted drug problem as an individual concern. Main sources in addition to governmental ones (Ministry of Social Affairs, NIHD etc.) were treatment institutions (13%), NGO's (12%), media (10%), citizens own information (6%) etc. A couple of articles on addiction treatment appeared with source information provided by the drug abuse prevention conference (e.g. EPL, 19. Nov. 2010).

Spread of diseases among IDUs. In 2000, AIDS as yet another critical drug-related problem moved to the spotlight of media. 18% of articles all of a sudden devoted plenty of attention to this evil. The number of infected people that were discovered started to increase rapidly during the 2000s and the media's reaction to that was quite panic stricken (e.g. EPL, 7. Sept. 2000). A number of analytical opinion pieces and problem articles appeared (EPL, 6. Sept. 2000; PM, 7. Feb. 2000; EPL, 3. March 2000; EPL, 21. Oct. 2000 etc.). Several editorials appeared on this subject (e.g. PM, 12. Oct. 2000; EPL, 21. Oct. 2000 etc.) which indicated that the issue was quite important for the press. Besides HIV, also tuberculosis and hepatitisin relation to drug addiction were discussed. However, when examining the media coverage from 2010 and 2014, it seems that this "ghost" no longer haunts Estonia.

Contrasting to crime thematic, problems were more often discussed related to addiction and diseases on individual (24%) or group level (13%). However, most often the issue was discussed in the state level (40%) which reflects the importance of the problem for the press. Articles were more analytical and profound. Important source of information besides state institutions has been the AIDS prevention center (9%).

Drug problem in schools. This topic was under-reported until 2000 when 12% of analysed articles reflected drug problem among adolescents. The results of a research were introduced in public in 2000 (e.g. EPL, 2. Feb. 2000). In contrast to some other topics (e.g. drug related crime) scientific sources were used quite often (23%). Scientists have been active to comment this problematic. e.g. in 2005, a sociologist (A.-A. Allaste) published several articles on adolescents and drugs (EPL, 26. Aug. 2005; PM, 2. May 2005; PM, 3. Sept.; EPL, 16. July, 2005). In 2014 drug abuse among students was discussed sporadically. Several events played an important role in activating media attention. First, cases of synthetic cannabis use made headlines as they resulted in several adolescents being admitted to the ER (PM, 7, 19, 21, 24 and 27 Nov. 2014). Secondly, the police revealed the results of the study on the drug habits of young people in Estonia. Apparently, the young turned out to be more avid cannabis users than initially suspected (PM, 4. June 2014). Thirdly, police raids in schools generated both praise as reluctant. In many cases (45% of articles on school topic) the police was used as the main source of information. Incidentally, the fact that marijuana was grown in a vocational school's dormitory made the news (PM, 19. Dec. 2010).

Lately, the topic of school children and drugs has taken on a more sinister criminal undertone. The focus has shifted from doing drugs to dealing in drugs at schools, adults trying to take advantage of youngsters and the countermeasures introduced by the police (EPL, 13. Feb. 2014; EPL, 5. June 2014).

Drug induced deaths. Despite the seriousness of the problem, the issue has been underreported in the main dailies. Articles on drug deaths comprised only 2% during the period 1990-2014. In 2014, eight articles were launched. The interesting fact for the journalists was that the United Nations Drug Report referred that Estonia is fifth in the world for its population in the number of drug related deaths (EPL, 15. July 2014). Already in the beginning of the year it was argued by Estonian prevention experts in press that the national prevention strategy has not worked so far and the state must now start to take action in this field (EPL, 3. Feb. 2014). The articles published in 2014 on drug-induced deaths were not too analytical, instead they conveyed mere statistical data.

Marijuana proponents' attempts at legalization. A novel and a rather distinct issue from the above is cannabis which has been generating considerable publicity for the past years now. The possible legalization of cannabis was the crux of 16 articles published in 2014.Journalists asked—how has the relaxation of cannabis laws in a number of US states affected Estonia's drug policy (PM, 1. February 2014)? On the one hand, public officials in general tend to oppose liberal drug policies (PM, 5. Feb. 2014; WPL, 23. July 2014 etc.), on the other hand, various cannabis activists and humanists openly call for more lenient drug reforms (PM, 1 Feb. 2014; PM, 21. Apr. 2014; PM, 15. Dec. 2014; EPL, 10. Feb. 2014 etc.). By the second half of 2014, journalists were somewhat astonished by the fact that the legalization of cannabis in some US states did not result in chaos after all (EPL, 6. Sept. 2014).

Topics compelling the latest media attention include online purchasing of narcotics constituting a criminal offence (e.g. PM, 15. Apr. 2014, 25. June 2014 and 5. July 2014) non-medical use of prescription drugs (e.g. PM 18. June 2014), minor changes in drug legislation (PM, 16. Dec. 2014), drug use in the army (PM, 24. Oct. 2014 and 25 Oct. 2014) etc.

In conclusion one can say that some issues (problem drug use, diseases) were more prone to cyclic coverage than the others (drug crime, drugs in schools). Cyclic press coverage emerged with regard to the whole drug issue. The decrease in press attention by 2010 could be explained probably by the impact economic crisis. e.g. Djerf-Pierre (2011: p. 502) has noted, that public concern for certain social issues diminish in times of economic recession. Secondly, apparently some fresh and more interesting topics caught media attention more. Thirdly, the press and the public could be tired of drug issues.

One can surmise that various evils concerning drugs enter and then fade from the media focus with the exception of drug-related crime which never loses its urgency. If the issue is new and interesting it naturally receives media attention for a while. As soon as a more novel and thrilling concern emerges, it assumes priority. For no apparent reason the indisputably pressing social ills in Estonia do not warrant must interest in the media.

DISCUSSION AND CONCLUSIONS

The results indicate that the trajectories reflecting press attention for various drug related issues are not similar. Significant fluctuations have taken place in the press interest with regard to different issues. The first problem to receive more intense coverage was drug-related crime which leaped into prominence due to sensational cases in 1995. Contrary to drug-related prevalence of AIDS in respect of which Estonia takes the lead in Europe but the media has failed to sustain interest in for too long, since 1995, drug-related crime has always been and probably will remain in the public eye. This is no surprise as delinquent behavior has been one of the favorite subjects of the press for ages. Placing the sensational aspects of drug issues centre stage has been mostly evident with regard to drug related crime. Arrests, confiscations, convictions are newsworthy for the press and seem exciting for the public. Police have been a good source of information and partner for the media in constructing drug problem. By 2000, press attention to drug crime has diminished, but has risen again by 2014.

Press concern for other drug issues has not stayed long. Cyclical attention by the newspapers emerged especially in connection with drug addiction and HIV. By 2000, a new issue—spread of HIV among drug users led to different approaches in the media. Massive HIV recording frenzy among IDUs in 2000 and the growing panic that this illness can eventually be contracted by the so-called decent people propelled the mounting concerns to the center of attention as the year came to a close. It is interesting to note, that concern to addicts and spread of HIV did not crowd out issue of drug crime at the turn of millennium and in the beginning of the new century. The press remained focused upon problem drug use issue as well in 2005. By 2010 the print media's interest had waned considerably despite the HIV incidence rate in Estonia still being one of the highest in Europe. The current situation where drug-related issues besides crime receive little media attention does not seem to correspond to the real conditions. Media interest to drug issues seems to depend more on news values, freshness of the issue, agenda setting processes, wider economic conditions etc. than on real world indicators. Due to modest media attention on some drug issues the average Estonians indeed might not fully grasp the urgency of these problems.

More intense periods of coverage have been generally triggered by out of ordinary events. In 1995, so-called Thailand case and "poppy war" triggered news wave. In 2000, spread of HIV among IDUs caused "spike". In 2013 and 2014, arrest of two young Estonian women in Peru made headlines in major newspapers. The experimental use of softer drugs among students has shifted to the focus of newspapers during the years in which either the findings of relevant studies and reports have been released or something else out of the ordinary has happened. Driven by the legalization of marijuana in some US states, cannabis captured the attention of Estonian newspapers in 2014. It seems that reporting on drug problems is geared more to commercialization of newsworthy events which apparently takes precedence over serving the common good by addressing critical social issues.

Coverage of drug related issues is, to a considerable degree, dictated by the profit-making ambitions of journalism characterized by the greatest regard for newsworthiness. Novelty, dramatization and other values of profit driven journalism seem to be the main driving forces in coverage of the important social issue.

REFERENCES

1. Bell, P. (1985). Drugs and the Media. Australian Alcohol/Drug Review, 4, 235-242.http://dx.doi.org/10.1080/09595238580000401
2. Bright, S., Marsh, A., Smith, L., & Bishop, B. (2008). What Can We Say about Substance Use? Dominant Discourses and Narratives Emergent from Australian Media. Addiction Research & Theory, 2, 135-148.http://dx.doi.org/10.1080/16066350701794972
3. Chermak, S. (1997). The Presentation of Drugs in the News Media: The News Sources Involved in the Construction of Social Problems. Justice Quarterly, 14, 687-718.http://dx.doi.org/10.1080/07418829700093551
4. Coleman, C. (1993). The Influence of Mass Media and Interpersonal Communication on Societal and Personal Risk Judgments. Communication Research, 20, 611-628.http://dx.doi.org/10.1177/009365093020004006
5. Craig, R. (1981). Drug Themesin Metropolitan Newspapers: Review and Analysis. Substance Use & Misuse, 16, 1087-1093. http://dx.doi.org/10.3109/10826088109038915
6. Crano, W. D., & Burgoon, M. (2002). Mass Media and Drug Prevention: Classic and Contemporary Theories and Research. Mahwah, New Jersey, London: LEA.
7. Deseran, T. A., & Orcutt, J. D. (2009). The Deconstruction of a Drug Crisis: Media Coverage of Drugs Issues during the 1996 Presidential Campaign. Journal of Drug Issues, 39, 871-891. http://dx.doi.org/10.1177/002204260903900405
8. Djerf-Pierre, M. (2011).Green Metacycles of Attention: Reassessing the Attention Cycles of Environmental News Reporting 1961-2010. Public Understanding of Science, 4, 499-516. http://pus.sagepub.com.ezproxy.utlib.ee/content/22/4/495.full.pdf+html?http://dx.doi.org/10.1177/0963662511426819
9. Edwards, G. (1995). Alcohol Policy and the Public Good. Oxford: Oxford Medical Publications.
10. Elliott, A., & Chapman, S. (2000). "Heroin Hell Their Own Making": Construction of Hero in Users in the Australian Press 1992-97. Drug & Alcohol Review, 19, 191-201.http://dx.doi.org/10.1080/713659328
11. EMCDDA (2005). Youth Media: Thematic Papers. Lisbon: European Monitoring Centre for Drugs and Drug Addiction.http://www.emcdda.europa.eu/attachements.cfm/att_34038_EN_TP_Youth_media.pdf
12. EMCDDA (2014). European Drug Report: Trends and Developments. Luxembourg: Publications Office of the European Union.http://

www.emcdda.europa.eu/attachements.cfm/att_228272_EN_TDAT14001ENN.pdf

13. ESPAD (2012). The 2011 ESPAD Report: Substance Use among Students in 36 European Countries. Stockholm: ESPAD.http://www.espad.org/Uploads/ESPAD_reports/2011/The_2011_ESPAD_Report_FULL_2012_10_29.pdf
14. Fan, D. (1996). News Media Framing Sets Public Opinion That Drugs Is the Country's Most Important Problem. Substance Use and Misuse, 31, 1413-1421.http://dx.doi.org/10.3109/10826089609063984
15. Gonzenbach, W. (1996). The Media, the President and Public Opinion: A Longitudinal Analysis of the Drug Issue, 1962-1991. Mahwah, NJ: Erlbaum.
16. Hansen, A. (1998). Content Analysis. In A. Hansen, S. Cottle, R. Negrine, & C. Newbold (Eds.), Mass Communication Research Methods (pp. 91-129). Houndmills: Palgrave Macmillan.
17. Hellman, M. (2010). From Myth of Marginality to Portrayals of an Addictive Society: Reporting on Addictions in the Finnish Press (1968-2006). Addiction Research & Theory, 18, 224-242. http://dx.doi.org/10.3109/16066350902836382
18. Hoffman, L. H., & Slater, M. D. (2007). Evaluating Public Discourse in Newspaper Opinion Articles: Values-Framing and Integrative Complexity in Substance and Health Policy Issues. Journalism & Mass Communication Quarterly, 84, 58-74.http://dx.doi.org/10.1177/107769900708400105
19. Hughes, C. E., Spicer, B., Lancaster, K., Matthew-Simmons, F., & Dillon, P. (2010). Media Reporting on Illicit Drugs in Australia: Trends and Impacts on Youth Attitudes to Illicit Drug Use. Monograph 19, Drug Policy Modelling Program (DPMP) Monograph Series, Sydney: National Drug and Alcohol Research Centre.http://www.dpmp.unsw.edu.au/DPMPWeb.nsf/resources/Monograph+16.pdf/$file/DPMP+MONO+19.pdf
20. Lawrence, G., Bammer, G., & Chapman, S. (1999). "Sending the Wrong Message": Analysis of Print Media Reportage of the ACT Heroin Prescription Trial Proposal, August 1997. Australian and New Zealand Journal of Public Health, 24, 254-264.http://dx.doi.org/10.1111/j.1467-842X.2000.tb01565.x
21. Manning, P. (2006). There's No Glamour in Glue: News and the Symbolic Framing of Substance Misuse. Crime, Media & Culture, 2, 49-66.http://dx.doi.org/10.1177/1741659006061711

22. McArthur, M. (1999). Pushing the Drug Debate: The Media's Role in Policy Reform. Australian Journal of Social Issues, 35, 149-165.
23. McComas, K., & Shanahan, J. (1999). Telling Stories about Global Climate Change: Measuring the Impact of Narratives on Issue Cycles. Communication Research, 26, 30-57.http://dx.doi.org/10.1177/009365099026001003
24. McCombs, M., & Reynolds, A. (2002). News Influence on Our Pictures of the World. In J. Bryant, & D. Zillmann (Eds.), Media Effects: Advances in Theory and Research (2nd ed., pp. 1-18). Mahwah: LEA.
25. McQuail, D. (2010). McQuail's Mass Communication Theory (6th ed.). London: SAGE.
26. Ministry of Justice (2015). Registreeritud kuriteod Eestist (Registered Offences in Estonia). http://www.kriminaalpoliitika.ee/et/registreeritud-kuriteod-eestis-2003-2014-excel
27. Ministry of the Interior (2014). Eesti uimastitarvitamise vähendamisepoliitika. Valgeraamat. (Estonia's Drug User Educing Policy. The White Paper).
28. Murji, K. (1998). The Agony and the Ecstasy: Drugs, Media and Morality. In R. Coomber (Ed.), The Control of Drugs and Drug Users: Reasonor Reaction? (pp. 69-85). London: Harwood. http://www.psychedelic-library.org/murji.htm
29. NIHD (2002). National Report on Drug Situation in Estonia 2001. Tallinn: National Institute for Health Development.
30. NIHD (2005). Narkomaania Eestis 2005 (Drug Addiction in Estonia 2005). Tallinn: National Institute for Health Development.
31. NIHD (2009). 2009.a. riiklik raport (2008. a andmed) EMCDDAle REITOXi riiklikult narkoteabekeskuselt (National Report to EMCDDA). Tallinn: National Institute for Health Development.
32. NIHD (2011). 2011.aasta riiklik raport (2010. Aasta andmed) EMCDDAle REITOXi riiklikult narkoteabekeskuselt. Uus areng, suundumused ja süvainformatsioon valitud teemadel. (National Report to EMCDDA, 2010 Data). Tallinn: National Institute for Health Development. www.tai.ee/terviseandmed/uuringud/download/169
33. NIHD (2014). 2014. Aasta riiklik raport (2013. Aasta andmed) EMCDDA-le REITOX-i riiklikult narkoteabekeskuselt. Eesti. Uued arengud ja suundumused (National Report to EMCDDA on Drug Situation in Estonia 2014, 2013 Data). Tallinn: National Institute for Health Development (NIHD).

34. Noto, A. R., Pinsky, I., & Mastroianni, C. (2006). Drugs in the Brazilian Print Media: An Exploratory Survey of Newspaper and Magazine Stories in the Year 2000. Substance Use & Misuse, 41, 1263-1276. http://dx.doi.org/10.1080/10826080600754868

35. OECD (2014). Health at Glance: Europe 2014. http://www.oecd-ilibrary.org/docserver/download/8114211e.pdf?expires=1423235691&id=id&accname=guest&checksum=0E5F99FFA808CA2BFAD369907622241D

36. Paimre, M. (2013). Narkoprobleemide kajastamine Eesti ajakirjanduses (1993-2009) (The Representation of Illicit Drugs Related Issues by the Estonian Press, 1993-2009). Academic Dissertation, Jyväskylä: Jyväskylä Studies in Humanities, University of Jyväskylä.

37. PHARE (1998). National Report Estonia. Sub-Regional Report Estonia. Phare Project on Drug Information System Final Phase. European Commission.

38. Riffe, D., Lacy, S., & Fico, F. (2005). Analyzing Media Messages: Using Quantitative Analysis in Research. Mahwah, NJ: Lawrence ErlbaumAssociates.

39. Saar, A. (2012). Võitlus narkomaaniaga ei saa olla vaid politsei rida. Postimees 18.

40. Sato, H., & Campbell, R. (2014). Newspaper Reports on BSE around the Time of the Japan-US Trade Conflicts: Content Analysis of Japanese and US Dailies from 2002 to 2006. Advances in Journalism and Communication, 2, 20-34.http://dx.doi.org/10.4236/ajc.2014.21003

41. Schäfer, M. S., Ivanova, A., & Schmidt, A. (2014). What Drives Media Attention for Climate Change? Explaining Issue Attention in Australian, German and Indian Print Media from 1996 to 2010. International Communication Gazette, 76, 152-176.http://dx.doi.org/10.1177/1748048513504169

42. Shanahan, J., & McComas, K. (1997). Television's Portrayal of the Environment: 1991-1995. Journalism and Mass Communication Quarterly, 74, 147-159.http://dx.doi.org/10.1177/107769909707400112

43. Shoemaker, P. J. (1989). Communication Campaigns about Drugs: Governmet, Media and the Public. Hillsdale: Lawrence Erlbaum.

44. Sznitman, S. R., & Lewis, N. (2015). Is Cannabis an Illicit Drug or a Medicine? A Quantitative Framing Analysis of Israeli Newspaper Coverage. International Journal of Drug Policy, 26, 446-452. http://dx.doi.org/10.1016/j.drugpo.2015.01.010

45. Taylor, S. (2008). Outside the Outsiders: Media Representations of Drug Use. Probation Journal, 55, 369-387. http://dx.doi.org/10.1177/0264550508096493

46. Törrönen, J. (2004). Finnish Newspapers' Positions on Drug Policy between 1993 and 2000. Contemporary Drug Problems, 31, 59-88.

47. UNODC (2011). World Drug Report 2011. New York: United Nations. https://www.unodc.org/documents/data-and-analysis/WDR2011/World_Drug_Report_2011_ebook.pdf

48. UNODC (2013). World Drug Report 2013. New York: United Nations. http://www.unodc.org/unodc/secured/wdr/wdr2013/World_Drug_Report_2013.pdf

49. UNODC (2014). World Drug Report 2014. New York: United Nations. http://www.unodc.org/documents/wdr2014/World_Drug_Report_2014_web.pdf

50. Watts, R. (2003). "Headlining Heroin": Policy Change and Reporting the Heroin Problem. Media International Australia, 108, 67-68.

Chapter 14

DEMOCRACY, CITIZENSHIP AND LOCAL PRESS: THE CASE OF THE USA "LOCAL PRESS IN BOULDER"

Fatma Gürses

Department of Journalism, University of Kastamonu, Kastamonu, Turkey

ABSTRACT

Nowadays, democracy discussions including a variety of different approaches are made due to the impact of globalization. In this respect, local press comes to the fore as a significant element in the development of participatory citizenship and democracy values from the periphery to the center in a way to reflect differences. This research aims at examining the relationship amongst democracy, citizenship and local press using the local media Boulder, a city in Colorado state of the USA, as a case study. The study is composed of two parts. In the first part, we are going to discuss theoretical frameworks that will help us to better understand the concept of democracy and citizenship, the impact and importance of participatory citizenship on democracy and democratization. The second part includes the historical development of Boulder city and Colorado state. Their sociological and economic features in order to understand the local background of the geography in which the newspaper we examine in our case study are located. The significance of local media and press in Boulder for the state in general and its historical development are analyzed also including examples including the flow of information rendering the participation of citizens possible. In this respect, the importance of local press for the participation of citizens and its impact on democratization are examined.

INTRODUCTION

Democracy has operated throughout history via direct democracy in the Ancient Greece as citizens' governing themselves or representative democracy with the advent of nation-states via citizens' being governed by elected representatives.

Nation-state has claimed that citizens bound through the citizenship status under the roof of a nation are free through representative democracy.

Until the First World War, nation was considered as a tool to protect what is really human in people, i.e. their autonomy represented by "equality and freedom" values. Democracy of this time defends freedom more than equality, contrary to today's democracies. With the advent of the industrial society, although this model amends, its very nature remains unchanged. It indeed takes the most mature form it has ever expressed itself through industrial democracy and welfare state. This social model resulted in the "West"[1] to enjoy inner development and hegemony over the world for centuries (Touraine, 2005: 34-38) . According to Huntington, (1996) global democratization has historically developed in "three waves." The first, long wave (1828-1926) corresponds to Britain, France and the USA's taking basic rights and freedoms under constitutional guarantee via general and equal right to vote; the second (1943-1962) to Germany, India, Israel and Japan's adopting democracy, while the third wave to Greece, Portugal and Spain as well as Latin American countries as Mexico, Chile and some old Eastern Bloc countries' adopting democracy (as cited Gürcüoğlu, 2007: 30). The thesis of Huntington indicates that democracy advanced through these three waves with the advent of nation-states. In this respect, nation-state has used democracy as a means to unite its citizens around common values within the liberal system.

The fact that liberal democracy is established on "common principles and values" is based on the assumption that a pluralist society is found by citizens. Liberal democracy assumes the existence of citizens enjoying certain rights and liberties as subjects of social relations. The concept of citizenship melting down individual differences and thusly creating certain "sameness" normalizes the contradictions of liberal democracy and contributes to both individualization of social relations and their integration through the category of citizenship. Nation pointing to homogeneity ignores demands of the individual struggling to form its own identity within the existing diversity. This results in a legitimacy crisis in the liberal democracy implemented by the nation-state. The main reason for this legitimacy crisis is that the concept citizen based on "sameness" excludes difference(Keyman, 1997:291) Nevertheless, although nation-state attempts to overcome this crisis via democracy, citizens have developed dynamics to limit the sphere belonging to the state.

Hence, modern democracy is born out of individual's demand for freedom acting as an economic agent in the society and the power to assure freedom of humans. Again a second intellectual tradition narrowed the scope of state intervention via citizens' active participation in public affairs without suggesting any limitations to state power (Schnapper, 1995: 101) . The status of citizens in liberal approach is determined according to subjective rights towards the state and other citizens. Subjective rights are negative rights of right holders enhancing the right to choose freely from outside pressure. Political rights provide citizens of the state to realize their special interests via voting. All citizens as citizens of the state can thus monitor whether state administration abides by social interests. Disintegration between state mechanism and the society cannot be overcome according to liberal approach, but it can be resolved through a democratic process (Habermas, 2005: 152-159) . In this context, liberal democracy is regarded as a conciliative attempt. Normative gaps in the establishment of a balance between power and interest shall be covered by the concept of law state.

Limiting democracy through state might transform it. This is an element complicating the applicability of democracy which requires a pluralist understanding. The concept of "we" established by the nation-state via the bond of citizenship provides the basis for belonging to a nation and excludes the ones outside us." When we define "us" and "others" not ideologically[2] but anthropologically based on cultural data, "others" become objects of knowledge, not political rivals for "us." In that case, the conflict between identity and difference might be overcome. According to liberal approach, the function of democratic process is to program the state according to the interests of the society. The basic commitment of a liberal democracy is the freedom and equality of its citizens as individuals. Liberal democracy was partially developed as a reaction to feudalism that defines political rights and economic opportunities of individuals based on the group they pertain to(Kymlicka, 1998: 71) Therefore, individual is defined as citizens of the state having equal rights with others not based on the group or segment s/he pertains to.

Hence, three necessary conditions of every democracy are as follows: restriction of power, representation of political governors and citizenship (Touraine, 2005: 333) . Citizenship as a political status and equality of citizens require a democratic administration (Heater, 2007: 208-212)Citizenship has always been considered as an indicator of elitism in almost all phases of history. Rousseau, one of the Enlightenment thinkers, emphasizes that citizens shall be more or less close to one another in terms of knowledge and welfare for the democracy to operate healthily. If some are very knowledgeable and others are completely ignorant, if some are rich enough to buy many citizens and others are poor enough to sell themselves, which democracy cannot function in a healthy manner (Akşin, 1996: 27) . Hence, democratic society includes balance in income distribution and relations between individuals and the society; the socialization of a citizen is inescapably related to democratic socialization and the role of citizenship.

According to an interactive structural perspective for a democratic society, the role of a citizen legally defined so as to include equality based on certain minimum standards is envisaged. Contrary to participatory democracy, representative democracy defines the "good citizen" within the scope of regional, socio-economic and ethnic differences. In line with the interactive perspective, citizenship is not rigidly defined and structured but it is rather non-formal, developed in an interpersonal context based on subjective choices and voluntarism (Iclihov, 1990: 12-13). In other words, a citizenship definition including democratic dynamics within the perspective of participatory citizenship is envisaged.

The critics towards this approach are based on the fact that although the individual has certain gain through basic rights and citizenship consciousness with the phenomenon of globalization, it does not have much chance to implement these rights practically within daily life. Especially nation-states witness important contradictions and complications in this matter. It is indeed difficult and prone to conflicts and challenges to both abide by the changes and conditions imposed by IMF, World Bank and the global capital and sustain social integrity, solidarity and institutions required by nation-states (Gürcüoğlu, 2007: 25) . In this respect, press is an important feature that has enhanced the participation of citizens and the functionality of democracy since the foundation of the nation-states. Therefore, local press is the unique instrument enhancing these democratic values to expand from periphery to the center. Relationship between local press and democracy remains its significance despite all adverse dynamics of globalization.

Within the scope of the above perspective, this study aims at examining the experience of the creation of citizens in the participatory democracy via local press with respect to the historical development of local press in Boulder city of Colorado, USA. The main purpose of the research is to examine the importance of local press in the foundation and advance of democratic values based on the case study in Boulder. Our research is composed of two parts. Firstly, we explained the relationship between democracy and citizenship as well as local administration and local press. Secondly, historical development, sociological, economic features, the foundation of local media and press, their importance for the estate and the information flow enhancing the participation of citizens are examined via a historical development line of Boulder city, Colorado. In this respect, the role of local press in the participation of citizens and democratization is evaluated. The study is important in the sense that it is the first investigation at local level on the democratic struggle in the USA being, in contrast to Europe witnessing the birth of nation-states, a newly founded country based on multi-culturalism. Hence, it aspires to be a model for other similar studies.

THE RELATIONSHIP BETWEEN DEMOCRACY, CITIZENSHIP AND LOCAL PRESS: FROM PERIPHERY TO CENTER

The thought that democracy will enhance a wider range of freedom and welfare, gave way to the concept of "participatory citizenship" including arguments going beyond the right to vote, a basic democratic right of citizens. Participatory citizenship is rendered possible through the political socialization of citizens[3]. Political socialization is based on strengthening democracy in the orientation of citizens. Therefore, it goes hand in hand with democracy, democratic citizenship and democratic participation of citizens to administration (Iclihov, 1990: 1) . Hence, political socialization is established and developed via information gathered at schools, in the family and via communication tools.

Many studies reveal the fact that what is learned in the family and ideological identity of the family have important roles in the ideological harmonization of children. This model ignores identity formations or state that they are unrealistic defending that children's interest in news, their discussions with peers and family members were important cognitive functions in the interpersonal process. Schools are other important factors in such stimulations. Schools are indeed unique spaces where the state can incessantly convey its political message overcoming cultural and socio-economic obstacles. Schools enhance a level of social interaction unparalleled to that of home (Kiousis & McDevitt, 2008: 483) . Another factor as important as family and school in political socialization is information enhanced by mass communication channels. Macro and micro organization of the state has a role in this information type. Information flow enhanced by local administrations, as micro-level institutions, to mass communication tools provides the participation of citizens as knowing subjects.

Hence, the participation of citizens, the principle of pluralism and responsibility to be accountable to electors are minimum requirements of democratic local administrations. Participation of citizens to local administrations enhances problems to be more healthily determined and solutions to be more effective and consistent. Democracy, in today's world, is not only representative but includes the participation of citizens to solution processes regarding their issues. In this respect, democracy envisages local communities' freely governing themselves in issues closely related to themselves via democratic means and methods. Therefore, the functionality and sustainability of democracy is possible through wider participation of people. The modern management understanding envisages people's participation in the decision-making procedures regarding streets, parks, squares, infrastructure, cultural and social life, technology, economy and history of a city. The identity of a city is further developed, sustained and settled through technological, economic, social structure and activities, as well as the democratic culture of citizens. Democratic processes play a significant role in the formation of economic, political, social and cultural spheres (Gürcüoğlu, 2007: 44-46) . Hence, the relationship between local administrations and the local press is important in the functionality of these democratic processes.

There are various approaches in journalism with respect to press' freedom and transfer of information to citizens. Citizenship journalism[4], the significance of alternative press and local press are among these issues. "Alternative Media Theory" being a part of these discussions is based on certain common grounds at various levels between wider national and social movements in global arena and small groups in micro and macro conjectures. This approach orients towards alternative media movements at macro levels. Traditionally, alternative media theories are classified in two groups. The first group defines alternative media in macro social perspective and aims at struggling with mainstream media in hearts and minds of citizens. It adopts a counter-hegemonic approach in social project. Alternative media sets targets for itself via small groups and communities and adopts certain practices accordingly. It has a role in the representation of women, workers and young people. The second type of theories examines impacts of alternative media broadcasting in daily life(Fontes, 2010:382) . Local and alternative media acting as areas to enhance the participation of wider and more variable people provides participatory democracy to develop.

Alternative press was born in the USA at the beginning of 1960s[5]. Hippi groups and journalists against Vietnam War started to publish cheap newspapers with different contends and styles at the end of 1960s and beginning of 70s in the USA. These newspaper as alternative means against traditional commercial journalism had a local impact. They had similar characteristics to national press until the mid-70s. In 1980s, titles and circulation gained significance as main income channels (Franklin & Murphy, 1991: 25, 84-85) . In fact, this was not limited to alternative press. Generally, the main income of the press in the USA in 1970s was advertisements. As to local media, it was basically local companies (Sim, 1969: 50) . Ironically, local press employees and newspapers are similarly more intertwined with local business circles nowadays. In times of internet, news and editorial models have changed[6] (Anderson, 2013: 166) . This created local media institutions having direct ties with the market. In other words, in terms of Serge Halimi, the follower of Noam Chomsky in France, "market journalism"[7] is highly common.

We might mention two incompatible opinions regarding local press. The first claims that local press has come to be related to wider investment and thusly national press chains within the scope of monopolization and that it became a part of this chain in local level. Second is related to the change in local press with regard to new technologies (Franklin & Murphy, 1991: 21) . Another problem with respect to local journalism practices unique to the USA is that laws change from one state to another. A situation regarded to violate "the confidentiality" of citizens in a state can be considered as legal in yet another state. It is the same with respect to categories as liars, gamblers etc. Hence, different decisions can be taken in similar cases. In that case, the case is appealed to a higher court. For instance, in a similar case in the USA, a decision was taken in a lawsuit claiming that newspapers do not violate private life as citizens are not public or official figures. In that case, questions as, "Who is a public figure," "Who is an official figure," "Is it possible to separate them from private life" come to mind (Berry, 1976: 21-22) . Thus, such different applications affect local and national publishing policies of newspapers.

The news includes transfer of an event within an ideological process and situation. Western countries and the USA more easily acquire popular images when compared to East. Citizens of countries like India, Brazil etc. cannot easily travel to West, for instance. These countries acquire news concerning European Union, legal ameliorations, US defense politics and the World Bank via "Western" mass communication channels that do not belong to them (Stanton, 2007: 32) . Another example claiming that the news is ideologically constituted is that the news itself is a fiction-imagination. For instance, terrorist attacks in North America, Indonesia or Spain, earthquake in Japan, flood in South America are recreated, "fictionalized" through terms of local actors from the other edge of the world. For CNN, Israel-Lebanon War in the Middle East can be a "fiction," but this event is "painful" for a US citizen living there (Stanton, 2007: 2-3) . That's why local elements of news-making are important in the expansion of democratic values from the periphery to the center.

One of the main elements and perhaps the most important one in the creation of a democratic culture is freedom of expression and press. In places where the citizens gradually become desperate, timid and ignorant against political power, the government somehow ignores this to sustain its political power, the dependency/in- dependency of the media, one way or another benefiting from this government, becomes problematic, democratization and the culture of democracy is complicated; democratic sustainability is either retarded or deliberately halted. Citizens in democratic societies have two information sources. First are information and documents pertaining to administration and the second are information and documents attained through mass communication channels (Gürcüoğlu, 2007: 126-127) . The second is only attainable through freedom of expression and press. Therefore, freedom of expression and press are indispensable elements of democracy and participatory citizenship.

Local press contributes to the propagation and settlement of the culture of democracy in local level. According to Vural (1999), local newspapers being the oldest and most significant tools of local communication are key tools for mass communication. These newspapers sometimes regulate the daily lives of people and therefore published to inform the public, but they also have the power to influence opinion and mold public opinion. They have a more important position than other mass communication channels with their power to regulate local people. In an ever shrinking world where borders are being eliminated, society and individuals within that society, on one hand, experience the feeling of being a citizen of the world through news coming from around the world via hundreds of channels and on the other hand, approaches to its close surrounding, culture and community via sentiments of devotion and solidarity. At this point, local press becomes the most important reference guide of individuals. Press is the biggest socialization tool for the local culture. Local newspapers are the most significant utilization, sharing and communication tools in the social life of the area (as cited Gürcüoğlu, 2007: 16).

A strong democracy can only be attained through efficient and participatory citizens who are not mere spectators, but consider politics as a way of life. Local press contributes propagation and settlement of democracy culture in local level. Local people are in need of information concerning what is going on in the town, social, political, cultural and economic developments. People are more concerned about developments in their close surroundings rather than events at the national level. The biggest task of local press is to adequately and sufficiently inform people concerning the problems in the city and enhancing the follow-up of initiatives taken to solve these problems(Atabek, n.d.: 47-49) . Therefore, it provides the necessary democratic environment for participatory citizenship.

Every political system creates political ideas appropriate to the membership of their young citizens. Therefore, training of citizens has been applied since the ancient times. Political education and learning are still central today. Today in US culture, children meet with the flag of their country at early ages. Patriarchal myths regarding the founders of the USA shape the "American lifestyle." Similar to tribal bonds, large communities encourage young members to know these myths; interiorize them via wide range of applications and a political harmony is thus attempted to be created. In this respect, citizenship attempted to be shaped in the USA is based on the perspective to sustain the functionality and sustainability of the state through a "homogeneous" society. Although this is a pessimistic outlook, it is witnessed that such an approach is adopted in cities and campuses of the USA. The first indicator of a certain alienation from this homogeneity is uprisings stemming from the distress caused by goods produced by the system. Second is the rejecting stance of the black population. Uprisings sustained by black Americans have had wide support. Political scientists orient towards groups at a larger dimension, including Mexican-Americans, indigenous people, and poor whites (Greenberg, 1970: 8-12) . Hence, local press is an important factor in the US having a wide geographical territory in the advance of democratic values from the periphery to the center.

LOCAL PRESS IN COLORADO AND BOULDER

Up to now, we tried to explain concepts as democracy, citizenship and local press in general. In the following part of our study, we will attempt to examine historical foundation and development of Boulder local press, alongside with its relations to other local elements in the country. In this respect, we are going to dwell on the sociological, historical and economic structure of the local region. Then, we are going to take a look at the foundation of the local press, its influence and status in the region the means it adopts to make use of democratic elements.

Short History of Colorado State

Colorado located at the mid-west of the USA corresponds to the geographical area including the highest peak of the country Elbert Mountain. The state whose capital is Denver has a very cold climate. It is named after Colorado River, meaning red in Spanish. It is also known as the centennial state. Colorado having a wide indigenous population where the first settlements date back to 13 thousand years is a state uniting different cultures. The first settlers were Apaches from the southwest of the state, Comanches from the northern Wyoming, Araphoe and Cheyennes from Minnesota having similar languages, indegenios tribes coming from Utes on the west living in Utah(Noel, 2011: 14, 21-24) . Colorado having hosted different cultures includes Hispanics composed of Spanish people and Mexicans and Italians and the French to be called European-American. Spanish people came before English speaking communities from New Mexico and Rio Grande and settled in South Colorado, especially in San Luis Valley close to Santa Fe. It is a difficult region with a cold temperature and high altitude. A short while later, Anglo-Saxons settled in central and northern regions. Railway installed in 1870s changed the life in the valley and a new town called Alamosa was established. Colorado increased its population with the discovery of valuable mines. English speaking community, though coming later, belittled significant contributions and influence of Mexican Americans to the history of the state due to the political power they attained. However, Mexican Americans giving their name to the state had undeniable amount of contribution to the country. Many Mexican towns indeed disappeared by now. The Spanish names of these towns were changed to English. Until European-American settler arrived in 1850, civil war between Spanish people coming from New Mexico and indigenous people continued for 230 years (Noel, 2011: 67-77). Colorado received official state status in 1876 (Runnells, 1976: 6) .

Colorado whose population reached 1.670,000 in 1957 with the economic advance through agriculture, cattle and ovine farming has attracted the attention of thousands of tourists with its natural beauties, mountains and lakes. Gold and silver are main minerals, while lead and zinc are other significant minerals. The state having a coal yard is the most significant region producing molybdenum. It also has uranium and wide oil reserves. Although it is a relatively small state, it has six state universities and colleges. Moreover, the state also has United State Air Force Academia and other higher education institutions (Kobre, 1959: 248) .

Life has changed in Colorado after the Second World War with television, wide highways enhancing transportation with other states, water projects, advancing economy and air transportation. Denver started to accommodate federal agents in Denver Federal Center and the city was called, "the second national capital." (Ubbelohde, Benson, & Smith, 2006: 333-334) . The capital of Colorado Denver had 35 thousand of population in 1880, while today this number reached 133 thousand at the beginning of the century and 415 thousand later on. It almost doubled its population in 1958 to 700 thousand as a metropolitan city. Denver is the business and financial center of Rocky Mountain region. Apart from being a cultural center, it is an important city also in education. It has important airports, railroads and highways for the USA and the world (Kobre, 1959: 248) . Boulder-Denver Turnpike was opened in 1952 between Boulder and Denver. 13,774 people passed through this highway until 1966 by paying 25 cents. It has the Office of National Standards (now called the Institute of National Standard and Technology) and National Air Research Center. The saying "workers in Colorado are 'happy campers' imply that people in the region do not have problems in finding jobs and they are economically comfortable. Nevertheless, according to latest reports (2003), 17% of workers are not "satisfied with their job." This ratio is 22% in general in the USA. Workers are paid very poorly and have stated their discomfort due to poor salaries and not being able to work in good and desirable positions (Ubbelohde et al., 2006: 333-348, 400-401) . Colorado, preserving its natural beauty at Central America, has witnessed lively journalism activities throughout its history.

Boulder: Athens of Colorado State

Boulder, being one of the most developed cities of the state, is located around 1 mile away from Arkansas River at the 40th latitude and 38th longitude (Abbott, Leonard, & McComb, 1994: 477) . Being at the hillsides of Rocky mountains having 1655 meters of altitude, Boulder is situated at the northwest of Colorado's capital Denver, 40 km away from it. Hills known as Flatiron are symbols of the city. Boulder Creek (river) flows at the west of the city. Boulder is the best business and career center of the USA. It has bicycle paths, pedestrian paths and connections. It mostly has liberal democratic electors. It is the most crowded eleventh city of Colorado State (Boulder, Colorado, USA, n.d.) . Accommodating many companies, Boulder is connected to other parts of the state through railroads and highways. Boulder is governed by a city council and nine council members are elected amongst well-educated residents (Runnells, 1976: 31) .

Boulder was founded at the end of the 19th century. 15 miners from Nebrasca camped in Boulder Canyon known as "Red Rocks." The leader of the group Captain Thomas Aikins agreed with Niwot Arapahoes and settled down in the region (Runnells, 1976: 5, Ubbelohde, Benson, & Smith, 2006: 60) . The discovery of gold in 15 January 1859 caused new settlements to emerge in the region. Areas at the north of Boulder River (creek) were separated into 56 shareholder in 10 February 1859 for 1000 dollars each and 4044 dollars in total (Center for Colorado & The West, n.d.) . Gregory Gulch[8] organized the first mining camp in 8 June 1859 (Abbott et al., 1994: 56). The first school of Colorado was established in 1860 and the first church in 1872, both in Boulder. The first high school of Colorado started giving education in 1876 again in Boulder. Commercial centers were established in 1877 and a university was established under the initiative of residents (Runnells, 1976: 5) .

Education is important for Boulder. In 7 November 1861, the mayor William Gilpin officially allowed the establishment of the first big university of the state, namely the University of Colorado Boulder[9]. Nevertheless, it was only 15 years later due to the adverse conditions caused by the war that the old building now located in Colorado University campus was established in 20 September 1857. Within the same year, it became the first higher education institution of the state. The foundation of the university was completed in 1876 through a budget of 15,000 dollars from the state parliament with the efforts of the mayor Charles F. Holly and 45,000 dollars allocated from the residents. It was officially opened in 2 September 1877 with a faculty composed of 44 students under the administration of Dr. Joseph A. Sewall. With the participation of 12 new employees to the staff in 1878, the university started to give regular education (Runnells, 1976: 67-68; Center for Colorado & The

West, n.d.) . At the end of the 19th century, Boulder became self-sufficient in education (Pettem, 2010: 39) . Nowadays, The University of Colorado Boulder is a public university with 46,000 students, while the private Naropa University adopting Buddhist principles has 1000 students. Despite having started to give education as a small university, the University of Colorado rapidly developed. Boulder County News published an advertisement of the university under the title, "coming together in a nice society, nice houses and a nice university." Denver Republican, on the other hand, published an advertisement of the university in 1882 under the title, "almost a Western University with few awards and a great assertion" (Abbott et al., 1994: 126) . Cincinati (Ohio), Lexington (Kentucky), Nashville (Tennessee), Ann Arbor (Michigan), Faribault (Minnesota), Berkeley (California) are the biggest cities of their respective states. In 1880s, Boulder was also known to be "the Athens of the Western World" as the most developed city of its state (Pettem, 2010: 41) .

With the advance of railroad transfer in Boulder in 1873, the number of settler substantially grew. The population grew from 300 to 3000 within a couple of years. Many buildings were established via briquettes made up of wood and slime. In 1871 the first bank, in 1874 the first national bank and again in 1874 the first water system was established. Texas-Colorado Chautauqua[10] was founded in 1898 to serve as the recreation center for Texas residents. Smallpox epidemic in 1880 was the biggest disaster of the city, while a great flood occurred in 1894. Many people in 1893 lost their jobs due to the economic crisis. Boulder people with a great cultural and historical heritage having first established their library in 1906 were involved in commerce and farming. The population was six thousand in 1900 and 11 thousand in 1910. The real population boom occurred after the Second World War. The timberland including Araphoe glaciers was purchased in 1929. Therefore, Boulder became the second city of the USA deriving water from glaciers. A program including the support of the federal government was implemented in 1930s during the times of economic tremor (Runnells, 1976: 6-7) . The foundation of the highway connected Denver to Boulder in 1950 and its launch in 1952 are among the historical events of the advance of Colorado (Abbott et al., 1994: 334) . Until 1966, daily 13774 people used this railroad paying 25 cents (Ubbelohde et al., 2006: 348) . It became a settlement for hippies in 1960s. At the beginning, the democrats had the highest votes in Colorado (Abbott et al., 1994, 76, 334) . Nowadays, on the other hand, it is one of the most well-known liberal democrat cities. In April 2012 elections, 69.5% voted for democrats, 28% for republicans, 1.5% for liberal party (The Denver Post, 2012 Elections Colorado, n.d.) .

Local Press in Boulder

Boulder is the media center of the northern Colorado. Boulder whose population increased and economy boosted with the incoming students has significant functions in the incorporation of citizens in local administration via local press. The local press has broadcasts aiming at informing residents so as to contribute to the participation of Boulder citizens in decision regarding problems of the city.

Denver Post a weekly newspaper published in Denver is one of the newspapers making local news. Boulder Magazine published three times a year was founded in 1978. Boulder having TV stations in the market has many radio receivers in Forth Collins and Denver. It is the center of Soldier of Fortune magazine and Paladin Press found in 1970. Apart from The Daily Camera, Boulder County Business Report published two times a month, Boulder County Kids and 50 plus Marketplace News are among the local publications of Boulder (City- Data.com: Cities of the United Satates: The West, n.d.) . Rocky Mountain News still being the most important newspaper of Colorado is amongst the mostly sold newspapers of Boulder. The competition with Denver Post was finalized in 2001 with a Joint Operating Agreement (JOA). In 26 February 2005, the journalist Joyn Temple used to say, "Two offices are still in fight as if their lives depended on it" (Vaughn, 2008: 455) .

Local press in Colorado state (see. Appendix 1) was born in the second half of the 19th century coinciding with the foundation of the state. The oldest newspaper of the state Rocky Mountain News was founded by William Byers in April 1859. The Colorado Daily published five times a week was first founded in 1892 for CU-Boulder as a campus newspaper (Colorado Online Historical Newspapers, n.d.; Boulder County Colorado GenWeb, 2011). Similarly, local press in Boulder coincides with the foundation of the city. The Daily Camera is the mostly read local newspaper.

The Daily Camera

Daily Camera was launched in 17 March 1891 as "one of the unique newspapers of the USA if not of the world." In April 1892, Bert Ball sold the newspaper to Boulder Publishing Co. established by L. C. Paddock and Valantine Butsch (Center for Colorado & The West, n.d.) (see Figure 1). From 1892 to 1940, L.C. Paddock was the editor of Boulder Camera (see Figure 2)[11]. Having a highly expensive infrastructure with high-speed stamping and linotype machines, Camera attracted attention in Colorado press with its advertisements and sales success. Revolutionary printing inspired all newspapers in Denver (Ubbelohde et al., 2006: 237) . L.C. Paddock started to use the slogan “science is the lamp of life” for its newspaper (Pettem, 2010: 40) .

The newspaper having at first been published weekly started to be printed nightly in 1893. Paddock became a name in not only Boulder but the state and overall journalism world. The newspaper was sold in 1 July 1931 to a printer from Kansas Oscar Stauffer. However, this printer failed to become successful and Paddock returned to the newspaper and continued its publishing life in 1931 under the name Boulder Daily Camera. When Paddock was deceased in 10 July 1940, his son Alva Adams Paddock started his career in Camera that would last for 52 years (Center for Colorado & The West, n.d.) .

After the Second World War, Camera was awarded with one of the most prestigious awards of the USA, F.W. Ayer typographical printing in 13 March 1947 among around 10.000 US newspapers. When Alva Adams Paddock deceased in 7 November 1961, his wife Annie Laurie became the president of Boulder Press and managed the newspaper from February 1960 to June 1992 for 32 years. Ridder Publishing became one of the partners of the newspaper in April 1969 and Lu Monroe and Norm Christiansen became members of the executive board. In 1970s, Camera started its career under an a lot less known name, Daily Camera Extra. Monroe retired in Marc1970 and Christiansen in 1976. The successful editor J. Edward Murray 1976-1982, Janet Chusmir 1982- 1987, John L. Dotson, Jr. 1987-1992 and Harold Higgins 1992-1995, Barrie Hartman 1995-2007, Scripps (1997- 2009) were the following editors of the newspaper (Center for Colorado & The West, n.d.) .

Camera has been prepared in the same building in Pearl Street 11 since its foundation. This building was then renovated into a two-floored house (see Figure 3). A new publishing room was annexed in 1973. In 2008, a new building was annexed in Walnut Street. The newspaper was moved to 5450 Western Avenue in 20 August 2010 (Snider, 2011) .

News Samples from Boulder Local Press

At the beginning of the 20th century, Colorado residents witnessed historical journalism practices of American press history through information from the local press. These years coincided with the peak of tabloid newspapers. Important events were conveyed to people through attractive titles. One of them was on the great influenza epidemic erupted after the First World War (1918). Newspaper frequently published news about this deadly disease known as Spanish flu spread to Boulder, Colorado Springs, Pueblo and Denver. Rocky Mountain News used intriguing titles as “more fruits and vegetables,” “Elect republicans, eradicate the fear of flu.” Schools and churched were closed to public and various measures were taken. From September 1918 to January 1919, around 8 thousand people lost their lives (Abbott et al., 1994: 268) .

Another event was in the limelight of the local press. Concerning the rise of Bolsheviks to power in Russia and Hungary, Rocky Mountain said, "Bolshevik administration found having involved in the worker strike in Seattle." Thousands of strikes erupted in the state. Many Colorado residents were exhausted and angry. Denver Post, used headlines supporting the federal government as "Bolsheviks and anarchists destroying the state take their lesson." Colorado administrators were targeting people by saying that having red flags meant being communist saying that such demonstrations would not be tolerated for the security of the state. In October 1919, a law was issued with the suggestion of mayor Oliver Shoup to repress anarchism envisaging over 20 years of jail sentence, a series of detentions by General Mitchel Palmer known as "Palmer raids" followed the law.[12]" 4 thousand communists are arrested in 33 cities including 249 activists. Denver city council penalized the freedom of speech. Speeches that might evoke uprisings were penalized. Only 8 activists were arrested before 2 January 1920, while this number substantially increased after the coming into effect of the law. The news covering the events in Denver Catholic Register, Denver Post and Rocky Mountain News were censured. They joined forces with the federal government to break the strikes of politicians and organized radical demonstrations supporting them (Abbott et al., 1994: 268-269) .

Figure 1: From left, Camera staff members Charles Butsch, Fannie Snell and Valentine Butsch stand in front of the newspaper s building around 1892. The name of the

fourth person is not known. The Camera began operations in downtown Boulder on March 17, 1891 (Snider, 2011) .

Figure 2: Camera staff members, including longtime editors A. A. Paddock and L. C. Paddock, stand in front of their downtown building in 1935 (Snider, 2011) .

Figure 3: After years of remodels and additions, the historic building at 11th and Pearl streets was demolished and replaced by this new building with two floors and a basement in 1963. That structure remains as the eastern part of the present Camera headquarters. (Snider, 2011) .

Boulder local press was highly efficient in informing the residents with news also covered by the national press. Events with national repercussions were also covered by the local press, while local news enhances the flow of information from periphery to the center. Global events were included in the agenda of the local press; national political news was presented to citizens with titles suitable to broadcasting policies of the local press.

CONCLUSION

Nowadays, democracy discussions including a variety of different approaches are made due to the impact of globalization. Participatory democracy may be the first of them, though radical democracy seems to be more convenient for the estimates of globalization. In this respect, press created by nation-state ideology is an important element in our times to enhance democracy since the 19thcentury. While the press has been shaped in Europe, the center of nation-state ideology, under the influence of such dynamics, local press has had an important role in the USA having a multi-cultural society being established via different dynamics in settling and sustaining democratic values. Participatory citizenship is one of the basic elements of today's globalization with respect to democracy and democratization. The press needs to have information to enhance citizens' participation in the administration and use of democratic means. National and global presses are not sufficient to bridge this gap. Therefore, information means of local press shall cover this gap and enhance the development of a participatory citizenship and democracy from the periphery to the center.

Boulder local press situated in mid-Colorado state we examined in our study had a role in the establishment of such democratic values. It had a significant role in establishing institutions and system of a newly found country, informing people and enhancing their participation. Local press has had a noteworthy influence in the establishment of a country via then materially non-existent institutions, creating a regime assuring the unity of various nations in this country, integrating them under the roof of a nation-state. Boulder created its own local press to create this multi-cultural structure with its diverse ethnic features, natural beauties and welfare. Examining the impact of local press on the participation of citizens' to decision-making processes via news analyses and spectator analysis in this multi-cultural structure will be complementary to the research. The study envisages being a model for other researches on local press, democracy and citizenship.

APPENDIX 1: THE PUBLICATION IN BOULDER

1) Valmont Bulletin, est. January 1, 1866-September 1868.
2) Boulder Valley News April 3, 1867-September 1868.
3) Boulder County Pioneer February 10-September 14, 1869.
4) Boulder County News October 12, 1869-November 8, 1878.
5) Boulder County News and Courier November 15, 1878-October 26, 1883.
6) Boulder News & Banner Nov. 1883-June 5, 1888.
7) Boulder News June 12, 1888-November 1914. the paper June 1, 1914 and turned it into a morning daily: Boulder Morning News November 10, 1914-February 17, 1916, when it merged with the Herald.
8) Boulder County Bee April to November 1875. It is believed that the Bee was the result of a merger of the Boulder Eagle and Longmont Inter-Ocean, both of which ceased publication in April 1875.
9) Colorado Banner September 30, 1875-September 1883.
10) Boulder Herald February 18, 1880-1916. It was followed shortly by a sister daily:

Boulder Daily Herald April 17, 1880-February 14, 1916.

11) Boulder News-Herald February 18, 1916-February 29, 1932, daily. A weekly News-Herald was also issued. Arthur Parkhurst, known as a crusading editor, brought new life to the News-Herald.
12) Boulder Sentinel 1 July-September 1871. A Longmont Sentinel was published in the same period.

Boulder Sentinel 2 June 1884-November 29, 1890.

13) Boulder Miner 1888-1889. It was absorbed by Boulder Tribune October 18, 1889-September 21, 1921.
14) Boulder Camera September 27, 1890-1891, weekly, Frederick P. Johnson and Bert Ball, founders.

Daily Camera March 17, 1891 to present.

15) Boulder County Miner #2 July 8, 1901-December 30, 1920.

Boulder County Miner & Farmer 1920-June 1949. (In 1940 the Miner & Farmer and the Journal combined their plants but issued separate papers.)

16) Boulder Sentinel #3, April 4-18, 1946, only two issues.
17) Rocky Mountain Eagle September 17, 1873-April 18, 1875.
18) Home Mirror 1880, a literary monthly.

19) Colorado Representative June 10, 1897-December 12, 1903

Boulder Representative (The name was changed back to the original name in 1898.) The Representative es- poused Free Coinage. Donald Oehlerts says it was continued as the Semi-Weekly Times.

20) Boulder Times, 1897-1907. The name was changed to Semi-Weekly Times February 17-September 29, 1903. It continued as Weekly Times or Times or Boulder County Times October 8, 1903-February 14, 1907.

21) Friday Social & Industrial Review 1899, short lived.

22) Labor Leader 1900-1902.

23) Oil News 1901-1902, absorbed into the Camera.

24) Boulder Advertiser 1903-1904.

25) Saturday Truth 1903-1904.

26) Free American September-October 1904.

27) W.C.T.U.Messenger 1905-?,

28) Boulder Citizen May 27-April 4, 1909.

29) Coloradoan 1915-1918, a weekly magazine of comments with an occasional dash of condemnation.

30) Progressive Citizen March 23-April 17, 1917, daily.

31) Rocky Mountain American January 31-July 31, 1925; William Francis, ed. The paper was a voice for the Ku Klux Klan.

32) Boulder Free Press 1931, briefly.

33) Boulder Advertiser 2, April 15, 1932-November 1932.

34) The Remainder 1932.

35) Boulder County Journal September 22, 1932-September 29, 1933.

36) Journal October 3, 1933-April 20, 1944. In 1940, it merged its plant with the Miner & Farmer, but the two papers were issued separately. It was revived as Boulder County Journal May 8, 1947-1952.

37) Wall Paper November 1932-1933.

38) Boulder Star November 24, 1932-January 19, 1934 semi-weekly.

39) Broadcaster 1938-1939.

40) Boulder Mirror October 7, 1942-1944. It was begun as a theatre advertiser, known as the Skipper.

41) Trailerite 1948.

42) Boulder Forum June 23-October 15, 1950, Frank Swerer.

43) Boulder Reporter July 10-November 30, 1952.

44) Lens-Leader May 1954-?, D.H. Loving, founder. Merged into Lafayette Leader.

45) Downtown Shopper 1963-1979, begun as a monthly in 1963 but changed to a weekly about two years later, then to every other week. In 1966 the name was changed to Town & Country, a weekly and discontinued spring 1979.

46) Boulder County Commercial Ledger . The June 11, 1970, issue is listed as Vol. 90 in Colorado Historical Society Records. It hasn't been found in other newspaper lists.

47) Express, 1970, Community Free School; underground press.

48) Boulder County Business Report January 1980 to present. It is a monthly.

49) Boulder County Courant September 24, 1983-?.

50) Boulder Courier 2, May 21, 1987.

51) Boulder Weekly August 1993-to present, "an alternative-style newspaper.

52) University of Colorado Newspapers.

53) Portfolio 1882-1892. The first University of Colorado publication was a four-page, magazine-sized paper issued quarterly.

54) Silver and Gold September 13, 1892-May 2, 1952.

55) Colorado Daily February 5, 1952 to present, though not an official university publication after 1971.

56) Working Press, later Campus Press, 1978-present. When the Press foundered in 1993, the Journalism and Mass Communications School suggested a joint venture with the Colorado Daily, with the Campus Press becoming an insert in the Daily.

57) Colorado Daily Sun dates unknown. Inter-Mountain Press said in 1922: Colorado Reporter, a second CU newspaper 1949 (Boulder County Colorado GenWeb, 2011) .

NOTES

[*]https://kastamonu.academia.edu/fatmagürses

[1] Stanton (2007) , in this study regarding the definition of the West attempts to answer the question, "How to be Western" and then poses the question of the journal Economist asking whether Turkey can establish a legal framework paving the way for its EU membership. Another question is, do we need a certain "language" to be Western? This is not the case for French, English, and Italian etc. Is the culture then? "Stanton states that this cannot be the binding

value, neither "economy" nor "democracy" can be this common feature because many other countries are now ruled by democracy. Why cannot we imagine countries like Taiwan, South Korea etc. as a part of the Western world? Our response to this question is "freedom of press." Freedom of press might not be necessary for the democracies of respective countries, but it is indispensable to be "Western." Free press seems to be the only criterion to be "Western." Freedom of press enhanced public discussions and the promoting of thought. Stanton states that countries like Turkey have had many reforms, but public discussions and feedback was missing." (Stanton, 2007: 46-47) .

[2]Ideology is a contradictory term. Herman and Chomsky used this term to understand what is going on in the world. They consider it as a Marxist term. Anti-communist ideology was for instance used by the US media discourse. However, overall media discourse is obviously related to economy.(Muhlmann, 2010) .

[3]In their recent study on determining the agenda in political socialization, Kiousis, McDevitt and Wu (2005) state that political tendencies of adolescents were shaped within ideological devotion and partisan identities, but such factors had less influence on their choices (Kiousis & McDevitt, 2008: 482-483) .

[4]American press has been separating journalism for people and journalism for citizens for the last 20 years. Anglo-American studies are generally on freedom of speech, cultural-political issues and information and communication (Muhlmann, 2010: 6) .

[5]Being a geographically large country changes the structure of news broadcasting in radio, newspapers and press in general. Canada broadcasts to the country in five regions, the USA to four. Canada has strongly used broadcasting system being partially public in the formation of a nation(Aldridge, 2007: 23) .

[6]Nowadays, a higher organization established through the union of differ rent organizations and a news media come to forefront. Complex institutions like World Trade Center and International Monetary Fund have adopted to this model (Stanton, 2007: 11, 179-189) .

[7]Serge Halimi from France being a follower of Noam Chomsky defined in 1997 the columnists of Le Monde Diplomatique as "the new watchdogs" of the new order. He states that they economically and politically act as the watchdogs of the system. He defines the journalism of Bob Woodward and Carl Bernstein in Watergate scandal as "watchdog journalism" (Muhlmann, 2010: 13) .

[8]John Gregory was the first to discover gold in Colorado known as "Greogory's Gulch" (Western Mining History, n.d.) .

[9]University of Coloroda Boulder ranked 97 in 2013-2014. (The World University Rankings, n.d.) .

[10]Chautauqua was a program as an adult education movement in the USA becoming popular especially at the end of 19th century and beginning of 20th century. Named after Chautauqua Desert, the program has raised important musicians and speakers. Chautauqua has become a successful education movement. Chautauquas, had religious functions in many states giving summer school training. At the end of 1919 it also gave training on political issues of the time as the rights of child workers and women movement. Chautauqua education movement was especially efficient in rural parts of the state. With the advance and development of mass communication channels, its impact was gradually declined (Chautauqua Trail, n.d.) .

[11]The founder of Daily Camera Lucius Carver Paddock (10 August 1859-31 July 1940) was the editor-in-chief of the newspaper for the last 49 years. His son Alva Adams Paddock (1867-1961) worked in the same post office for 21 years (Runnells, 1976: 5; Lucius Carver Paddock, n.d.) .

[12]Palmer raids is a term coined to describe the detentions of radical leftist militant at the end of 1919 and the beginning of 1920. Detentions under the rule of General Mitchell Palmer caused great reactions and revolts (Spartacus Educational, n.d.) .

REFERENCES

1. Abbott, C., Leonard, S. J., & McComb, D. (1994). Colorado, A History Of The Centennial State. Niwot, CO: University Press of Colorado.
2. Akşin, S. (1996). Uluslaşma Sürecinde Devlet ve Yurttaş (State and Citizens in the Nation-Building Process). In Çileli, M., (Ed.), Yurttaşlık ve Eğitim Türk Eğitim Derneği XX. Eğitim Toplantısı (Citizenship and Education Turkish Education Association XX. Education Meeting) (pp. 23-45). Ankara: Türk Eğitim Derneği Eğitim Dizisi.
3. Aldridge, M. (2007). Understanding the Local Media. Maidenhead: Open University Press.
4. Anderson, C. W. (2013). Rebuliding the News: Metroplolitan Journalism in the Digital Age. Philadelphia: Temple University Press.
5. Atabek, N. (n.d.). Yerel Basın ve Yerel Demokrasi (Local News and Local Democracy). Journal of the Faculty of Communication, 47-54.http://www.journals.istanbul.edu.tr/iuifd/article/viewfile/1019012673/1019011901
6. Berry, T. E. (1976). Journalism in America: An Introduction to the News Media. New York, NY: Hastings House.

7. Boulder, Colorado, USA. (n.d.). About Boulder.http://www.bouldercoloradousa.com/about-boulder/
8. Boulder County Colorado GenWeb. (2011). Boulder Newspapers: Dates, Founders, Publishers and Editors.http://theusgenweb.org/co/boulder/newsclips/boulder_newspapers.html
9. Center for Colorado & The West. (n.d.). Boulder. https://coloradowest.auraria.edu/content/boulder
10. Chautauqua Trail. (n.d.). A North American Cultural Renaissance.http://www.chautauquatrail.com/faqs#Frequently-Asked-Questions
11. City-Data.com: Cities of the United States: The West (n.d.). Boulder: Communications.http://www.city-data.com/us-cities/The-West/Boulder-Communications.html
12. Fontes, C. (2010). The Global Turn of the Alternative Media Movement. In K. Howley (Ed.), Understanding Community Media (pp. 381-390). Thousand Oaks, CA: SAGE Publication. http://dx.doi.org/10.4135/9781452275017.n33
13. Franklin, B., & Murphy, D. (1991). What News? The Market, Politics, and the Local Press. London, New York: Routledge.
14. Greenberg, E. S. (1970). Consensus and Dissent: Trends in Political Socialization Research. In E. S. Greenberg (Ed.), Political Socialization (pp. 1-16). New York: Atherton Press.
15. Gürcüoğlu, M. F. (2007). Demokratikleşme Sürecine Katkı Sağlayan Bir Araç olarak Yerel Basının, Yerel Yönetim Meclisleri Bağlamında Kamuoyunu Bilgilendirme Düzeyi: Eskişehir SAkarya ve İstikbal Gazeteleri Örnekleminde (Powered Contribution to the Democratization Process as a Tool Local Newspapers, Public Disclosure Level of Local Government Councils Context: The Future of Newspapers in Eskişehir Sakarya and Samples). Ph.D. Thesis, Eskişehir: Anadolu University, Institute of Social Sciences.
16. Habermas, J. (2005). Öteki Olmak, "Öteki"yle Yaşamak (Being the Other "Other" Is Meant to Live). İ. Aka, Trans., İstanbul: Yapı Kredi Press.
17. Heater, D. (2007). Yurttaşlığın Kısa Tarihi (A Brief History of Citizenship). M. Delikara, Trans., Ankara: İmge Press.
18. Iclihov, O. (1990). Dimensions and Role Patterns of Citizenship in Democracy. In O. Ichilov (Ed.), Political Socialization Citizenship Education and Democracy (pp. 11-25). New York: Teacher College Press.
19. Keyman, F. (1997). Globalleşme ve Türkiye: Radikal Demokrasi Olasılığı (Globalization and Turkey: Radical Democracy Chance). In N.

Bilgin (Ed.), Cumhuriyet, Demokrasi ve Kimlik (Republic, Democracy and Identity) (pp. 281-294). İstanbul: Bağlam Press.

20. Kiousis, S., & McDevitt, M. (2008). Agenda Setting in Civic Development Effects of Curricula and Issue Importance on Youth Voter Turnout. Communication Research, 35, 481-502. http://crx.sagepub.com http://dx.doi.org/10.1177/0093650208315978
21. Kobre, S. (1959). Modern American Journalism. Ph.D. Thesis, Tallahassee, FL: Tallahassee Institute of Media Research, Florida State University.http://hdl.handle.net/2027/uc1.b3555096
22. Kymlicka, W. (1998). Çokkültürlü Yurttaşlık (Multicultural Citizenship). A. Yılmaz, Trans., İstanbul: Ayrıntı Press.
23. Lucius Carver Paddock (n.d.). http://www.findagrave.com/cgi-bin/fg.cgi?page=gr&GRid=11111050
24. Muhlmann, G. (2010). Journalism for Democracy. J. Birrell, Trans., Malden, MA: Cambridge.
25. Noel, T. J. (2011). Colorado: The Highest State. Boulder, CO: University Press of Colorado.
26. Pettem, S. (2010). A Sense of Time & Place Revisited. Charleston, SC: Charleson History Press.
27. Runnells, D. D. (1976). Boulder: A Sight to Behold: Guidebook: Self Guided Tours of the Historic City, Geology and Scenery, University of Colorado, Plus Short Side Trips to Nearby Areas. Boulder, CO: Estey Printing Co.
28. Schnapper, D. (1995). Yurttaşlar Cemaati, Modern Ulus Fikrine Dair (Citizens Community, on the Modern Nation Intellectual). Ö. Okur, Trans., İstanbul: Kesit Press.
29. Sim, J. C. (1969). The Grass Roots Press: America's Community Newspapers. Ames, IA: Iowa State University Press.
30. Snider, L. (2011). Daily Camera. http://www.dailycamera.com/boulder-county-news/ci_17106735
31. Spartacus Educational (n.d.). The Palmer Raids. http://spartacus-educational.com/USApalmerR.htm
32. Stanton, R. C. (2007). All News Is Local: The Failure of the Media to Reflect World Events in a Globalized Age. Jefferson, NC: McFarland & Co.
33. The Denver Post, 2012 Elections Colorado (n.d.). Boulder County 2012 Elections Results.http://data.denverpost.com/election/results/county/boulder/2012/

34. The World University Rankings (n.d.). University of Colorado Boulder.http://www.timeshighereducation.co.uk/world-university-rankings/2014-15/world-ranking/institution/university-of-colorado-boulder

35. Touraine, A. (2005). Birlikte Yaşayabilecek miyiz (Can We Live Together)? O. Kunal, Trans., İstanbul: Yapı Kredi Press.

36. Ubbelohde, C., Benson, M., & Smith, D. A. (2006). A Colorado History. Portland, OR: West Wind Press.

37. Vaughn, S. (2008). Encyclopedia of American Journalism. New York: Routledge.

38. Western Mining History (n.d.). Central City, Colorado.http://www.westernmininghistory.com/towns/colorado/central-city/

Chapter 15

THE USAGE BEHAVIORS, MOTIVATIONS AND GRATIFICATIONS OF USING USER-GENERATED MEDIA: THE CASE STUDY OF TAIWAN'S YOUTUBE

Tai-Li Wang

The Graduate Institute of Journalism, National Taiwan University, Taiwan

ABSTRACT

Video sharing websites have become an indispensable online service to Internet users. We aim to investigate the relationships between motivations of using video-sharing websites, online reputation management, innovation orientation, and video-sharing website usage behaviors, and how these factors affect gratification obtained from video-sharing website usage. This study employs focus group interviews and online questionnaire surveys. The research findings reveal that the higher the interpersonal media related motivations, such as participating or sharing, the higher the level of involvement of video-sharing website usage behaviors is. However, the mass media related motivations, such as browsing or consuming, are irrelevant to the level of usage involvement. The earlier users adopt video-sharing websites, the higher level of usage involvement is. The more value video-sharing websites' users put for video sites' performance perception, the lower level of usage involvement is; on the contrary, the more value video-sharing websites' users put for impression management, the higher level of usage involvement is. Taken as a whole, the higher level of usage involvement, the higher level of gratifications acquired from using user- generated video-sharing websites is. This paper establishes a comprehensive behavior model of video-sharing websites, which is helpful both for online media research and business practice. It is worthy of noting that the findings are based on survey data from a single country, and may impact this paper's external validity.

INTRODUCTION

On March 11, 2011 an earthquake triggered a massive tsunami in Japan. The resulting natural disturbances were videotaped by a number of affected residents. Many of these homemade video clips were uploaded to YouTube by Taiwanese netizens to express concern for Japan. Not only did these videos spread rapidly on the Internet, they also caught the attention of the mainstream media. One particular example is "God Bless Japan" (2011). In this video, a netizen inspired others to write the words "God Bless Japan" on their palms. The footage was collated and edited into a clip. The clip attracted over 720 thousand clicks and more than 6 thousand comments in a short period of time. This is one recent event which once again brought attention to the propagation characteristics and the effectiveness of video-sharing websites.

In fact, YouTube has become an indispensable online service to Internet users. A survey reports that the number of people in Taiwan using online video sites in the previous month has increased to 70 percent (iSURVEY, 2010). Globally, there are 183 million users visiting YouTube monthly (Yang, Hsu, & Tan, 2010). These figures demonstrate the growing popularity of video sites, which have become a vital online medium of the Internet generation.

Despite the rise of online video sites, previous academic research has been primarily on the content genre or function (Harp & Tremayne, 2007; Ye, 2007), or tends to assume the traditional concept of mass media usage behavior, and takes the simplified view of video site usage as a single Web browsing behavior (Tsai, Tsai, Xie, & Chen, 2006 ; Lee, 2008). Some studies do differentiate watching and sharing behaviors, but lack an overall behavioral model of using video sites (Hanson & Haridakis, 2008 ; Yang et al., 2010). Moreover, past research also lacked a comprehensive study on users, with the subjects mostly made up of young students (Kao, 2006 ; Chen, 2008 ; Courtois, Mechant, Marez, & Verleye, 2009).

Therefore, one of the most prominent blind spots in past research on video-sharing websites may arise from the definition of video site usage behavior. User-Generated Media (UGM) is a new kind of media, as a user's role is beyond that of a mere user. This paper posits that an encompassing model of user behavior needs to be proposed for the study of video-sharing website usage.

As such, this paper assumes atheoretical UGM model proposed by Shao (2009) , which identifies three video site usage behaviors: consuming, participating, and producing, and attempts to substantiate the model by empirical study.

Since past studies did not thoroughly explore the motivations and satisfaction of multiple aspects of production and usage, focus group interviews were first conducted to test the suitability of the UGM model. The results of the interview also aided in the development of the online survey questionnaire for the second phase.

The outcome from the focus group yielded two aspects previously unconsidered aspects, namely reputation management and innovation. It was discovered that many respondents described their retrospective experience in the pursuit of innovative communication technology, and their experiences of managing online impression. In the process, it has been found that their behavior may well be influenced by the Diffusion of Innovation theories. Therefore, this paper applies both the Uses and Gratifications and Diffusion of Innovation perspectives, in order to enhance our prediction on user behavior.

To sum up, the purpose of this paper is to establish an over all behavior model of the usage of user-generated video sites, in order to explore the relationships among the motivations, reputation management, innovation orientations, and user behaviors concerning video sites. This paper further attempt to investigate how these factors affect the gratifications obtained from using video-sharing websites.

LITERATURE REVIEW

This paper will firstly exam previous studies on user generated media models to explore users' involvement of their video website usage. Then the uses and gratification perspectives and reputation management theories on websites are proposed to sketch this paper's theoretical frameworks. Finally, a few potential demographic factors which may affect users' involvement level in video website usage are discussed in details.

UGM—User Generated Media Model and Users' Involvement Level of Video Website Usage

User-generated video sites have multiple functions; therefore, users may have to take on multiple roles when using these sites, and these roles need to be distinguished.

Shao (2009) established a UGM model based on uses and gratification theories. The three video-website usage behaviors of the model are consuming, participating, and producing. Consuming behaviors refer to the individuals who only watch, read, or view for information and entertainment. Participating behaviors include both user-to-user interaction and user-to-content interaction (such as scoring, adding to a playlist, sharing, commenting), primarily for social interaction and community development. Producing behaviors refers to the creation and publication of one's personal work such as text, images, audio, and video, mainly based on self-expression or self-actualization motivations.

These three usages of UGM activity can be analyzed separately, but they also can be viewed as dependent units to suit different needs of users in any combination. Therefore, in addition to separately considering these three types of user's behaviors concerning video-sharing websites, this study considers another significant issue: how these behaviors will be integrated in the Web 2.0 era.

This study suggests that the user behaviors concerning video-sharing websites cannot only be divided into three levels (including browsing, commenting, and producing) upon the levels of involvement, but they are also integrated into a comprehensive "Produsage Behavior" based on users' free will (Bruns, 2008).

When producers and users combined into "produser", the producers and distributors lost their position from the production value chain. Users have become a part of content production, extending the process of creating common information. In this value chain, participants play a dual role as users and producers, and thus becoming "produsers" (Bruns, 2008).

The idea of produsage can be traced back to 80 s. Alvin Toffler (1980) in Third Wave mentioned the concept of prosumer and prosumerism. The consumption pattern of online content is a process of users' gradual involvement. In the process, users' different levels of involvement are caused by different levels of use. The levels of involvement of consuming behavior in video-sharing websites are lower than producing. Regarding this, Toffler (1980) did not distinguish the difference between producing and participating behavior, but took them both as a productive behavior. After the rise of video sites, the concept of Internet content usage involvement has also been used to study video-blog usage behaviors (Örnebring, 2008). The current paper argues that, combining with the concept of Shao's (2009) UGM model and the concept of online video behavior from Toffler (1980)and Bruns (2008) , it is better to analyze users' different levels of involvement in using video-sharing websites with the concept of the level of involvement of video-sharing website users' behaviors, for more precise exploration of a comprehensive user's behavior of video-sharing websites.

USES AND GRATIFICATION PERSPECTIVES

The centrality of the individual audience member suggests the value of applying audience-centered perspectives to studying media use in an environment in which users can receive, publish, and modify Web content freely. The predominant research framework for studying media use from the audience's perspective is uses and gratifications, which assumes that people use media to satisfy underlying needs.

Proposing uses and gratification, Katz, Blumler, and Gurevitch (1974) hypothesized that audience members are conscious when selecting media, are able to identify their reasons for choosing media, and motives for media use are shaped by audiences' particular social and psychological characteristics. Five major motivations for media uses were proposed out of the social and psychological functions of the mass media: cognitive needs, affective needs, personal integrative needs, social integrative needs, and tension release needs (Katz, Gurevitch, & Haas, 1973).

The Internet not only blurred the boundaries between mass media and interpersonal communication, but it also combined characteristics of both media (Morris & Ogan, 1996). The user-generated video site is a medium where users can receive both mass media messages and send interpersonal messages. Therefore, motivations for using video-sharing websites should include motivations of both the traditional mass media and interpersonal communication media.

Prior Internet research has identified both traditional media-related motives, such as for entertainment (Ebersole, 2000 ; Wolfradt & Doll, 2001), information (Kaye, 1998 ; Papacharissi & Rubin, 2000), passing time, or distraction from boredom (Ebersole, 2000).

For browsing behavior on video-sharing websites, a great amount of content was originated from traditional media, especially from television. The majority of video-sharing website content is about entertainment (InsightXplorer, 2009 ; iSURVEY, 2010). As a result, the traditional media motivations of entertainment, information, and passing-time should also be motivations for using video-sharing websites.

Therefore, summarizing the perspectives of uses and gratifications theory, the UGM model, and users' involvement with video-sharing websites, this study proposes the first hypothesis:

H1: The motivations for using video-sharing websites will impact the levels of users' involvement in using video-sharing websites.

Because browsing behaviors on video-sharing websites are closer to viewing traditional mass media, this paper further assumes that browsing motivations should be based on entertainment or information-seeking needs, and users require less computer skills or effort than evidenced in participating or producing, thus users may have lower levels of involvement. Therefore, this study proposes that:

H1-1: The higher motivations for browsing video-sharing websites, the lower level of users' involvement with using video-sharing websites.

For commenting behavior on video-sharing websites, this paper posits that motivations related to interpersonal interactions, such as online community participation or belonging, should be closer to the characteristics of interpersonal communication media of video-sharing websites. For example,Baumer, Sueyoshi, and Tomlinson (2008) found that blog readers regard themselves as participants of a blog, rather than merely luring outsiders; moreover, community participation or belonging are all important motivations for using blogs. Kaye (2005) also pointed out that the blog is not an immediate interactive space, and among all kinds of interaction, self-expres- sion and personal fulfillment are usually significant motivations (Kaye, 2005).

Because participating is closer to the characteristics of interpersonal communication media, this paper assumes that participating motives should be out of the demand for social interaction or community involvement, and therefore, engage an advanced level of video-sharing website usage behavior. The study assumes that:

H1-2: The higher motivations of commenting on video-sharing websites, the higher level of users' involvement when using video-sharing websites.

For producing behaviors, YouTube users were found to employ various self-presentation strategies to manage their images to expand their online social networks (Chen, 2009). Users produce video content to manage their online image. One of the ultimate goals should be to obtain interpersonal gratification. Huang, Shen, Lin, and Chang (2007) identified the following four motivations: self-expression, life document, commenting, and community forum participation, which lead to interaction-orientation behavior on blogs. Interaction-oriented blogging behavior positively corresponds to the frequency of interacting with other bloggers and managing blogs.

This paper assumes that the producing motivation should come from self-presentation and social need, which involve higher levels of video-sharing website usage; therefore, the study establishes:

H1-3: The higher motivations of producing content on video-sharing websites, the higher level of users' involvement with using video-sharing websites.

DIFFUSION OF INNOVATION

The Diffusion of Innovation theory proposed that the "innovation-decision process" involves an individual or organization experiencing a series of steps before the innovation is adopted (Rogers, 1983). Rogers (1983) further defined five factors of innovations that influence an individual's decision to adopt or reject an innovation: Relative Advantage, Compatibility, Complexity, Triability, and Observability.

In addition, the Diffusion of Innovation model follows an S curve when plotted over a length of time. Rogers (1983) developed five distinct innovation "adopter categories" to classify individual attitudes towards technology: innovators, early adopters, early majority, late majority, and laggards. Innovators are the first individuals to adopt an innovation, to take risks and experience new ideas in the early adoption stages, and to play important roles in the diffusion process. This paper deems the Diffusion of Innovation model appropriate to investigate the diffusion process of video-sharing websites and their users' behaviors.

Recent Internet studies continually found that users' innovation orientation is positively correlated with the level of their Internet use. The higher the innovation orientation, the higher the Internet adoption level is (Busselle, Reagan, Pinkleton, & Jackson, 1999).

Oh, Susarla, and Tan (2008) applied the diffusion theory to social networks and found that centrally connected users take on opinion-leader roles in transmitting information, and have a great impact on other users in the spread of new videos. In the context of video-sharing websites, new videos usually do not acquire recognition from the overall users. Opinion leaders in this instance could promote new videos in the early stages of diffusion.

To summarize, a video-sharing website's innovative characteristics should include relative advantage, trust, interface, and perceived critical mass. The earlier adopters of video-sharing websites should present stronger characteristics of innovation, and demonstrate higher levels of involvement with video-sharing website usage. Therefore, this study proposed the second hypothesis:

H2: Innovation orientation will be positively related to the level of involvement of video-sharing usage behaviors.

H2-1: The higher the innovation orientation of video-sharing websites' users, the higher level of involvement with the usage.

H2-2: The earlier adopters use video-sharing websites, the higher level of involvement with the usage.

REPUTATION MANAGEMENT: SITE PERFORMANCE AND IMPRESSION MANAGEMENT

Video-sharing websites combine the characteristics of interpersonal and mass media. In terms of interpersonal media, the concept of "impression management" or "self-presentation" is closely related to usage behavior. As for the characteristics of the mass media, user behavior is closely related to a user's perception or satisfaction of video-sharing websites' performance. Taken together, users' perceptions of site performance and their impression management on the site could be theorized as reputation management of video-sharing websites.

The self-presentation concept, also referred to as impression management, was originally developed to explain that every individual performs a certain role while appearing in public. Goffman (1959: p. 17) explained it as "the ways individuals manage impressions of themselves on their audiences". Every individual's presentation in a socially interactive scene has some specific meaning; therefore, the process of controlling the formation of others' impressions is called impression management.Leary and Kowalski (1990) proposed that impression construction involved two processes: determining the type of impression one tries to make and choosing how one goes about it. This study conceptualizes impression management on video-sharing websites in accordance with scholars who have defined self presentation in terms of fostering an impression others hold of them.

The Internet enables people to develop and strengthen their interpersonal relationships, which not only provides opportunities for self presentation, but also provides new challenges. Although self presentation takes place offline as well, self-presentation online is much more manageable than it is offline because it is convenient for users to create, modify, and edit messages about themselves (Walther & Burgoon, 1992).

In this respect, participating or producing behaviors on video-sharing websites is relevant to strategic impression management because users periodically updated their personal video archives (in order to establish their ideal online identities) and frequently obtain comments from visitors (being validated by other people).

Visitors' participation affects the level of online users' impression management; users are encouraged to self- disclose more and to please other browsers if they have more visitors. Consistent with what Schlenker and Wowra (2003) argued, in the interactive process, individuals know what their external behavior shows, and that the behavior will lead others to evaluate them.

Another dimension of reputation management on video-sharing websites is the sites' performance, that is, user's perceptions of browsing video-sharing websites. Previous studies of users' perceptions of Websites usually focused on satisfaction of the sites (McKinney, Yoon, & Zahedi, 2002 ; Melone, 1989; Tsai, 2007) and investigated users' satisfaction along the dimensions of site designs, system functions, information content, and interaction (Ye, 2007). These dimensions were closely related to users' browsing behaviors, and greatly affect users' continuous uses of video-sharing websites.

Therefore, the third hypothesis is proposed:

H3: Reputation management will affect the level of involvement in video-sharing website usage.

H3-1: The more important users value the sites' performances, the lower level of usage involvement.

H3-2: The more important users value the reputation management, the higher level of usage involvement.

DEMOGRAPHICS AND THE USERS' INVOLVEMENT LEVEL IN VIDEO WEBSITE USAGE

The relationship between new computer technology development and demographic characteristics has attracted a significant amount of academic attention. Studies constantly revealed that male users outnumbered females, and they had higher tendency of Internet addiction. It also found that the stronger the Internet usage motives, the higher the levels of Internet gratification (Hsiao, 1998). Studies on home computers or electronic newspapers both showed that the adopters of new technologies tend to be male, better educated, and had higher personal income (Dutton, Rogers, & Jun, 1987 ; Li, 2003). Young and male users were more likely to show higher self- efficacy in computers and locus of control (Broos & Roe, 2006).

However, studies on video-sharing websites emerged divergent results. Younger and lower-educated users were positively correlated to the entertainment uses of video-sharing websites (Peter & Valkenburg, 2006). A Finnish study on teenagers showed that lower-educated users had a higher likelihood to produce video online; younger users are also more likely to participate than to produce. Compared with male users, female users participate and produce more on sites (Courtois, Mechant, Marez, & Verleye, 2009).

Chen (2008) found that age and educational levels were not significantly related to content creators on video websites. Content creation may be due to users' professional knowledge of editing software required to produce online content, regardless of educational levels.

As Livingstone & Bober (2005) emphasized, the Internet population has been ushered into the age of heterogeneity, and demographic characteristics will not last forever. As video-sharing websites are used for entertainment around the world, this study suggests that the level of education may not a determining factor affecting video-sharing websites' uses. However, based on users' demographic characteristics of video-sharing websites, we suggest that the males are more likely to have higher involvement in video-sharing website usage than females.

Therefore, the forth hypothesis is proposed:

H4: Male users will have higher levels of involvement with video-sharing website usage than female users.

Finally, the original hypothesis of the uses and gratifications theory proposed that audience members consciously select media to meet their psychological needs. Empirical studies also confirmed that stronger motivations for Internet use would lead to obtaining stronger gratification (Hsiao, 1998 ; Kaye, 1998 ; Charney & Greenberg, 2002 ; Song, LaRose, Eastin, & Lin, 2004).

Therefore, the final hypothesis is proposed:

H5: The higher level of involvement with video-sharing Web site usage, the higher level of gratification will be acquired from video-sharing Websites.

The conceptual model is illustrated in Figure 1.

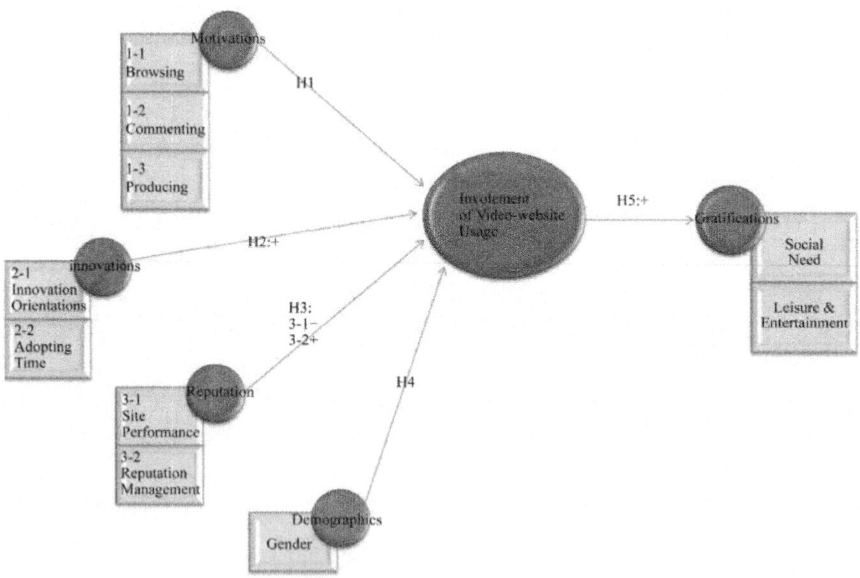

Figure 1: Conceptual model of UGM usage behavior.

METHOD

This study first obtained user's experiences and opinions from 4 focus group interviews. Based on both the literature and interview findings, we designed a questionnaire for online surveys. The question items are listed in Table 1.

The questionnaire includes variables of motivations for using video-sharing websites, innovation orientations, site performance, reputation management, gratifications, and demographics. Except demographic variables, all other items are measured on 6-point Likert scales from strongly disagree, disagree, slightly disagree, slightly agree, and agree, to strongly agree.

The primary variables are measured and defined as follows:

1. Motivations: There are seven browsing motivation-related items; two factors were extracted as "Seeking Information" and "Entertainment"; nine items were composed of commenting motivations, and "Interpersonal Interaction" and "Recommendation" were extracted; nine items of producing motivations, "Recording & Sharing Life" and "Self-Expression" were extracted.
2. Involvement of UGM: Involvement of video-sharing website usage distinguishes user-generated behavior into four levels, from the lowest-level "browsing only", "browsing and commenting", "browsing and producing", and finally the most high-end "browsing, commenting, and producing".
3. Gratifications: The gratifications were obtained from the experience of using video-sharing websites; two factors were extracted from the eight survey items: "Social Need" and "Leisure & Entertainment".
4. Innovation Orientations: Three factors were extracted from fifteen items of the users' characteristics and tendencies of innovations: "Popularity & Fun", "Adventure & Excitement", and "Convenience & Advantage".
5. Adoption Time of Video-Sharing Website Technology: Users were divided into five categories, including innovators, early adopters, early majority, later adopters, and laggards.
6. Site Performance: Aimed to understand how much users value the quality, speed, content choices, and content updating rate of video-sharing websites.
7. Reputation Management: Aimed to understand how much users value friends' or relatives' evaluations of their work, messages, or comment management, and how such feedback affect their work afterwards.
8. Demographics: Gender.

The formal online survey was held from June 18 to June 24, 2010 in Taiwan. There were 5800 respondents randomly selected from the member list of an Internet survey company. Survey links were sent to them, and 2173 respondents clicked the link, resulting in a participation rate of 37 percent. Among them, 108 were halfway out and 520 were unable to respond because of quota limits. After data clear-up, 950 samples were retained from 1114 valid samples.

The demographic information of the 950 qualified samples is as follows: Male respondents (51.4 percent) slightly outnumbered female respondents (48.6 percent). Respondents aged 20 to 29 years made up the greatest number of respondents (29.9 percent), followed by 30 to 39 years (27.9 percent), and 40 to 49 (18.3 percent), aged 19 and below (16.9 percent), and aged 50 and over (6.9 percent). The university education level accounts for 44.0 percent, followed by high school (24.1 percent).

The 950 respondents all had browsing experience, including 237 respondents (24.9 percent) had commenting experience, and 198 respondents (20.8 percent) had producing experience. The top three commonly browsed video contents are Entertainment & Sports (80.9 percent), Information & Learning (12.2 percent), and Life Document (6.9 percent).

Reliability analysis is used to examine the validity of the questionnaire. There were 59 items examined, and the Cronbach α values ranged between .825 to .903 with an average of o.864. KMO values range from .801 to .913, which is above a .70 statistical level, and the Bartlett test value is significant ($p < .001$). Therefore, all items are suitable for factor analysis.

Principal component analysis and Varimax rotation were used for factor analysis. Table 1 indicates the findings. Factor loadings of each factor are above .483, greater than the standard value of .3, and the explained variances of each factor are between 55.26 to 72.83 percent.

ANALYSIS AND RESULTS

This study applied path analysis to investigate the relationship between variables. The first hypothesis predicted that those who have higher motivations of browsing video-sharing websites will have higher levels of involve-

Table 1: Cronbach alpha of factors

Construct	Factors	Items	α
Motivations of Browsing	Seeking Information	I browse video-sharing websites because of work demands.	.843
		I browse video-sharing websites to learn new things.	
		I go to video-sharing websites for downloading various types of videos.	
		I like to seek similar opinions on video-sharing websites.	
	Entertainment	For me, browsing video-sharing websites is relaxing.	
		I have fun when browsing video-sharing websites.	
		Browsing video-sharing websites allows me to escape from real life.	
Motivations of Commenting	Internet Interaction	I would e-mail authors to express my opinion.	.847
		After watching videos, I would give comments on video-sharing websites.	
		I would give comments even if my opinion is different from authors.	
		I will add authors as friends.	
		When I comment on video-sharing websites, I would do it anonymously.	
		When I comment, I care about other users' opinions.	
	Recommendation	I would recommend my favorite videos or producers to others through social websites.	
		I would share good videos through the links of videos.	
		I would recommend video or producers to others on messengers.	
Motivations of Producing	Recording & Sharing	I produce videos on video-sharing websites to record life.	.903
		I love to produce video works on sites to share with like-minded friends.	
		I shoot online video because I want to keep records of life.	
		I produce online video out of personal interest.	
		I like to share life by shooting and uploading videos onto video-sharing websites.	
	Self-expression	It is important to make myself known to others by shooting online video.	
		It is important to draw people's attention to my work via shooting online video.	
		I love to expand interpersonal relationships via producing online video.	
		I would like to express myself via producing online video.	
Innovation Inclination	Popularity & Fun	The experience of using video-sharing websites is pleasant.	.871
		It is interesting to use video-sharing websites.	
		My family and friends have experience using video-sharing sites.	
		Most of the people I keep in frequent contact with have experience using video-sharing websites.	
		My family and friends have experience using video-sharing sites.	
	Popularity & Fun	Most of the people I keep in frequent contact with have experience using video-sharing websites.	
		I find no conflict between video-sharing websites and my previous computer-using experience.	
		My family and friends will continue to use video-sharing websites in the future.	
		Overall, it is easy to use the video-sharing website.	
	Adventure & Excitement	I like to learn new technology.	
		I like to follow the latest news of 3C technology products.	
		I like to learn new things.	
		I am willing to take a risk.	
	Convenience & Advantage	Learning to use video-sharing websites is difficult for me.	
		I think online video content is reliable.	
		In general, I think video content with better comments are more reliable.	
		The viewing rates and comments on video-sharing websites will affect my trust in video content.	

Site Performance		I care about the visual quality of video-sharing websites.	.825
		When I visit video-sharing websites, what I care about is speed.	
		For me, the content choice on video-sharing websites is important.	
		The updating frequency of content will affect my browsing frequency.	
Reputation Management		I care about users' evaluations of my online video work.	.897
		Reviews and feedback from other users affect how I produce online video work.	
		Users' ratings affect my selection of video production topics.	
		I care to win general viewers' appreciation of the quality of my online video work.	
		I care about my friends' and family's evaluations of my online video work.	
		I reply to comments on my online video work.	
		I will delete negative comments on my online video work.	
Gratifications	Social Need	The experience of using video-sharing websites met my work needs.	.883
		I felt satisfied due to the interaction with other people on video-sharing websites.	
		In general, the experience of using of video-sharing websites allowed me to identify myself.	
		The experience of using video-sharing websites met my learning needs.	
	Leisure & Entertainment	I usually find the videos I want on video-sharing websites.	
		The experience of using video-sharing websites met my leisure and entertainment needs.	
		The experience of using video-sharing websites allowed me to escape from real life.	
		The experience of using video-sharing websites met my searching needs.	

ment with video website usage. The path analysis showed that two factors of browsing video-sharing websites, "Seeking Information" ($\beta = .01$, $p = .15$), and "Entertainment" did not significantly affect users' involvement levels of video website usage ($\beta = .00$, $p = .98$). Hypothesis 1-1 is not supported. Table 2 summarizes the research findings.

For Hypothesis 1-2, two factors of commenting motivation, "Internet Interaction" ($\beta = .14$, $p < .001$) and "Recommendation" ($\beta = .28$, $p < .001$), both significantly affected users' levels of involvement of video website usage. Therefore, Hypothesis 1-2 is supported.

For Hypothesis 1-3, while "Recording & Sharing" ($\beta = .68$, $p < .001$) had a significant impact on users' involvement, "Self-Expression" ($\beta = -.04$, $p = .21$) did not have such effect. Therefore, Hypothesis 1-3 is partially supported.

Hypothesis 2-1 predicted that those who have higher innovation orientations will have higher levels of involvement with video website usage. However, three factors of innovation orientations, "Popularity & Fun" ($\beta = -.03$, $p < .05$), "Adventure & Excitement" ($\beta = -.02$, $p < .05$), and "Convenience & Advantage" ($\beta = -.02$, $p < .05$) have significant but negative effects on users' levels of involvement with video website usage. Therefore, Hypothesis 2-1 is not supported.

Hypothesis 2-2 predicted that those who adopt video-sharing website technology earlier will have higher levels of involvement with video website usage. Results confirmed that the adopting time has significant and positive effects on users' levels of involvement with video website usage ($\beta = .15$, $p < .001$), Hypothesis 2-2 is supported.

The third hypothesis predicted that reputation management will affect users' levels of involvement of video- sharing website usage. For Hypothesis 3-1, the performances of the sites ($\beta = -.02$, $p < .05$) did lead to lower level of users' involvement with video website usage. Hypothesis 3-1 is supported. For Hypothesis 3-2, reputation management ($\beta = .16$, $p < .001$) did lead to users' higher level of involvement with video website usage. Hypothesis 3-2 is also supported.

Hypothesis 4 stated that gender will affect users' levels of involvement with video website usage; male users will have higher involvement levels. However, different gender ($\beta = .00$, $p = .98$) did not differ in the levels of involvement. Hypothesis 4 is not supported.

Table 2: Summary of results

Hypothesis	B coefficient	Remark
Hypothesis 1. Higher motivations of to use video-sharing websites will lead to higher levels of users' involvement with video website usage.		Partially Supported
Hypothesis 1-1. The higher motivations to browse video-sharing websites, the lower level of involvement with video website usage.		Not Supported
(1) The higher "Seeking Information" motivation to browse video-sharing websites, the lower level of involvement with video website usage.	.01	
(2) The higher "Entertainment" motivation to browse video-sharing websites, the lower level of involvement with video website usage.	0	
Hypothesis 1-2. The higher motivations for commenting on video-sharing websites, the higher level of involvement with video website usage.		Supported
(1) The higher "Internet Interaction" motivation of commenting video-sharing websites, the higher level of involvement with video website usage.	.14***	
(2) The higher the "Recommendation" motivation for commenting on video-sharing websites, the higher level of involvement with video website usage.	.28***	
Hypothesis 1-3. The higher motivations of producing works on video sharing websites, the higher level of users' involvement with video website usage.		Partially Supported
(1) The higher "Recording & Sharing" motivation for producing on video-sharing websites, the higher level of involvement with video website usage.	.68***	
(2) The higher "Self-Expression" motivation for producing on video-sharing websites, the higher level of involvement with video website usage.	−.04	
Hypothesis 2. Innovation-orientation will be positively related to users' levels of involvement with video-sharing website usage.		Partially Supported
Hypothesis 2-1. The higher users' innovation orientations, the higher levels of involvement with video website usage.		Not Supported
(1) "Popularity & Fun" will be positively related to levels of usage involvement with video-sharing websites.	−.03***	
(2) "Adventure & Excitement" will be positively related to levels of usage involvement with video-sharing websites.	−.02**	
(3) "Convenience & Advantage" will be positively related to levels of usage involvement with video-sharing websites.	−.02**	
Hypothesis 2-2. The earlier users adopt video-sharing websites, the higher levels of their usage involvement.	.15***	Supported
Hypothesis 3. Reputation Management will affect users' levels of involvement with video-sharing website usage.		Supported
Hypothesis 3-1. The more important video-sharing websites' users value the sites' performances, the lower levels of the usage involvement.	−.02*	Supported
Hypothesis 3-2. The more important video-sharing websites' users value the reputation management, the higher levels of the usage involvement.	.16***	Supported

Hypothesis 4. Gender will affect users' levels of involvement of video-sharing website usage: Male users will have higher levels of involvement than female users.	0	Not Supported
Hypothesis 5. The higher levels of users' involvement with video-sharing websites' usage, the higher level of gratifications users will acquire from their experience using video-sharing websites.		Supported
(1) The higher levels of usage involvement, the higher levels of "Social Needs" gratifications will be acquired from using video-sharing websites.	.29***	
(2) The higher levels of usage involvement, the higher levels of "Leisure & Entertainment" gratifications will be acquired from using video-sharing websites.	.10**	

Finally, Hypothesis 5 proposed that users' higher involvement with video website usage would lead to higher levels of gratification. Results confirmed that users' levels of usage involvement had positive effects on "Social Need" ($\beta = .29$, $p < .001$) and "Leisure & Entertainment" ($\beta = .10$, $p < .01$). Hypothesis 5 is supported.

Path analysis confirmed the direct effect of users' involvement with video-sharing websites' usage and gratification. According to the principles of path analysis, we further verify the indirect effect of users' involvement with video-sharing websites' usage and gratification to clarify the relationship between them.

Via the mediation effect of users' levels of involvement with video website usage, we particularly found that the indirect effect ($\beta = .2$, $p < .001$) of "Recording & Sharing" on the "Social Needs" is greater than the direct effect ($\beta = -.012$, $p < .001$); therefore, the total effect ($\beta = .188$, $p < .001$) turned out to be positively related to "Social Needs". The higher "Recording & Sharing" motivation for browsing video-sharing websites, the higher level of "Social Needs" gratification acquired from using video-sharing websites. All other independent variables did not impact users' gratification because of the indirect effects.

RESEARCH CONCLUSION AND DISCUSSION

This paper originally hypothesized that the degree of attention or effort required for browsing behavior is lower than that of other UGM behavior; therefore, the greater the browsing motivations, the lower the level of involvement. However, research has shown that these two factors are unrelated. Although in the process of conducting a video search, a certain level of initiative is required, compared to the level of initiative of participating and producing, the passive nature of browsing behavior becomes more apparent. This could be one of the reasons why browser motive is unrelated to the level of involvement.

In relation to participation, the higher the motivations for participation in commenting, regardless of whether the motivation stems from online interaction or a recommendation of a good piece of work, the higher the level of involvement on video sites. Due to the participative and interactive nature of video sites, whether it is commenting or discussing, or even taking the initiative to recommend work, these actions can be considered as social interaction and community involvement. At the same time, they also require one to put in more attention, focus, and time as compared to purely browsing alone. As such, the level of involvement may be higher.

As for producing, it has also been confirmed that the higher the motivation for record-sharing, the higher the level of usage involvement with video sites. It was originally hypothesized that producing and uploading is due to the need to present oneself as well as to establish personal relationships. As such, the level of involvement may be higher. However, the findings show that the motivation for recording-sharing, as a predictive variable on the level of involvement, far exceeds that of self-expression.

In the past, research on predominantly text-based blogs suggests that self-presentation is often a crucial motivational factor. The main focus of this study is video sites that deal primarily with videos or images, and this shift in focus has yielded different results. Haridakis and Hanson (2009) pointed out that "co-viewing" is a unique aspect of video sites, and is distinct from typical text-based blogs. This feature of co-viewing fully reflects the characteristic social linking of the Internet. Rather than stating that video sites are the composites of the mass and interpersonal media, it may be more accurate to view them as a new type of social media (Fernando, 2007). From this perspective, the motive for recording-sharing may indeed be more effective in predicting the level of involvement with video sites than the motive for self-presentation.

With respect to the overall research results, it seems that it is easier to predict video site users' behaviors in using the video site, as compared to interpersonal communications-related motives, such as social interactions, community involvement, and sharing. This finding, together with some past research, suggests that though the motivations for using video sites and traditional electronic media (like television) do not differ significantly (Haridakis & Hanson, 2009), there is nonetheless a clear distinction. The motivation for using a video site is closer to the motivation for using interpersonal communication media, but it is less related to that of traditional media. This distinction may stem from cultural differences of the video site usage environment. It may also be possible to further deduce if the dissemination characteristics of video sites and the characteristics of interpersonal communication are closer. These two queries merit further research in the future.

In relation to users' orientations towards innovation, this paper predicts that there will be a positive correlation between users' orientations towards innovation, and the level of usage involvement with the video site. However, the empirical results suggest the exact opposite. It is speculated that the lower level of involvement that is required of browsing may be in line with the inclination towards risk-taking or the desire to try new experiences, among other characteristics. On the other hand, a higher level of involvement requires profound thinking when participating, or more time, skill, and patience are needed for production. As such, this cannot be explained simply by the orientation towards innovation. However, in terms of when the users start using video sites, it is confirmed that the earlier video sites are used, the level of involvement is indeed higher.

In terms of demographics, it was found that the level of involvement for the genders do not differ much. This is in stark contrast with the impressions of gender differences stated by the majority of research on the Internet. This paper argues that videos sites are a product of Web 2.0. If videos sites are compared to other communication platforms on the Internet of an earlier period, they are technologically less sophisticated and more interactive media. Video-sharing sites emphasize users' participation and collective knowledge. Even if the content-making requires more expertise, such as shooting or editing software knowledge in film-making, with the proliferation of numerous digital video technologies into household appliances, and the simplification of equipment and software, the stereotypical impressions of the gender difference in computer literacy, at least in relation to video sites, may no longer exist. However, the Internet population has been ushered into the age of heterogeneity. The variables of the demographics of past Internet research may have to be considered more meticulously in the future.

In conclusion, this paper confirms that the greater the level of usage involvement, the higher the level of gratification obtained from video-sharing sites. From past findings on gratification of Internet usage, the sum of all the predictor variables often does not exceed 10 percent (LaRose & Eastin, 2004). However, all these variables in this study on the degree of involvement after adjustment, is $R^2 = .974$. Therefore, this paper extends and furthers existing research through the integration of Uses and Gratifications and Diffusions of Innovation theories.

This study has its limitation because it only conducts surveys and interviews in a single country, thus the findings may have cultural differences when generalizing to other regions of the world. In addition, this study does not apply more advanced statistical methods due to nominal and ordinal natures of some variables.

Future research can base on this article and further statistical models to add to the theoretical foundations of communication behaviors on video-sharing sites.

NOTE

In total, Taiwan's donation to the earthquake amounted to approximately NT $5.9 billion (about $205 million) and topped the world's total contribution (Ko, 2001) https://www.youtube.com/watch?v=MltKxmQpB2A.

REFERENCES

1. Baumer , E., Sueyoshi, M., & Tomlinson, B. (2008). Exploring the Role of the Reader in the Activity of Blogging. In M. Czerwinski, & D. S. Lund (Chair), Shared Authoring. Meeting of Proceedings of the 2008 Conference on Human Factors in Computing Systems (CHI, 2008), Florence, 9 April 2008, 1111-1120.
2. Broos, A., & Roe, K. (2006). The Digital Divide in the Playstation Generation: Self-Efficacy, Locus of Control and ICT Adoption among Adolescents. Poetics, 34, 306-317.http://dx.doi.org/10.1016/j.poetic.2006.05.002
3. Bruns, A. (2008). Blogs, Wikipedia, Second Life, and beyond: From Production to Produsage. Digital Formations, 45. NY: Peter Lang.
4. Busselle, R., Reagan, J., Pinkleton, B., & Jackson, K. (1999). Factors Affecting Internet Use in Asaturated-Access Population. Telematics & Informatics, 16, 45-68.http://dx.doi.org/10.1016/S0736-5853(99)00018-0
5. Charney, T., & Greenberg, B. (2002). Uses and Gratifications of the Internet. In C. Lin, & D. Atkin (Eds.), Communication, Technology and Society: New Media Adoption and Uses (pp. 379-407). New York: Hampton Press.
6. Chen, C. P. (2009). Exploring Interpersonal Communication and Self-Presentation of Users on YouTube. National Science Council Project Reports, Taoyuan: Yuan Ze University.
7. Chen, H. T. (2008). Understanding Content Consumers and Content Creators in the Web 2.0 Era: A Case Study of YouTube Users. Annual Meeting of the International Communication Association, Montreal, 22 May 2008, 11.http://citation.allacademic.com/meta/p_mla_apa_research_citation/2/3/3/7/0/p233709_index.html
8. Courtois, C., Mechant, P., Marez, L., & Verleye, G. (2009). Gratifications and Seeding Behavior of Online Adolescents. Journal of Computer-Mediated Communication, 15, 109-137. http://dx.doi.org/10.1111/j.1083-6101.2009.01496.x

9. Dutton, W. H., Rogers, E. M., & Jun, S. (1987). Diffusion and Social Impacts of Personal Computers. Communication Research, 14, 219-250. http://dx.doi.org/10.1177/009365087014002005

10. Ebersole , S. (2000). Uses and Gratifications of the Web among Students. Journal of Computer-Mediated Communication, 6. http://jcmc.indiana.edu/vol6/issue1/ebersole.html

11. Fernando, A. (2007). Social Media Change the Rules. Communication World, 24, 9-10.

12. Goffman, E. (1959). The Presentation of Self in Everyday Life. New York: Doubleday.

13. Hanson, G., & Haridakis, P. (2008). YouTube Users Watching and Sharing the News: A Uses and Gratifications Approach. Journal of Electronic Publishing, 11, 6.http://dx.doi.org/10.3998/3336451.0011.305

14. Haridakis, P., & Hanson, G. (2009). Social Interaction and Co-Viewing with YouTube: Blending Mass Communication Reception and Social Connection. Journal of Broadcasting & Electronic Media, 53, 317-335. http://dx.doi.org/10.1080/08838150902908270

15. Harp, H., & Tremayne, M. (2007). Programmed by the People: The Intersection of Political Communication and the YouTube Generation. Annual Meeting of the International Communication Association, San Francisco, 23 May 2007, 11-16.http://citation.allacademic.com/meta/p_mla_apa_research_citation/1/7/3/0/6/p173067_index.html

16. Hsiao, M. C. (1998). An Exploratory Study of Taiwan College Students' Internet Using Behaviors, Motivations, Gratification Levels, and Internet Addiction. Master's Thesis, Hsinchu: Department of Communication, Chiao-Tung University.

17. Huang, C. Y., Shen, Y. Z., Lin, H. X., & Chang, S. S. (2007). Bloggers' Motivations and Behaviors: A Model. Journal of Advertising Research, 47, 472-484.http://dx.doi.org/10.2501/S0021849907070493

18. InsightXplorer (2009). Internet Usage in Taiwan: A Basic Investigation in December 2009.http://www.insightxplorer.com/specialtopic/crossmedia_200912.html

19. iSURVEY (2010). E-ICP 2010 Professional Electronic Yearbook of Full Products. Taipei: ISURVEY.

20. Kao, N. Y. (2006). Uses and Gratifications Theory on Web 2.0 Application—A Case of Online Video Sharing Websites. Master's Thesis, Taipei: National Taiwan University of Science and Technology.

21. Katz, E., Blumler, J. G., & Gurevitch, M. (1974). Utilization of Mass Communication by the Individual. In J. G. Blumler, & E. Katz (Eds.), The Uses of Mass Communications: Current Perspectives on Gratifications Research (pp. 19-31). Beverly Hills: Sage Publications.

22. Katz, E., Gurevitc, M., & Haas, H. (1973). Use of Mass Media for Important Things. American Sociological Review, 38, 164-181. http://dx.doi.org/10.2307/2094393

23. Kaye, B. K. (1998). Uses and Gratifications of the World Wide Web: From Couch Potato to Web Potato. New Jersey Journal of Communication, 6, 21-40.http://dx.doi.org/10.1080/15456879809367333

24. Kaye, B. K. (2005). It's a Blog, Blog, Blog World: Users and Uses of Weblogs. Atlantic Journal of Communication, 13, 73-95. http://dx.doi.org/10.1207/s15456889ajc1302_2

25. Ko, S. L. (2011). Intricate Bonds behind Taiwan's Donations to Japan. Kyodo News, May 26.

26. LaRose, R., & Eastin, M. (2004). A Social Cognitive Explanation of Internet Uses and Gratifications: Toward a New Model of Media Attendance. Journal of Broadcasting and Electronic Media, 48, 358-377. http://dx.doi.org/10.1207/s15506878jobem4803_2

27. Leary, M. R., & Kowalski, R. M. (1990). Impression Management: A Literature Review and Two-Component Model. Psychology Bulletin, 107, 34-47.

28. Lee, F. C. (2008). The Motivations and Identification of New Internet Media Users—A Case Study of Video Blog. Master's Thesis, Taipei: Chinese Culture University.

29. Li, S. S. (2003). Electronic Newspaper and Its Adopters: Examining the Factors Influencing the Adoption of Electronic Newspaper in Taiwan. Telematics and Informatics, 20, 35-49. http://dx.doi.org/10.1016/S0736-5853(02)00002-3

30. Livingstone, S., & Bober, M. (2005). UK Children Go Online. London: Economic and Social Research Council.

31. McKinney, V., Yoon, K., & Zahedi, F. M. (2002). The Measurement of Web-Customer Satisfaction: An Expect Ion and Disconfirmation Approach. Information Systems Research, 13, 296-315. http://dx.doi.org/10.1287/isre.13.3.296.76

32. Melone, N. P. (1989). A Theoretical Assessment of the User Satisfaction Construct in Information Systems Research. Management Science, 36, 76-91.http://dx.doi.org/10.1287/mnsc.36.1.76

33. Morris, M., & Ogan, C. (1996). The Internet as a Mass Medium. Journal of Communication, 46, 39-50. http://dx.doi.org/10.1111/j.1460-2466.1996.tb01460.x

34. Oh, J. H., Susarla, A., & Tan, Y. (2008). Examining the Diffusion of User-Generated Content in Online Social Networks. Mimeo, Seattle, WA: University of Washington.

35. Örnebring, H. (2008). The Consumer as Producer of What? User-Generated Tabloid Content in The Sun (UK) and Aftonbladet (Sweden). Journalism Studies, 9, 771-785.

36. Papacharissi , Z., & Rubin, A. M. (2000). Predictors of Internet Use. Journal of Broadcasting & Electronic Media, 44, 175- 196.http://dx.doi.org/10.1207/s15506878jobem4402_2

37. Peter, J., & Valkenburg, P. M. (2006). Adolescents' Internet Use: Testing the "Disappearing Digital Divide" versus the "Emerging Digital Differentiation" Approach. Poetics, 34, 293-305. http://dx.doi.org/10.1016/j.poetic.2006.05.005

38. Rogers, E. M. (1983). Diffusion of Innovations. New York: Free Press.

39. Schlenker, B. R., & Wowra, S. A. (2003). Carryover Effects of Feeling Socially Transparent or Impenetrable on Strategic Self-Presentation. Journal of Personality and Social Psychology, 85, 871-880. http://dx.doi.org/10.1037/0022-3514.85.5.871

40. Shao, G. (2009). Understanding the Appeal of User-Generated Media: A Uses and Gratification Perspective. Internet Research, 19, 7-25.http://dx.doi.org/10.1108/10662240910927795

41. Song, I., LaRose, R., Eastin, M. S., & Lin, C. (2004). Internet Gratification and Internet Addiction: On the Uses and Abuses of New Media. CyberPsychology & Behavior, 7, 384-394. http://dx.doi.org/10.1089/cpb.2004.7.384

42. Toffler, A. (1980). The Third Wave. New York: Bantam Books.

43. Tsai, C. R. (2007). The Study of User Gratification for Participators of Online Video Sharing Websites. Master's Thesis, Taipei: National Taiwan Normal University.

44. Tsai, P. R., Tsai, C. C., Xie, T., & Chen, J. J. (2006). The Factors Affecting Students' Use of Video Blog in Taipei. Master Thesis, Taipei: National Taiwan University of Arts.

45. Walther, J. B., & Burgoon, J. K. (1992). Relational Communication in Computer Mediated Interaction. Human Communication Research, 19, 50-88.http://dx.doi.org/10.1111/j.1468-2958.1992.tb00295.x

46. Wolfradt, U., & Doll, J. (2001). Motives of Adolescents to Use the Internet as a Function of Personality Traits, Personal and Social Factors. Journal of Educational Computing Research, 24, 13-27. http://dx.doi.org/10.2190/ANPM-LN97-AUT2-D2EJ

47. Yang, C., Hsu, Y. C., & Tan, S. (2010). Predicting the Determinants of Users' Intentions for Using YouTube to Share Video: Moderating Gender Effects. Cyberpsychology, Behavior and Social Networking, 13, 141-152. http://dx.doi.org/10.1089/cyber.2009.0105

48. Ye, J. S. (2007). The Study of Service Quality and Gratification of Audio Video Web—Use YouTube and Noname Blog as Examples. Master Thesis, Taipei: Chinese Culture University.

CITATION

CHAPTER 1

Moeller, J. (2015) Economics Forged by Mass Communication and Scarcities. New Theoretical Framework—New Policy Prescriptions—New Scientific Thinking Modern Economy, 6, 1279-1284. doi: 10.4236/me.2015.612121.

CHAPTER 2

Kurt Lang Gladys Engel Lang, Mass Society, Mass Culture, and Mass Communication: The Meaning of Mass, file:///C:/Users/tri/Downloads/597-2847-1-PB.pdf.

CHAPTER 3

Lhamo and Oyama T, Public Policy Program, National Graduate Institute for Public Policy, Tokyo 106-0032, Japan Professor of Public Policy Analysis, National Graduate Institute for Public Policy, Tokyo 106-0032, Japan, doi:10.4172/2165-7912.1000266.

CHAPTER 4

Han, F. , Ge, Z. and Zhou, R. (2016) Reconfiguration and Empirical Study on the Evaluation System of WeChat Communication Effect of Sci-Tech Periodicals. Advances in Journalism and Communication, 4, 8-15. doi: 10.4236/ajc.2016.41002.

CHAPTER 5

Obama, C. (2016) Normativity and the Problem of Look in the Emergence of Citizen Journalism. Advances in Journalism and Communication, 4, 1-7. doi: 10.4236/ajc.2016.41001.

CHAPTER 6

Pavolik, B. , Piwinsky, M. and Fulton, L. (2015) News Crawls in Local TV News: Do They Help or Hinder Information Recall and Retention. Advances in Journalism and Communication, 3, 139-150. doi: 10.4236/ajc.2015.34015.

CHAPTER 7

Chinnasamy, S., & Roslan, I. (2015) Social Media and On-Line Political Campaigning in Malaysia Advances in Journalism and Communication, 3, 123-138. doi: 10.4236/ajc.2015.34014.

CHAPTER 8

Nguegan, J.-F., & Essono, T. (2015) An Ethnomethodological Perspective on the Conflict between Magistrates and Journalists in Cameroon. Advances in Journalism and Communication, 3, 115-122. doi: 10.4236/ajc.2015.34013.

CHAPTER 9

Tang, J. Q. (2015) Analysis on the International Situation and Evolution of Research: Quantitative Analysis on the SSCI Theses from 2005 to 2014. Advances in Journalism and Communication, 3, 100-109. doi: 10.4236/ajc.2015.34011.

CHAPTER 10

Alves, D. and Weber, M. (2015) Social Merchandising: Human Trafficking in Brazilian Soap Opera. Advances in Journalism and Communication, 3, 89-99. doi: 10.4236/ajc.2015.34010.

CHAPTER 11

Bummara, V. and Choi, J. (2015) Exploring the Effectiveness of Distracted Driving PSA (Public Service Announcement). Advances in Journalism and Communication, 3, 71-78. doi: 10.4236/ajc.2015.34008.

CHAPTER 12

Kwon, S. , Cha, M. and Lee, S. (2015) Hierarchical Value Maps of Smart Phones, Portal Sites, and Social Network Services Based on User Involvement. Advances in Journalism and Communication, 3, 56-70. doi: 10.4236/ajc.2015.33007

CHAPTER 13

Paimre, M. (2015) Mapping Trajectories of Attention to Drug Related Issues in Estonian Main Dailies. Advances in Journalism and Communication, 3, 39-48. doi: 10.4236/ajc.2015.32005.

CHAPTER 14

Gürses, F. (2015) Democracy, Citizenship and Local Press: The Case of the USA "Local Press in Boulder". Advances in Journalism and Communication, 3, 19-32. doi: 10.4236/ajc.2015.31003.

CHAPTER 15

Wang, T. (2014) The Usage Behaviors, Motivations and Gratifications of Using User-Generated Media: The Case Study of Taiwan's YouTube. Advances in Journalism and Communication, 2, 137-150. doi: 10.4236/ajc.2014.24015.

INDEX